SAS

THE SOLDIERS' STORY

SAS

THE SOLDIERS' STORY

Jack Ramsay

MACMILLAN

First published 1996 by Macmillan

an imprint of Macmillan Publishers Ltd
25 Eccleston Place, London SW1W 9NF
and Basingstoke

Associated companies throughout the world

ISBN 0 333 66102 8

Copyright © Arlott Services Limited 1996

1 3 5 7 9 8 6 4 2

A CIP catalogue record for this book is available from
the British Library

Typeset by CentraCet Limited, Cambridge
Printed and bound in Great Britain by
Mackays of Chatham plc, Chatham, Kent

Contents

List of Illustrations *vii*
List of Maps *ix*
Collect of the Special Air Services *xi*
Publisher's Note *xii*
Acknowledgements *xiii*
The Soldiers *xv*

1. THE EARLY YEARS *1*

2. SELECTION AND TRAINING *13*

3. BORNEO *65*

4. OMAN *97*

5. THE IRANIAN EMBASSY SIEGE *135*

6. NORTHERN IRELAND *167*

7. THE FALKLANDS WAR *193*

8. THE GULF WAR *221*

LIST OF ILLUSTRATIONS

SECTION ONE

On Continuation Training you have to find lunch as well as cook it. (*Military Picture Library/Tim Fisher*)

Johnny Two-Combs, river-crossing drill in Belize.

A 'brew-stop' on navigation training, Malaya.

Johnny Two-Combs, squadron training in Malaya.

The Iban taught us jungle skills. (*Telegraph Picture Library/S. Flynn*)

With two local youths during a 'hearts and minds' operation in Borneo. (*Brown Packaging*)

Snapper: 'In front of the Batt House in Mirbat, a week before the battle.'

Laba in full fighting mode: 'He deserved a VC for what he did.' (*TRH Pictures/Republic of Fiji military forces*)

Roger and Bob in the .5 Browning *sangar* at the top of the Batt House. The DG fort is in the background.

The young *firqa* troops relaxing in Mirbat between operations.

Snapper: a few weeks after the battle, back on hearts and minds ops, having tea with one of the locals.

SECTION TWO

RF: 'This is the plan of the upper floors of the Iranian Embassy which we were given as part of our briefing packs.'

RF: 'Before we knew that the terrorists' leader was called Salim, we were given this ID poster. It turned out to be a pretty good likeness.'

Abseiling down the back of the Embassy, Tom the Fijian troop commander got tangled in his rope and the whole operation was put in jeopardy.

RF: 'Going in at the back of the Embassy. I'm in the middle with no gloves on.'

RF: 'The telex room after we'd eliminated three of the terrorists.'

RF: 'The aftermath. You can see bullet holes in the table on the right of the picture.'

RF: 'The Embassy after we'd finished with it.'

On patrol in South Armagh's 'bandit country'. (*Pacemaker*)

David: 'The Pucaras and Aermacchi MB-326s on Pebble Island after we'd seen to them.' (*TRH Pictures*)

Matt: 'An hour into enemy territory and one of our Land Rovers was written off due to the arduous terrain.'

Matt: 'After our first contact we had to camouflage the Iraqi vehicle while we waited for a chopper to take it out. Of course, it proved to be too difficult to do that and we had to dispose of it on the ground.'

Matt: 'Two and half weeks inside enemy lines. It was freezing most of the time, especially at night, and these Arab coats proved a lifesaver after the resupply.'

Matt: 'Me in my woolly hat behind enemy lines about twenty-five miles north of the Iran–Iraq border. The operation had been satisfactorily concluded and we were having a brew before heading back to base.'

Matt: 'Safely on our way home.'

LIST OF MAPS

Borneo 1963–1966
66

Oman 1970–1976
98

Northern Ireland
168

The Falklands Islands 1982
194

The Gulf
222

COLLECT OF THE SPECIAL AIR SERVECES

O Lord, who didst call on thy disciples to venture all to win all men to thee, grant that we, the chosen members of The Special Air Service Regiment, may by our works and our ways dare all to win all, and in so doing render special service to thee and our fellow men in all the world, through the same Jesus Christ our Lord. Amen.

PUBLISHER'S NOTE

The mixture of Imperial and metric units throughout the book is not the product of editorial dereliction: the SAS use the units interchangeably. Systematic conversion, it was considered, would have been intrusive and otiose.

ACKNOWLEDGEMENTS

The author chiefly wishes to thank the soldiers whose stories made this book possible. He would also like to thank Martin Lloyd-Elliot for his considerable assistance and who, together with Rhodri Philipps, was the originator of the *SAS: The Soldiers' Story* project. Also, many thanks to Gordon McGill and Peter Darman.

If readers are interested in the history of the SAS, they might find the following works of interest: *The SAS at War*, Anthony Kemp; *The SAS – Savage Wars of Peace*, Anthony Kemp; *The SAS at Close Quarters*, Steve Crawford; and *Who Dares Wins*, Tony Geraghty.

THE SOLDIERS

David Served in the Falklands and the Gulf

'I had known about the SAS all my life, but I decided I wanted to go into the Marines and signed up to do so as a young cadet. Soon after I realized I had made a mistake so I went for the Army instead. It was my clear intention to make my way into the SAS as soon as possible.'

R.F. Served in Northern Ireland and took part in the storming of the Iranian Embassy

'I heard about the SAS in 29 Commando, which classes itself as also being in the special forces. You'd hear stories in the pub. It was the sense of something even more exciting, something even more élite.'

Jock Thompson Served in Aden and Borneo

'I was a coal miner although it wasn't my choice. I just had to because my dad died when I was twelve and I was the eldest of five and that was the only place to get money. My mother didn't want me to go down the pits because that's what killed my dad, so I promised her that as soon as my youngest brother left school we would join the Army. We left at Christmas 1959 and on 6 January 1960 I reported for Selection.'

Johnny Two-Combs Served in Northern Ireland

'I was the eldest of nine and my family was very poor, so when my cousin who was in the Green Jackets suggested I join up, I realized it was the only way out – that or football, because Villa were interested. So I joined on my seventeenth birthday. A few years later my RSM said I could go to Sandhurst and get made up to colour sergeant, but I'd become determined to try for the SAS. I'd seen the Embassy thing. It was a challenge, an intense desire to better myself.'

Lofty Large Served in Aden and Borneo

'I'd served in Korea, and was badly wounded at the Imjin River battle. It took me four years to get fit again. I didn't fancy being told when to die or when not to die. I'd rather tell myself. So the idea of the SAS appealed to me. I applied for Selection in 1957.'

Mack Served in Northern Ireland and took part in the storming of the Iranian Embassy

'I did two and a half years with the Army Youth Team, based in Worcester. One of the places were visited regularly was the TA Centre at Hereford. One day in a Hereford pub I came across an old mate who had just finished Selection. I knew hardly anything about the SAS, so I asked him and what he told me got me thinking. After several weeks I said to myself, "I'm going to go for this."'

Matt Served in Northern Ireland and the Gulf War

'I joined the infantry in 1977 and spent the next eight years learning normal soldiering in Northern Ireland, Germany,

Canada and Cyprus. I have served the last ten years in the SAS all over the world. My uncle was in the SAS in Malaya. I joined because I wanted to be in the best there is.'

Pete Scholey Served in Borneo

'My grandfather was in the Army in the First World War. My father was in the Royal Air Force. After the war, my dad ran a barrow stall at the market. One of the old boys there had been in the SAS during the war and he used to tell me about his adventures, though I never thought then that I'd join the regiment.'

Sek Served in Aden, Borneo, Oman, Northern Ireland and took part in the storming of the Iranian Embassy

'I joined the King's Own Borderers when I was seventeen. I was part of the battalion recruited after the Malayan campaign when Fiji was still a British colony. An NCO told me I would never pass Selection. He was wrong.'

Snapper Served in Oman, Northern Ireland, the Falklands and took part in the storming of the Iranian Embassy

'I was never a civilian. My father had gone through the war from Dunkirk to Anzio and right through to Berlin without a scratch. I joined the Royal Engineers when I was fifteen. I just fancied the life. I heard about the SAS after Aden, where I met members of the regiment who told me things were about to happen. They didn't go into details, but that was enough for me. As soon as I got back to the UK, I put in for Selection.'

1
THE EARLY YEARS

In summer 1941, in the Scottish Military Hospital, Alexandria, David Stirling, a twenty-six-year-old Scots Guards lieutenant, lay paralysed in both legs as a result of an accident on his first parachute jump. Two panels of his canopy had ripped as he exited and he landed hard and fast, injuring his back. For an hour he had been blind. Now – during June and July – he had time to study the Desert War; and all the news from the front was bad.

Rommel's Afrika Corps was rampant and was at the Egyptian frontier. An attempt by British forces to relieve Tobruk had failed, and General Wavell, the Commander-in-Chief, had been dismissed. A number of seaborne raids undertaken by a commando brigade called Layforce against Rommel's communication lines had been unsuccessful. Stirling, a member of No. 8 Commando, one of the units in Layforce, had taken part in these raids. He talked at length to his visitors, and as a result he came to the conclusion that the failure of the raids was due to lack of surprise. In hospital he scribbled notes. The commando units had been too big. David Stirling began to think small.

'I argued the advantage,' he wrote later, 'of establishing a unit based on the principle of the fullest exploitation of surprise and of making the minimum demands on manpower and equipment ... a sub-unit of five men to cover a target previously requiring four troops of a commando, i.e. about 200 men. I sought to prove that, if an aerodrome or transport park was the objective of an operation, then the destruction of fifty aircraft or units of transport was more easily accomplished by a sub-unit of five men than by a force of 200.'

In addition, he proposed that each unit must be self-sufficient, responsible for its own training and operational planning.

Furthermore, he suggested that forty units be recruited and trained to arrive on the scene by land, sea or air as the occasion demanded.

Having come up with the theory, he then, in late summer, formulated a specific operation to be put into practice when the Eighth Army struck back. All he had to do was convince the top brass. He was no longer paralysed; he could move on crutches and he could drive. He left the hospital and drove to the head-quarters of General Claude Auchinleck, the new Commander-in-Chief Middle East. He told the sentry at the gate that he had forgotten his pass. The sentry didn't buy it. Stirling looked around, hobbled to a gap in the fence, dropped the crutches and squeezed through. Sentries yelled and began to chase after him, but he made it to the building. He pushed through one door and started talking. The major behind the desk threw him out. He tried another door and found General Neil Ritchie, Auchinleck's Deputy Chief of Staff. Despite the sentries' noisy pursuit of the intruder, Ritchie listened and promised to read the hand-written memo Stirling gave him and to pass it on to his superior.

Two days later, Stirling was promoted to captain with a brief to recruit six officers and sixty men, the force to be known as L Detachment, Special Air Service Brigade. There was no such brigade. It was an invention of Brigadier Dudley Clark, whose role was to mislead the enemy. In order to fool the Italians into believing that there was a large airborne force in the Middle East, he had been having dummies dropped by parachute near Italian prisoner-of-war camps. Now he had sixty live soldiers to play with.

The SAS was born – conceived by a cripple and christened by a practised deceiver.

Based at Kabrit near the Suez Canal, Stirling began his recruitment drive, drawing upon volunteers from the old com-mando force, men who subsequently became known as the 'Originals'. Stirling later described them as a 'bag of vagabonds ... escaping from conventional regimental discipline who didn't fully appreciate that they were running into a much more exacting type of discipline'.

After three months' training, during which two men were killed when their parachutes failed to open and his men had carried out a successful dummy raid against an RAF airfield, L Detachment was ready to go. They had their insignia – the winged dagger cap badge having been the winner of a competition among the men – and they had their motto, dreamt up by Stirling and which, over the next fifty years, would become a byword for the extraordinary courage and determination exhibited by SAS men: 'Who Dares Wins'.

The first SAS operation was planned for November 1941 to coincide with a British offensive codenamed Operation Crusader. Stirling planned to hit five airfields around Timini and Gazala on the North African coast. His units would blow up enemy aircraft on the ground just before the British push was due to begin. Five aged Bristol Bombay aircraft were to drop the five units near their target on the night of the 16th. They were to lie up the next day until nightfall, when they would place their bombs on enemy aircraft just before the start of the offensive. The job done, they were to meet at an agreed spot, rendezvous with a patrol of the Long Range Desert Group, a British reconnaissance and intelligence-gathering unit, and be driven back to base in the LRDG's Chevrolet trucks.

The one joker in the preparation pack was the weather. When night fell on 16 November, a gale was blowing. None the less, the five aircraft took off as scheduled from an airstrip at a place called Bagoush. After a two-hour flight they reached their targets and came under attack from anti-aircraft fire. One plane was shot down, killing two of the crew and one soldier; the survivors were taken prisoner. A second aircraft vanished, having either crashed or been shot down.

Three units jumped into the gale, unsure where they would land, as the sandstorm that had been whipped up had obliterated the pilots' landmarks. Two men were so badly injured on landing that they had to be left behind. Supplies were missing. Stirling, who had been knocked unconscious on landing, found the bombs but no detonators. Without them the mission had to be aborted, and in bedraggled groups the survivors eventually made their way back to the rendezvous. Only twenty-two of the original sixty-five men dropped were picked up by the LRDG.

From this disaster Stirling drew one positive conclusion. He figured that if the LRDG patrol could get his men out, then it could also get them within walking distance of their targets. There was no need for aircraft. This slight change of procedure brought immediate success. In December 1941 the rump of the 'Originals' launched attacks against enemy airfields at Sirte, Agheila, Tamit, Nofilia and Marble Arch (the latter so named because of a massive arch erected there by Mussolini to mark the border of Tripolitania). Over 100 aircraft, plus stores, petrol and vehicles, were destroyed.

•

With success came the need for more recruits, and L Detachment was increased to two troops of sixty men. Throughout the summer of 1942 these units attacked airfields and harried road traffic in operations described by a Chief of Staff as 'small raiding parties of the thug variety'. In September the 'thugs' were raised to full regiment status – 1 SAS Regiment – with a headquarters squadron and four combat squadrons – A, B, the Free French and the Special Boat Section (SBS), the latter two known respectively as C and D Squadrons. By December Stirling, now a lieutenant-colonel, had over 650 men under his command. The new year began well for the British: Rommel was in full retreat after El Alamein and the SAS was launching many hit-and-run raids. But then disaster struck: Stirling was taken prisoner at the end of January 1943.

The SAS organization split up, with the Free French and Greeks who had joined returning to their respective armies and the maritime section, the SBS, hived off to Palestine. The 250-strong 1 SAS was now renamed the Special Raiding Squadron (SRS). However, David's brother Bill had created another SAS regiment – 2 SAS – and both it and the SRS fought in the Allied invasions of Sicily and Italy in 1943 until being recalled to England to take part in the D-Day landings. David Stirling had created an organization that could fight in all theatres, and during the last phase of the war SAS units fought in Italy, Holland, Belgium and Germany. They crossed the Rhine in advance of the ground forces, and it has even been suggested that SAS men were the first soldiers to reach Belsen.

•

In April 1945 Stirling was liberated from Colditz. On his return to England he immediately presented a detailed plan for the SAS to continue the war in the Far East, which was approved by Churchill. But in August Hiroshima and Nagasaki rendered it redundant.

With the war over, the remaining units were disbanded. And, but for the persistence of former members who refused to let the idea die, the exploits of the SAS might have amounted to no more than a series of footnotes in the general histories of the Second World War. However, ex-SAS men swiftly began to lobby the War Office and so, in 1947, an SAS unit was formed within the Territorial Army. It was attached to a unit named the Artists Rifles to become the 21 SAS (Artists) TA, and many wartime members of the SAS, including former SBS men, joined up.

In 1949 the new CO, Lieutenant-Colonel Brian Franks, who had commanded 2 SAS during the Second World War, wrote to the War Office, stressing the importance of Stirling's original idea: 'The fundamental difference between SAS "units" and other units of the army, which must be grasped if the special needs of the SAS are to be understood, is that the former are not "units" in the sense generally accepted for the latter. The SAS regiments are NOT organized and CANNOT be employed as units; all operations undertaken by SAS troops are carried out by parties especially picked and equipped for the occasion. The strength, composition, equipment and method of employment of each party depends on the exact circumstances of each operation and are only decided when the operation is allotted and examined in detail.

'It will be seen therefore that the term "unit" is a misnomer in this case and that the SAS regiment is not a tactical unit. It is merely a force of SAS troops from which a large number of SAS parties can be found, controlled and maintained.'

He further argued that SAS troops would be required in the early stages of any future war and that planning must be constant in anticipation of trouble anywhere.

That was the theory. However, by 1950 the SAS was reduced to two squadrons and a signals detachment. It was little more than an appendage of the Parachute Regiment, complete with red beret.

Then came Malaya.

•

The British-dominated Malay peninsula was moving towards independence in the aftermath of the Second World War. The British attempted to accommodate nationalist sentiment by setting up, in 1948, the 'Federation of Malaysia', a step towards full independence. However, the Chinese minority resented Malay dominance of the Federation and some Chinese Communists turned to violence to right their grievances.

In June 1948 three British rubber planters were brutally murdered. This atrocity marked the beginning of a Communist-led insurrection that was to last for the next twelve years. The Malayan Races Liberation Army (MRLA), an 8,000-strong force comprising mainly Chinese, made a concerted effort to redress the balance of power in the peninsula in favour of the Chinese.

Despite a number of casualties – a total of 229 soldiers were killed in 1949, along with 344 civilians – the security forces managed to push the Communist Terrorists (CTs, as they were known) deeper into the jungle. It became clear that a deep-penetration unit was needed that could remain in the jungle for longer than three weeks at a time – the maximum period thought possible for regular troops – to defeat the CTs. General

Harding, the Commander-in-Chief Far East Land Forces, sent for 'Mad' Mike Calvert, a veteran of the Chindit campaigns in Burma who had ended the war as commander of the SAS Brigade and one of those who had lobbied for the rebirth of the SAS regiment. Calvert's report proposed deep-penetration units that could exist in the jungle for lengthy periods. He also proposed making contact with the native tribes to win them over by kindness, by setting up medical clinics, and generally to render them unsympathetic to the enemy. In the words of the High Commissioner, General Sir Gerald Templer, it was a 'hearts and minds' campaign. It was to be the first of many.

The special force was named the Malayan Scouts (SAS), and the first 100 men were recruited in the Far East in 1950 to form A Squadron. The idea was to train them to fight and live in the jungle in small groups of three or four men. As Calvert said: 'The fewer you are, the more frightened you are, therefore the more cautious you are and therefore the more silent you are. You are more likely to see the enemy before he will be able to see you.'

It was to be something of a false start. Later recruits from Britain reported back on indiscipline, and one of Calvert's officers admitted that 'numerous widely publicized, sensational and mainly true stories circulated' and almost caused the disbanding of the unit. Calvert, though, was sympathetic to his men, comparing them to a building site, 'which can be a rough-and-ready place until construction is finished'.

Construction was finally completed in 1952 with the addition of B company from members of 21 SAS and reservists and C Squadron from Rhodesia. Calvert had been invalided home a year before, but the new commander, Lieutenant-Colonel John Sloane, ably assisted by John Woodhouse and Dare Newell, tightened up discipline. This paved the way for the creation of 22 SAS, which was formed from the Malayan Scouts in 1952. The men had to fight in appalling conditions – something with which subsequent generations of SAS men would become only too familiar.

Johnny Cooper, one of David Stirling's 'Originals' and a troop commander of B Squadron, tells of soaked clothing in dark terrain, the sun obliterated by the jungle canopy, of the constant threat of ambush and booby traps of sharpened bamboo, of moving slowly through swampland, being lucky to cover two hundred yards in an hour, of elephants and snakes, tigers and angry buffaloes, of hornets and mosquitoes.

'Apart from the enemy, leeches were our main adversary. They would fall off the leaves and latch on to one's softest areas, around the neck, behind the ears, under the armpits, and on a long patrol they would even find their way to one's private parts. You couldn't feel them, but as they slowly sucked blood they enlarged into horrible black, swollen lumps.'

Despite these privations, operations continued and the occasional contact was made with the enemy, but the Malayan jungle was no place for pitched battles. The reckoning was 1,800 man-hours of patrolling for one kill. By now a fourteen-day ration of dehydrated food had been adopted. The good news was that the soldiers could remain undetected for a fortnight without the need for regular supplies by helicopter. The bad news was that men would lose on average 10 pounds per patrol, while their clothes rotted, their sores festered and they were plagued by leeches.

Meanwhile, the 'hearts and minds' campaign was stepped up. The soldiers lived with the tribespeople, became their dentists and their midwives and built jungle forts which were then handed over to the local police and troops.

By 1956, with the addition of British paratroopers and 140 New Zealanders, including a number of Maoris, the regiment was up to a strength of 560 men and had become so effective that it had made a significant contribution towards the containment of the Emergency. Murders of civilians still took place but had fallen to five or six a month and the leaders of the MRLA had fled to Thailand.

'It was in the jungles of Malaya,' says the military historian Anthony Kemp, 'that the foundations of the modern regiment were laid down by an enlightened series of officers ... and a completely new set of skills had to be learnt the hard way by practical experience, [the men] having been locked in combat with what was essentially a terrorist force motivated by Communist ideology.'

The future for the SAS was still uncertain, except as part of the Parachute Regiment. But the Suez Crisis in 1956 led the Government to re-evaluate Britain's military role worldwide, and in January 1957 the SAS's link with the Parachute Regiment was severed. After seven years of wearing the red beret, the SAS men could again don the beige. At last their role was clearly defined. The regiment was to collect intelligence, to conduct small-party offensive operations, to cooperate with foreign partisan and guerrilla groups and to assist combat survivors and escaped prisoners of war.

The War Office assumed that the regiment's future lay in Germany, where the forces of NATO and the Warsaw Pact faced each other, but the reality, as we shall see, turned out to be very different.

2
SELECTION AND TRAINING

A sign over the door of the training-wing *basha* (sleeping quarters) at Hereford reads: 'Many are called but few are chosen.' Instructor Lofty Wiseman has amended this to: 'Death is Nature's way of telling you that you've failed Selection.'

An American guy came over to test out Selection. A real John Wayne, with the crew-cut and everything. A Colonel Charlie Beckworth. He got through okay. At the end he said that if the Americans had this sort of training, they wouldn't have lost in Vietnam. Delta Force was based on the SAS and this guy became the head of it.

I failed the first time because I fell down a hill with the Bergen on and did my back in. I wasn't going to fail the second time. You only get two chances. The first time I'd been stationed in Germany, and it was flat. This time I got fitter, trained on the Brecons. Each night I'd put on the Bergen with about 50 pounds in it and watch television for a couple of hours, doing step-ups on the coffee table. It was a strong coffee table.

Johnny Two-Combs

While the men of the SAS fought the insurrection in Malaya, Major John Woodhouse, the commander of D Squadron, returned to England to set up a selection course. He based it initially at the Parachute Depot in Aldershot but then began to look for somewhere that men could be tested to – and beyond – the limits of their endurance. The bleak terrain of the Brecon Beacons on the borders between Wales and Herefordshire – and particularly Pen-y-fan, at almost 3,000 feet a God-given endurance test – seemed perfect. This desolate place was to be make-or-break for potential SAS men. Of those soldiers who volunteered for selection, most would fail; some would die in the attempt.

According to Major Dare Newell, 'Selection is designed to find the individualist with a sense of self-discipline rather than a man who is primarily a good member of a team. For the self-disciplined individualist will always fit well into a team when teamwork is required, but a man selected for teamwork is by no means always suitable for work outside the team.'

The qualities that the Training Wing look for have remained consistent since then: good judgement in spite of stress and fatigue and the ability to think – alone – under conditions of extreme isolation and hardship. Supreme fitness is a pre-requisite and taken for granted.

As Peter Watson, in his book *War on the Mind*, puts it, 'The psychologists look for those who ... are: above average in intelligence; assertive; happy-go-lucky; self-sufficient; not extremely intro- or extroverted. They do not want people who are emotionally unstable; instead they want forthright individuals who are hard to fool and not dependent on orders. The psychologists do acknowledge that occasionally, with the SAS, there are problems of too many chiefs and not enough Indians.'

Any male member of the Army, Navy, RAF and Territorial Army SAS is eligible to apply for Selection. Officers must be between twenty-two and thirty-four, other ranks between nineteen and thirty-four; all must have at least three years and three months left to serve from the date when, if successful, they pass Selection Training.

Having applied, the men then undergo a three-week build-up period followed by Test Week. Selection starts with a standard Army Battle Fitness Test followed by a daily regime of road marches across the Brecon Beacons. Initially these are team efforts, but on the third week the candidates are left to go solo.

In the 1960s the Bergens (rucksacks) were filled with bricks. Today they are filled with more useful items, such as a sleeping-bag. The men are also issued with a 57-pattern webbed belt, a poncho for wet-weather protection, two one-and-a-half-pint water bottles, a standard army compass and maps (map references to be memorized, never written: after use, each map must be folded along its original seams so that it cannot betray your destination), a brew kit and three twenty-four-hour ration packs (to be used in the first three-day trial) and an old-fashioned Self-Loading Rifle with no sling. Every day the weight carried increases from a basic 25 pounds to an eventual 55 pounds.

The route marches are set day and night so that candidates are fighting the clock as well as the elements. Marches are routed via rendezvous (RV) points, and only when the soldiers reach one RV are they told where to find the next. And so it continues, with sleep deprivation thrown in; on Selection you are up at four and don't get to bed until well after ten.

During Week One comes the first 'sickener' – three days of moving from point to point as the crow would fly. Except that crows can fly over ditches filled with stagnant water and the entrails of long-dead sheep. Men on Selection must crawl through everything in their path.

During this first week, those whom the instructors deem to be passengers, 'lambs' (the physically weak) or 'mouths-on-sticks' are summarily RTUd (returned to unit). Crap-hats once more, they are just squaddies waiting on Platform 4 of Hereford Station for a train out. Back at the training wings, their photos will be desecrated by a red line scarring their faces, a ritual known to those remaining as 'SAS plastic surgery'.

For the officers during the first week there is the additional hazard of 'staff exercises' every evening. A candidate will be asked to plan a commando raid or deep-reconnaissance patrol, then has to defend it under interrogation by senior NCOs and troopers. The plan is usually rubbished; on average only 6 per cent of the officers make the grade.

Those who survive the first week continue the forced marches up and down Skirrid, a 500-metre peak, for another fortnight, then move on to the Test Week, in which each soldier is on his own. Distances and Bergen weights are increased daily. The men are disorientated by last-minute changes of plans, sudden extra distances, late nights and unexpected early-morning calls.

They march three times up and down Pen-y-fan, at 2,900 feet the tallest peak in the Brecon Beacons, a distance of thirty miles. At any point an instructor might appear and ask them to solve a mathematical problem or reassemble a foreign weapon. To compound their difficulties, they have to swim naked across the River Wye, carrying rifle, Bergen and clothes.

At the end of the course comes a 46-mile endurance march known as the 'Fan Dance', to be completed in under twenty hours. The time limit means the men have to jog most of the way with their Bergens loaded up to 55 pounds. Candidates are given no dispensation if the weather is bad. In winter men have died.

If, at the end of all this, a man survives, he is given a weekend break and told to report back to Stirling Lines, the SAS's UK base in Hereford, for first parade on Monday morning and the start of fourteen weeks of Continuation Training. This involves two weeks of basic skills training: weapons; Immediate Action (planning for an assault, known to the men as IA); becoming accustomed to working in four-man patrols; learning how to operate behind enemy lines, with the focus on intelligence gathering, sabotage, ambush and, where required, causing civil unrest. During basic skills training, the men also learn how to move with a 50-kilogram Bergen on their backs without being seen and how to survive in a metre-deep hide, lying on plastic sheets beneath camouflaged chicken wire.

Continuation culminates in learning combat and survival, which ends with escape and evasion. Candidates are on the run from trackers and when caught, and they inevitably are, the men are put through the rigours of interrogation.

Those who are left then undertake six weeks of jungle training in the Far East. Finally they take a four-week parachute course at RAF Brize Norton, where – after eight jumps – they receive their 'Sabre' wings. Those who are left at the end of this then return to Hereford, where they are 'badged' SAS. They are now

SAS soldiers, though their advanced training is yet to begin. The final pass rate ranges from 5 to 17 per cent.

Within each squadron there are four sixteen-man troops, each with a specialist role: the boat troop concentrates on amphibious warfare; the mobility troop operates Land Rovers, fast-attack vehicles and motor cycles; the air troop goes in for freefall parachuting; and the mountain troop works on Arctic warfare as well as mountaineering. And each troop is composed of four four-man patrols; even after they have passed men can still be RTUd if they don't keep up to standard.

Peter Scholey, an SAS veteran, sums it up: 'The point of all this Selection and Training is that the SAS are trained very well. They have very good staying power. They always put in that little bit extra that makes the difference. Very flexible. Any war situation, in any part of the world, in any environment, and we are ready to cope. That's why we are called Special.'

The stories that follow show just how true his words are.

•

Mack I left school at sixteen and wanted to join the Army. The old man OKd it, but my Maw said no. In those days you had to get the written permission of both parents in order to be able to join. So that was that down the tubes. You know what Maws are like. I was the youngest of the family, the baby. As well as my twin brother I had an elder sister.

I did lots of sport, especially running and football. Even as a kid I was always doing things like climbing trees and swimming and stuff. I had a multitude of jobs but I just couldn't settle down. Four years later I was passing by one of the locals and I just popped in for a quick pint. I met one of my mates in there, Jim, and we got chatting. I said to him, 'What are you doing?'

'I'm going off to join the Army.'

'What do you mean?'

'I'm off to the old recruiting office at Grangemouth' – which was about a mile away.

I looked at my watch. It was five to two. In four years I hadn't once thought about the Army. Without hesitation I said to him,

'Tell you what. Wait for me to finish my pint and I'll come with you.' And so off we went together, with me riding on the back of his motorbike.

Thirteen days later I was in the Army, the Royal Engineers. That quick.

I'd served for a couple of years when the sergeant-major called me in one day. He'd seen an advertisement requesting volunteers for the Army Youth Team (AYT), and he asked me if I fancied the idea. I had never even heard of it. He explained that you wear a tracksuit all day and go around schools and colleges recruiting people and telling them about the Army. He asked me how I felt about the idea. I said, 'Yeah, it sounds good.'

'That's good,' he said, 'because I've already sent off your application.'

I did two and a half years with them. We were based in Worcester. One of the places on our regular visits was the TA Centre at Hereford. We would work in teams of two. I partnered a guy called Paul, who didn't drink, so he did the driving. We would go and set up a film to be shown to potential recruits. Once the film was rolling, I would pop down the road to the local for a couple of pints. It was here that I first met people from the SAS. A couple of times Paul didn't pick me up because he couldn't find me, so I would set off from Hereford, blind drunk, and arrive back in Worcester sober after a six-hour walk. I was young. I didn't worry about such things.

One day in a Hereford pub I came across an old mate called Tommy who had just finished Selection. Tommy came from Falkirk, same as me. We joined up on the same day and only found out on the train going south.

'Where are you going?' I'd said.

'Tae jine the Army.'

'Christ. So am I.'

And here he was again. I knew hardly anything about the SAS, so I asked him, and what he told me got me thinking.

After several weeks I said to myself, 'I'm going to go for this.' I started studying and asking guys I knew in the regiment what was required to pass Selection. I was already reasonably fit because part of our job in the AYT was to take the young lads running in the hills and such like. Anyway I soon got into training wearing a heavy backpack. In total I spent a year getting fit. After that I applied and got a place on Selection almost immediately. At the last minute I decided I just wasn't quite ready. I wrote and apologized. They said, no problem, when you are ready reapply. Instead I applied for 59 Commando.

I went to the Engineer commando training centre in Plymouth. There were sixty of us. At least twenty dropped out during the initial weeks. It was tough, but I passed and got my green beret. I did several years as a commando. It was good fun, but the time came when I knew I was going to end up getting posted to Germany and I really didn't want that.

So, with a close friend called Ginge, I started heavy training a few days later. We would fill our Bergens with wet sand. Every night we would have our tea and then make our way down to a local site where they were constructing a ski-slope. I used to read trashy novels as I walked up and down this slope for a couple of hours every night. Sometimes I would do it backwards. Try walking backwards up a ski-slope with a Bergen full of wet sand on your back. That really gets your thigh muscles going. It paid off. Every Sunday morning we would do a 30-mile walk. We had a set route. Our friends knew what we were training for and they were good about it. One of the lads in our section had failed Selection the previous year, so we knew what we were in for.

The sergeant-major at 59 Commando was my mate and, thanks to him, I got a month off to train full-time before I went for Selection. Together with Ginge and two other lads, I went up to Hereford. We were given a room and rations. On Monday mornings we all got in a car and drove up to the Brecons. We went walking every day and camped out overnight the whole week. We did that for three weeks running, getting very fit and getting to know the area. Then we took one week off before Selection started.

I arrived and the feel of the camp was completely different

from anywhere else I had been with the Army. It was a hot day, and when I went to book in, I saw all these guys sitting around in old armchairs, sunbathing, wearing shorts and flip-flops, and others, scruffy-looking, wandering about. Even those in uniform weren't walking ramrod-straight. Then when I went for a meal I was amazed. In the green army you got one egg, one slice of bacon and a sausage if you were lucky. Here you just helped yourself to as much as you liked and no one said a word.

I thought: This'll do for me. When Selection started I was quite ready.

Day one involves a mile-and-a-half walk. You have to run back within a certain time. You then do a map-reading test. Day two, you are given a Bergen with 45 pounds in weight, I think – anyway, it's not much. You are put into four groups, two on one side of the Fan, two on the other. As long as you can stick with the instructor you're going to make it back in time. You have to run right over the top of the Fan, reach a certain point, change instructors and then run back again. It's about 8 kilometres each way. We had to do it in four hours.

One young lad, from the Military Police, had brand-new boots and a nice pair of new nylon football socks. On the morning of the third day a lot of people were hobbling, but this guy, his blisters were unreal. They were the size of oranges. We were laughing so much. He was in agony.

I said to him, 'So what happened? You know, did you finish?'

'No,' he says, 'it took me nearly five hours just to go one way.'

He was actually crying, but he kept saying he was going to come back. Off he went. Back to his unit. We never saw him again. And he wasn't the only one either. About 30 per cent of the blokes failed the first hurdle. Gone after two days. It was a fair old benchmark as to your fitness. There were some blokes there who had been running five or six miles a day and they thought they would be fit enough. I've never been a runner but I am a plodder and a sticker. You put a house on your back for a few months and get used to it. When I started Selection I discovered that I had been carrying more weight on my back doing my own training.

During the walking section of Selection you do an average of five or six hours per day, which is between 24 and 30 kilometres. They would never set a specific timeframe or tell you exactly how far you had to cover, so that meant that you would just go for it each time to the best of your ability.

Then came a disaster. I injured myself on the Endurance March. I slipped on a stone as I crossed the river and I was taken off the course and sent on three weeks' leave to get fit again. When I returned, I was attached to what they call the Goon Troop. We were all people who had been injured on Selection but who they thought had a fair chance of getting through and were allowed to try again. I was attached to Training Wing, so for five months I trained every day. About three weeks before the next Selection started there were thirteen of us goons. Geordie, the instructor, lined us up and said to us, 'OK, today there are thirteen of you. By the end of three weeks I will have got rid of most of you.' And he did.

He took a ten-speed racing bike and on day one we went for a 5-mile run first thing in the morning. We had to keep up with him on the bike. Then we went straight into the gym and played two hours of five-a-side football. He just knackered us. After lunch he took us out for a 10-mile run. That got rid of a few.

In week two we did the same thing again but added to it were regular visits to the Fan. He would say, 'The truck will be at the far side of the Fan and will be leaving at exactly half past ten. Goodbye.' And, my God, if you weren't there on time, he would drive off and leave you behind. Sometimes blokes would be running down the hill, and we were in the back of the truck waving to them with big grins on our faces as we drove off without them. There were only three of us left at the beginning of the third week, and one of the other two injured his knee running down a hill, so only two of us Goons made it to the end. And then we had to go through Selection again.

On week three we were up in 'moon country' in the Black Mountains. The ground is terrible. Great big tufts that mean you cannot walk anywhere in a straight line. It was pissing down. There was a big coloured bloke who used to spar quite seriously.

We met Lofty Wiseman, one of the instructors, at the halfway RV. He told us to get a quick brew of tea from the back of the wagon, gave us our next grid reference and told us to bugger off. This big black fellow was whinging and whining and said he had had enough. Lofty said, 'No problem, mate. If you've had enough, you've had enough.' So this bloke finishes his cup of tea and goes to climb into the truck. Lofty calls out to him, all casual-like, 'What you doing, mate? You didn't come in that truck. Your truck is at the next RV.' So he had to complete the exercise anyway. The rest of us were laughing, of course. We never saw him again.

I said to myself, 'There is no way I am going to fail unless it is through injury.' As I was one of the smaller ones, I was all the more determined. Being with other blokes who were six foot eleven was an added incentive. I'd look at these massive blokes and say to myself, 'Nah problem. I can beat them.' It's all in the mind you know. Just the same, it's the voice in your head that says, 'I can't go on.' I did. It felt very good when I passed.

Thirteen of us made it out of about 160.

•

Johnny Two-Combs When my cousin, who was in the Green Jackets, suggested I join up, I realized it was the only way out. I was one of nine children, from a very poor family, so it was that or football, because Villa were interested – so I joined on my seventeenth birthday at Winchester and went straight into the battalion football team. Six months later I was in Belize. It had been a good decision. I played for the British Army in 1973 in the Aztec Stadium in Mexico City before 80,000 people and in 1977 I won the Queen's Jubilee Medal for best NCO in my company.

When I'd just turned eighteen I went to Northern Ireland and saw some bad things, then after a few years it seemed my career was mapped out. My RSM said I could go to Sandhurst and get made up to instructor (and colour sergeant), but I'd become determined to try for the SAS. I'd seen the Embassy thing. It was a challenge, an intense desire to better myself.

Selection is a very personal thing. Before you get to go on Selection, you have to seek permission from the commander of your unit, so even at that stage you face scrutiny. You must set yourself at least a six-month training period, and you work very hard. Eventually you arrive at Hereford and quickly become aware that you are there as an individual, and if you look around you, you see other really fit, motivated men. You wonder if you will make it because only about 10 per cent do.

On the Fan I saw people in front of me disappearing into the mist before I could even get into a starting position. I told myself all the time not to panic and to go at my own pace. I had to keep telling myself, 'I can do this, I am fit, I am trained for it. Go at your own pace.' After a while you start to see people sitting, exhausted, by the path. From each person I passed I drew great encouragement. Just before I got to the top of Pen-y-fan, on the first leg, I was near the lead group, and by the time I got to the bottom I was with them. There is real pressure to keep up with the lead group but most people are used to working up to their pain barrier and not beyond. I could go through it.

I did it twice and both times finished in the lead group of about fourteen or fifteen out of eighty who started. When you progress beyond the first four days' basic fitness and navigation tests, you move on to another phase.

Many people don't realize how hard and important it is to be able to navigate fast and under pressure when pushed to your physical limits. They will march you somewhere, give you a map and ask you where you are, you tell them, and then they read you out a grid reference and tell you that is where you have to get to. You have then to do a really rapid map appreciation. A great deal of time can be lost doing this if you are unsure, and you have to subconsciously visualize the map in three dimensions. That way you should see the best way to go, remembering that the most direct way is not necessarily the best.

Once I came to a checkpoint, and a couple of guys were heading off to the same place I was heading. They were a way in front of me anyway, so I could see how they had chosen to do it, but I knew that their path would lead to an almost vertical drop off some high ground.

I headed off in another direction, and as I came into the checkpoint, I looked for them ahead of me. Far behind me in the distance I could see two little dots, which gave my confidence a great boost.

In week three you must carry a weapon, a rifle, and it must be kept at arm's length at all times, whether you fall over or are at the checkpoint. One chap left his weapon at a checkpoint. I came in after him, and the DS kept me behind for a full five minutes, I suppose because he didn't want me racing off to tell him, but after we crested the hill, I caught up with the fellow and warned him. I never saw him again, and I guess it is because he jacked the whole thing in at that point instead of swallowing his pride, going back down, getting a lecture and getting on with it.

To save time when going from checkpoint to checkpoint, where you can take on water, I would carry a civilian bottle with a pipe leading to my mouth, so that instead of stopping to take a drink I could just keep going. This would give me the additional few seconds that, by the end of the day, were the minutes which could mean the difference between passing and failing. That and practically living on Mars bars. Those two things got me through Selection.

In the mountains your mind can play funny tricks on you, so to stay sane I would take a mini radio with an earpiece, and quickly take it out and hide it when I approached a checkpoint. It made it just a bit easier to push myself to finish.

I don't think that I even contemplated failure. If you refuse to think about failing, it helps you pass. You almost cannot pass without that attitude. You feed off other people's weaknesses – like, if you pass someone, or they are in difficulty, it gives you great courage and hope.

On Endurance itself, which is the ultimate test, I had to be convinced that I would pass. We set out at about 3.00 a.m., and the physical side of the march was extremely hard. Towards the end of it, I teamed up with a rupert [an officer], and we kept each other going. By then the pain in my feet was excruciating. Blisters really affected me, like they do everyone, and in the morning I would syringe them, put my boots on and get on with it. The first ten minutes were horrendous, but after that the pain was tolerable. Once you take your boots off, your feet swell and the blisters come up worse, sometimes septic, so when you get back to barracks in the evening, you syringe them again and try to ignore the pain.

Somehow we finished, and when I sat in the back of the van, only then did I truly feel the throbbing in my feet and the pain in my knee. I hadn't really noticed before. Despite the pain, the euphoria was amazing. Relief overwhelmed me, and I started sobbing. I looked over to the rupert and he was sitting there silently sobbing as well. You cannot imagine the sense of accomplishment and pain and relief.

When I was out tabbing, listening to my radio to stop my head getting into knots, I would think about the knockers – the people who'd smile as if to say, 'He'll be back,' when I told them I was going for Selection – and the thought of saying, 'I'll show you,' really plays on your mind. I used to visualize my children to keep me going and to think how proud they are of me and me of them, and in particular my daughter. I thought to myself constantly that there was no way I would fail them, and I just had to pass the test. I did.

•

Snapper I've never been a civilian. My father was at Dunkirk and went all the way through to Anzio and Berlin without a scratch. Only twelve of his battalion were left at the end. He told me about his experiences, and I never wanted anything else except to be in the Army.

I joined at fifteen as a boy soldier with the Royal Engineers in Chepstow and served with the regiment in Aden in 1967, the time of the so-called tactical withdrawal by the British Army. As far as I was concerned, it was a retreat, a disgraceful retreat. A lot of guys lost their lives – and for what? They're in silent valley now. Aden was given away by your 'darlin' Harold'. We marched out and the Russians marched straight in. I was there in the last few days and it was a débâcle. Kit and equipment, bulldozers, expensive engineering plant, all left behind for the Russians. As I climbed on to the aircraft to take us out, I thought, 'Never again.' This was my first operation theatre and we were retreating. 'Never again will I be in the situation where I am retreating.' That's what I told myself.

After that I was posted to RAF Shar-jah near Dubai, where I met members of the SAS who told me that things were going to happen in the region soon. I'd never heard of the regiment, and the guys didn't go into details. It was veiled speech, but they said: 'We're going to put it right.' That was enough for me. As soon as I got back to the UK, I put in for Selection, and now here I was, three years later, listening to the Colonel's pep talk.

'Nearly twenty-six weeks of exhaustive scrutiny,' he said. 'Half a year of uncertainty. You could get your marching orders at any point along the way, usually when you least expect them. We've been known to fail someone on the very last day.'

He told us that he was looking for men with initiative, stamina, intelligence, patience and – not least – a sense of humour, and I thought, Yeah, well, the last is guaranteed. Black humour mostly, from the gallows.

He told us that we wouldn't achieve fame or fortune and not to expect any parades or to be fêted as heroes. The regiment moved silently, did its job and melted away into the background. What he did promise those who made it was deep self-respect and a unique identity as part of a very exclusive family.

And that was it. We were told to get an early night because we were going to need it. I took his advice. Nine thirty, head down. But I hadn't counted on Geordie in the next bed. He'd sneaked a bird in, and they were at it all night, long and loud.

Fuck's sake. Who dares wins, I thought.

Our instructor was a veteran of Malaya called Tim, whose first words to us were that 'selection' really meant 'rejection'. The weeding-out process about to begin was essential because in a four-man unit one weak link spelled disaster. It was possible for an inferior soldier to hide in the regular Army. Not in the SAS.

We piled out of our Bedford truck and looked up a hill. It was like the side of a building. Sickener One. Three days of it. On with the Bergen and straight up.

My card had been marked. In addition to the standard issue, I'd bought twenty-four Mars bars, a bottle of olive oil to soak my socks, a Sivas compass, squares of foam padding for Bergen-burn on my shoulders, two large plastic bags and two essentials – curry powder and Tabasco sauce.

The three days on the hills were 'head down, arse up and keep going till you're told to stop'. You couldn't take the easy routes. You had to go direct from one trig point to another. It was called cross-graining the *bukits* (from the Malayan word for 'hill'). Just when you thought you'd reached the end of your rope, Tim would appear out of the rain and urge you to call it a day and go back to your regiment. If you just blinked as though you agreed, it would be a red-line job.

During a heavy squall on the first day, with a near-vertical cliff to climb, two guys alongside me looked at each other. One said, 'Sod this,' and the other one agreed – and there was Tim telling them to get back down the road. Platform 4 already.

Base camp in the woods that night. Sleeping-bag, and the poncho stretched over it to keep off the rain. I'd said nothing to the others over my mug of tea. Maybe talking was an RTU offence. You didn't know what the rules were. So I kept to myself.

Next day same thing, then towards the end we came to a ditch. It was 2 feet deep and 4 feet across, filled with stagnant water and sheep's entrails. It stank. Tim wanted us to get across it, on hands and knees, doing the leopard crawl – holding your rifle horizontal and pressed against your forehead. Of the four of us I seemed to be the only one to know about the leopard crawl, so I was in first. Halfway across, weighed down by the Bergen, my belt snagged on a rock and I had to wiggle free, my face in the muck.

We all stank that night.

The third day ended with a stretcher race, carrying Tim, complete with his Bergen and rifle, for the last mile, but we could see the Bedford trucks waiting for us at the RV point. Just as we were about 100 yards away, they took off. The rest of the lads straggled up from various points, and Tim told us that there had been a change of plan. New transport was 10 miles away.

One of the lads went nuts. He threw a punch, and that was the end of him. Platform 4.

We headed off for the last 10 miles, but Tim had conned us. The trucks were over the next hill.

Ninety made it through the first week, but on the second the Skirrid saw off quite a few more. The Skirrid is 500 feet of sore thumb sticking out of flat lands near a place called Llanfihangel. The top was ideal for map-reading exercises, but you had to get there first, and it was nearly vertical. Up and down all day with full kit. On the top one time my vision blurred and I couldn't read my map. I could imagine the indignity. Platform 4 because of double vision.

I shook my head and thought of Tim's survival rule: calmness and coolness at all times. My vision cleared and the map made sense – in the nick of time.

That day my leg muscles tightened until they were locked, and I got blisters on my blisters.

The third week we were on our own, and they tried all sorts of tricks to disorientate each one of us; plans and distances would change at the last minute. You couldn't fake it with bravado either, not with Tim around. Any deep personality flaws came to the surface. It was as if the instructors were scientists experimenting with accelerated-ageing techniques.

We were reduced to half the original number when we hit Pen-y-fan. Up at four, ready to go at six, out of the Bedford, 40 pounds in the Bergen, and off we went, up the path to the summit, down the other side, across the plain and start again – three times. At the top, on the last lap, an instructor appeared out of nowhere and asked me to do some complicated piece of mental arithmetic. I was knackered, soaked in sweat and nearly bowled over by the wind, and I had to multiply something by something else and divide by the number he'd first thought of. Put the brain into gear and think. I came out with a number. He nodded. Thank Christ – and all this just a dress rehearsal for the real thing.

Day five, week four, the endurance march. Forty-six miles' cross-graining to be done in under twenty hours; 55 pounds in the Bergen now with four one-and-a-half-pint water bottles on my belt. I had twenty-four Mars bars with me, one for each hill, but when I got the Bergen on, I could hardly move.

Then we went, the remaining thirty-seven.

And of course, sod's law, it had to be hot that day. Eight hours in and less than halfway round, I couldn't find the answer to carrying on.

The friction in my boots felt like someone pushing a hot, razor-sharp file across the skin of my ankles. Backwards and forwards relentlessly with each step, sapping my will-power and determination until it felt as if the file was sawing against raw bone. I was overwhelmed by feelings of isolation and loneliness.

I was on the point of jacking it in. So near and yet so far. Then, like Paul on the road to Damascus, I got the sign. The heat reminded me of Aden. The reason I was standing on this Welsh hill was a chance to get my own back. It was revenge that got my blistered feet moving again, and I made it back to the Bedford early in the evening, beating the deadline.

Seventeen of us passed out of the original 135.

•

Lofty Large I joined the band of the Wiltshire Regiment at the age of fifteen because that was the only way I could get into the infantry at that time – 1946. I'd have joined at fourteen if I could. I served for five years as a band boy, then as a drummer.

I didn't like being in the band. I wanted to be a real infantryman, so I volunteered for the Gloucestershire Regiment in Korea. A bad move. I was badly wounded at the Imjin River battle and spent two years as a prisoner of the Communists in North Korea for my trouble.

On my return I was graded P7, the lowest medical grade in

the Army, and I was in rather a mess, down to 9 stone 10 pounds then from my original 15 stone 8 pounds. The Chinese classified me as unfit for military service because of my arm, so I thought: I've got to stuff them somehow.

It took me four years to get fit again. I was a storeman at the Glosters' depot. I wasn't able to do much else as I had my arm all crippled up. At that time three blokes from SAS came back to us, their original unit, in order to be demobbed. This made me realize that the SAS Regiment still existed because until that time I thought it had been disbanded at the end of the Second World War. When I went to Korea they had been asking for volunteers for the 'ferret force'. Although I didn't know it at the time, they were to become part of the newly sparked SAS. I heard about the SAS through these men, who told me there was no bullshit and no drill, and I thought, That's for me! It sounded like the ideal regiment. I've never seen any point in all that drill. I think that all the emphasis in the Army on drilling is stupid, with the Guards doing twelve weeks a year on solid drills alone. Who can afford that much time out of a training year? It's not on. It's a waste of public money.

I didn't fancy being told when to die or when not to die. I'd rather tell myself. So the idea of the SAS appealed to me.

I applied for Selection in 1957. The medical specialist in charge of my case laughed in my face when I told him I wanted to join the SAS. 'Christ, they jump out of planes and all sorts of things. You'd kill yourself doing that.'

'No, no, it'll be all right. I definitely want to have a go.'

He persuaded me to train for a further six months. All through the training he was amazed at the improvement I made. He kept on saying, 'It's against all medical science and logic for you to be getting this fit.'

After those six months were up, I told him that I wanted upgrading. As a P7 I was excused everything bar breathing. He offered to put me up to P3, which means you are excused route marches or some such thing. I said, 'Oh, no, P3's no good. Put me right up to fully fit. Then I'll know where I stand.'

So during my last six months with the Glosters I was declared fit even though I wasn't. Everything had stood against me to get fit enough to apply for Selection, let alone survive the course.

I actually passed initial Selection, but in the final part, on the endurance march, I tore my Achilles tendon and had to hobble the whole way back. I was about half an hour late getting in, only reaching the cairn above Tallybont Reservoir as the truck took off. I was in a right state because I had gone all the way across the Beacons with my leg buggered. When I finally got into camp, into the office, I told them that I had seen the truck leave. They quizzed me about what time it took off and had to admit that I had made it. So I passed. We were six out of twenty-seven.

I jumped on my bike and headed for Gloucester. On the way a great big coach turned right in front of me. There was nowhere for me to go, and I spent two weeks in Newport hospital. To this day I still can't move the toes on my left foot. After a couple of months I did the first Selection march with a size twelve boot on my swollen left foot and a size eleven (my normal) on my other, with the officer saying, 'Just test your foot out.'

That evening another officer said to me, 'How did it go, Lofty?'

I said there had been no problems.

'Foot all right?' he asked suspiciously.

I assured him it was fine.

'Good,' he said. 'Join in again with the lads tomorrow. Give you something to do.'

It went on like this, day after day, until effectively they had made me do the whole Selection process again. The whole bloody lot. I thought: Shit. Just my luck to have to pass twice to get in once.

•

Pete Scholey Selection? These days I have no doubt the standard is as high as it's always been, but when I joined they ran Selection on two 4-tonners and a packet of fags.

I tried to get into the RAF but failed. I had about thirty different jobs but wasn't happy with any of them. Then my

National Service came due, so I joined Run Away, Someone's Coming [the Royal Army Service Corps]. Their motto was 'Remember Always Someone Cares'. I think that people should always be proud of their regiment and their badge, whatever it is.

I got demobbed from there, took one look at Civvy Street, didn't like it, so went into the Artillery because it was a 30-mile sniper and, given that I hate fear and am a coward, that seemed like a good idea. Then I was posted to 27 Guided Weapons Regiment (RA).

At this time I started cross-country running and potholing. My aim was to get into the Paras, but I knew my lack of education and exam skills would be fatal. Luckily I made the education corps sergeant laugh, and he liked me, so when I was sitting my exams he would mark me generously.

After about three years I volunteered for the 33rd Parachute Light Regiment (RA). But shortly after joining them, my Army service expired, so I was discharged from the Army. I walked out of the barracks and into the depot of the Parachute Regiment to join the Paras. The finest airborne infantry in the world. I worked bloody hard for my wings. I was terrified of jumping. I much prefer jumping at night when it's pitch-dark. Like that, you can't see anything to frighten you. I had many sleepless nights in the Paras over jumping, but I never told anybody and eventually I got used to it. I was driven to jump because I wanted to go flying so much. If I couldn't fly aeroplanes, I wanted to jump out of them. You can always conquer fear, especially with good comrades.

After winning my red beret, I was sent to Cyprus and, in 1961, to Kuwait. And always I trained in my spare time. Even on ten days' leave I would go up to the Brecons.

In 1964 I joined the SAS Regiment. That was the most terrifying thing I have ever done. When you go in through those gates, the frightening thing is the quietness. After the shouting and screaming and bawling I'd been used to, great big blokes like Lofty were whispering troop sergeants.

'OK, lads, tomorrow morning, eight o'clock, on parade.'

Next morning, on parade, there's one missing. Whispering as usual, the sergeant asks, 'Where's Edwards?'

Somebody replies, 'He'll be here in a minute.'

'Okay,' says the sergeant.

Five minutes later he turns up.

'Edwards, would you just pop down to the orderly room, please?' – all quiet and polite, like.

NEVER SEEN AGAIN. Platform 4.

People sometimes ask why no one with a police record is ever accepted by the regiment. It's simply impossible. Four-man patrols can't afford to have one missing. Twenty-five per cent of your fighting force gone off for a court case when he's been naughty? No time for that.

As far as Selection was concerned, they knew what they wanted. I had no idea what I was letting myself in for. I just took it a day at a time.

On my first day I managed to make two of the three RVs. I was worried because I wasn't good at navigation. Then I made a fundamental mistake. I followed some of the other blokes heading towards what they thought was the third. They were lost. So was I. Eventually I got to the third RV at one o'clock in the morning. I phoned in and told them where I was and the number of the phone box. They told me to get myself back. It took me another two hours. It was raining.

I walked into the little office. The instructor hardly looked up from his desk. 'Get your head down in there, son.'

The room was full of stinking, sweating, wet bodies, all snoring. I didn't even get undressed. I put my head down, and as I close my eyes I'm opening them again and it's morning.

An hour later, on parade, the sergeant-major calls out, 'Where's the lad who came in at three o'clock?'

I took one step forward.

'Right, you want to finish now, don't you?'

It was more of an order than a question.

'No, sir. I survived yesterday so I'm sure I can survive the rest.'

One hundred of us did Selection. I was so tired, my eyelids ached. My blisters were so bad that blood oozed out of my lace holes. Nine of us passed.

The colonel came into the room and gave us our winged-dagger badges and our wings. 'Welcome to the regiment. First, you are on a year's probation with your squadron. You won't be putting anything into the regiment until you have completed three years. Then you will be a trained trooper. You will enjoy life in the regiment if you remember one or two important things that make us different from the rest of them. First, pay. We don't go chasing claims. We don't have time. If you queue up, it will be outside the ops room for briefing. Two, rank. Only when you are capable of leading a four-man patrol will you be considered for the rank of lance-corporal. Three, medals. Forget them. You are SAS. More is expected of you. Four, whatever job you are doing, and wherever you are, make sure that you work longer and harder than any other person. If you do this, you will enjoy the regiment.'

I don't believe in giving accolades and medals away easily. For example, as far as I'm concerned, you're not a member of the airborne troops unless you have served with an airborne unit as a soldier. In the old days you only got a balloon on your sleeve if you had done a parachuting course, not your wings. I can tell you that winged-dagger badge did not come easy to me. I worked my guts out for it, and I was very proud at the end when I got to wear it.

•

Jock Thompson I come from a place called Glencraig in Fife. I was a coal miner, although it wasn't my choice. It was a case of just having to because my dad died when I was twelve and I was the eldest of five and that was the only place to get money.

I was fifteen and a half when I first went down the mines. My mother didn't want me to go because that's what killed my dad, so I promised her that as soon as Robert, my youngest brother, left school I was going to join the Army. He left school at

Christmas 1959, and on 6 January 1960 I reported for Selection at the Para Depot in Aldershot.

I chose the Paras because I always choose the most difficult. Start at the top instead of the bottom. My county regiment is the Black Watch. They are brilliant, but I always had this thing about going for the biggest challenge. So instead of going underground, I decided to go up in the air.

I did my Para course at RAF Abingdon and was posted to 2 Para, based in Cyprus. We used to do drops to Libya and Greece and Kenya. We were there for two years, and it was fantastic. I was really lucky because I caught the last seven months of EOKA (a Greek Cypriot terrorist organization) before Cyprus became independent.

We returned to Aldershot and things were just too tame for me. Road blocks and firing blanks were not for me. I said to myself, 'To hell with this.' I was looking for some action when this guy appeared at the barracks who had been RTUd from the SAS. He'd been in a punch-up. I think he had punched an officer, the adjutant, and got away with it, but that's another story. He was wearing a sandy-coloured beret with a winged-dagger badge, so I went up to him.

'What regiment are you?'

'Well, I was SAS, but now I'm back in 2 Para.'

I asked him to explain.

'Whereas the Paras are out-and-out aggression, pure killers – you know, fix bayonets and take no prisoners – the SAS specialize in explosives, booby traps, demolitions, languages, paramedic skills, advanced communications. In the SAS the killing is nice and quiet, subtle and silent, what the Malayans call *perlahan lahan*, which means "slowly slowly".'

The list went on. I was all fired up straightaway. I said to myself, 'This is for me.' I was pretty fit at the time. I was in the cross-country team, the boxing team, the swimming team. I won the Middle East Battle Trophy for shooting. The fact is if I could see it I could hit it. It was as simple as that. I could hit a 12-inch circle at 600 yards without a telescopic sight.

I went to see the CO of 2 Para. I told him that I wanted to try for SAS Selection.

He said, 'You can go for the course, but you had better not fail it. If you fail, you will not be welcome back with 2 Para.'

I appeared in Hereford in October 1962. The regiment had only been there a year. There were ninety-eight on the course. I and David Jones from the Shropshire Light Infantry were the only two to pass.

I remember the day I passed Selection. I went before the colonel, John Woodhouse. I was highly chuffed. He said, 'Well, Jock, I've sent a letter to Colonel King to tell him you have come top of the course and have done the Paras proud. Also, being a Para, I suppose you want to carry on jumping.'

'Oh, aye.'

'Right. Jolly good. I'm putting you in 16 Troop, the freefallers.'

'Thank you, sir. That'll do me just fine.'

Continuation Training started immediately. I did communications, survival, escape and evasion, explosives and so on, then on to CQB [close-quarter battle], advanced communications and a three-language course – Malay, German and Arabic. I became a fully trained paramedic and a qualified instructor in escape and evasion, including tracker-dog evasion, and resistance to interrogation.

If you know interrogation techniques and can anticipate what is coming next, you are better prepared. I went to the Military Intelligence training operation in Kent for three months. One of the things they did was throw me in a cell with another bloke who was all beaten up and covered in bruises and dried blood. He was a stool pigeon. He's the one who gets you talking, not the interrogators.

'Oh, fucking hell, mate. You've been caught as well. What a bastard. You've got to watch these bastards. They don't half put you through it.'

Then, a bit later, 'So who are you with?'

'The Black Watch.'

'Are you married?'

And so on. He's the guy who is actually interrogating you. He asks you innocent questions to get you used to giving true answers and then slips in a more significant one to try to catch you off guard. They teach you to recognize such techniques and overcome them.

Tracker-dog evasion is all about scent. The dogs are usually Labradors. If you are escaping, you always assume that they are using dogs to catch you. There are certain procedures that rely on a combination of common sense and specialist knowledge.

You ask yourself endless questions, analysing the situation all the time. What's the state of the ground? If it's dry, your scent won't hang around for long. Where is the wind? If a man runs straight up the middle of a field with a wind blowing from his left, tracker dogs will run in parallel to his route but fifty yards over to the left. If you see a field full of sheep or cattle, you can run through that, but you have to be careful because if you go up the side of a hedge, all the sheep in the field will stop grazing and look at you. Cattle are inquisitive and will come towards you. Birdlife can give away your position too. A blackbird or a thrush disturbed in a hedge will cackle like hell.

Now, when I was a lad I did a lot of poaching, so all of this stuff was natural to me. You learn to read every detail. For example if you watch a pigeon flying and it suddenly changes direction there is something or someone on the ground exactly beneath the point where it turned.

As far as training is concerned, I don't think you ever finish. By God, I had a lot of it and gave a lot of it to others as well.

I've seen armies all over the world. Most of them are rubbish. They stick a red beret on their heads and call them special forces, but they're not. The only ones who come close to us are the Germans, the French, the Israelis, some of the Soviets, but nobody touches the SAS. Sheer professionalism. We are the best.

•

Mack After two weeks on basic skills it's off to Brunei for six weeks of jungle training.

The jungle is a good equalizer. It is different from anywhere else on earth. The first time I went, I loved it. It was like being a kid again. As a kid I was always playing in the woods, making dens and tree-houses and all the rest of it. One of the ruperts had a little poetry book which he would read all the time. After a few days he started mumbling to himself and then he went round the twist. RTUd. Never to be seen again.

A lot of people go crazy because they feel so enclosed. Although it is daytime, it is never quite light because the canopy is so full and dense. You get beams of light filtering through here and there, but you don't see the sky. It gets to people.

Basically you are living in shit. As long as you don't fight it, you can make yourself really comfortable.

The first thing I used to do was find myself a suitable position for my bed. It had to be somewhere with good drainage, so usually on a slope and not too far to walk to replenish your water. Then I would set up my pole bed – two long poles which you feed through a piece of canvas with slats folded and stitched running the length of it on either side, so that it looks a bit like an old-fashioned stretcher. How you fix it is up to you, but I preferred being on a high rise, about six feet off the ground, slung between two trees, with my poncho over the top to try to keep out the worst of the rain. We were still always soaked through. It never used to bother me, being wet. It was like a home from home. I set up my cooking stuff underneath on the ground. Although it was rough as anything, you would make your own little area and that would be home.

Some blokes would even craft bamboo to make chairs and things. Any spare gear, like an old ammo box, would also be put to good use. I used one to keep my goodies in, as it helped to keep the animals and insects out. An old target nailed to four bits of wood served as a table top.

I got nicknamed Baldrick by one of my mates because I am a right scruffy git in the jungle. You have to be. No washing. One set of kit that you wear from day one. By the end of the trip you all stink to high heaven.

Once a week we would have what they called 'fresh day'. We would make our way to a particular RV and be given an egg and a couple of slices of bacon, a steak and some potatoes. The rest of the time we had to live off compo, which, no matter how much curry powder you put into it, is still compo. Anybody didn't want any food, or didn't want to carry it, I'd take it. I used to eat twice as much as anybody else. I think I must be the only guy in the regiment who would put on weight in the jungle. It really gets to you, not eating anything else, and you're bunged up to the eyeballs.

Patience is one of the things you need in the regiment and nowhere more than in the jungle. You can sometimes walk all day and only cover a single kilometre, maybe less, depending on what you are up against. If you are lucky, you find your way to a ridge line where you can cover much more ground in a shorter time.

A typical jungle trip would be two weeks' acclimatization and jungle skills, two weeks of more specialized battle, navigation and survival skills and then, in the last two weeks, a full exercise. Normally the squadron would be divided into two groups, one half against the other. You patrol against each other and attack each other's camp.

By the end you are really fit. You have burned off all your fat. Physically moving through the jungle is harder work than anything else. Another problem was that maps had been produced in 1944, and the detail was all wrong. There were rivers marked that no longer existed, and we would come across rivers, some quite large, that weren't even marked. One time I was leading the patrol, following a path on the map. The undergrowth was very thick. I pushed my way through. I stepped through this bush – *whoosh*, 30 feet straight down! The bloody cliff wasn't marked on the map. I was lying at the bottom in a heap when these two faces appeared up above me, Big Bill and Old Stew Fisheye. They were chuckling as usual, good old sick army humour.

•

R. F. My first jungle was Belize, for Continuation Training, and it is generally considered dirty, stinking training. It was a difficult time, difficult jungle.

Before we got there we had heard that an Irish Ranger had been eaten by a large snake. That put us on our toes, to say the least. The Irish Ranger was never found, though his belt kit, etc., was. Nobody knows whether the story is true or not. The extraordinary thing is the way the jungle affects different people.

The lads on my course, for example. One in particular screamed in his sleep for reasons unknown to us. Another kept imagining large green creatures in front of him. Even stranger, one man wanted to leave litter all over the place. They were all RTUd at some point during that trip.

Like everyone else, I was bitten by insects and still bear the scars. Never mind mosquitoes: there are others far worse. One in particular probably bit me in my sleep and laid its eggs in my neck. One morning Bernie, one of the instructors, said to me on parade, 'What's that on your neck?' I couldn't feel anything. He said, 'It's a white lump with two black things like eyes.'

Bernie, who was a qualified medic, cut open the lump in my neck with a scalpel and cleaned out the wound. He then gave me an intramuscular injection of penicillin to stop secondary infection. Because we were about to embark on the final exercise, I had to soldier on.

That was bad enough.

But then Taff S. was in front of me in our four-man patrol when we had a break and sat down on a bank, Bergens, belt kit and weapons still at hand. We got up to move on, and all I can think is that Taff must have covered a hornets' nest. As soon as he stood up, I could hear the hum and saw these things coming straight for me. I dived into the river. I was bitten twice on the face and a couple of times on the neck. As I fell down the river bank I had my watch torn off somewhere. I emerged to see a patrol of giggling soldiers. I was apparently in a right state. I was already dosed up with penicillin: now it was time for anti-histamines for the hornet stings. I can't recall the rest of the exercise because I was as high as a kite. But George F. did go back into the river and actually found my watch.

Despite all that, I made it through. A lot of the lads didn't. The way I see jungle duty, you have twelve hours of sleep and twelve hours of work, because once it is dark you can't move, but you do have to be patient and disciplined. The way to move in the jungle is slow and methodical. I sensed the lads who might fail. They would get caught up on the 'wait a while' plants, the ones that are like vines with sharp spikes that dig into clothing or skin. Once you get aggressive and angry, and start pulling, they dig deeper and deeper. Hence the name 'wait a while'. You can end up getting ripped to shreds. If you take it easy, take the time to untangle them, you are okay. The jungle is like that.

If you failed any part of the jungle training, you would be sent back to the UK as soon as possible. The training staff didn't want failures around, depressing others. Sometimes it was surprising to see who made it. Some lads who had done well in other areas of Selection, very big and strong, would suddenly flip and could not cope in the jungle. Others would come into their own and really seem at home in that new environment.

In Indonesia, at 6,000 feet, the jungle is known as 'moon country'. The snakes there don't move even if frightened. It's too cold. I used to go with the local snake man and collect bags of snakes in no time at all. I was called *orang ular* – 'snake man' in Malay. We would then get the whole squadron together and show them all the different types to be found. Some of these snakes were seriously poisonous.

In Botswana too we would go out and collect bags of snakes. Again the whole squadron would be taken outside in whatever they stood up in. The idea was to get the lads used to snakes and try to override the natural instinct of running from them. Keep still is the answer.

All the snakes were let go at once, and they went where they wanted. There was no movement apart from the snakes. Once one or two of the lads made it on to the top of a water bowser. That was the first mistake. A spitting cobra went for the bowser and stayed there. The local snake man tried everything to get it out. It was a really nasty piece of work. He did eventually get it out, ripping the skin from the snake in the process. It started spitting in our direction, although, so I was told, for humans the spit is dangerous only to the eyes. We had no anti-venom kits with us. If someone was bitten, you had to catch the snake for ID purposes and then get a medevac to a hospital as soon as possible.

•

Johnny Two-Combs Everyone refers to the jungle as the 'Green Hell' but I enjoyed it. We all knew that the jungle selection of four weeks is perhaps the hardest phase of Selection and, in my case, took place in Brunei.

I flew across and spent the first night in a transit camp, and next day I was helicoptered into the middle of the jungle. The first thing that gets you is the intense heat. You are immediately exhausted.

We had six teams, all commanded by ruperts, which takes a lot of pressure off you, removing the need for command skills. You only need soldiering skills to pass the unit. I was a sergeant of the Green Jackets and knew that all I had to do was keep my gob shut, learn all that was put in front of me and just soldier. It was great until one day when my world shattered.

I came back to the debrief area after doing jungle lane-shooting drills. The RSM was there. He told me, 'Your patrol commander has binned it and is now out of it. You are now the patrol commander. Your commander was due to take orders for a live-firing camp attack that was to take place tomorrow morning. You now have to lead it.' The RSM told me to go to the schoolhouse to take orders, which I did forty-five minutes later. It was make or break time.

We had two troops with three patrols in each. This means one person runs the troop in each attack. We had a two-troop attack on an enemy camp, and I had to lead the whole thing – extract the relevant bits from the orders and plan the attack. I made a model of the camp and briefed the men in the schoolhouse that night. The next day the attack went off perfectly. It was a great personal success. And I have never felt so relieved.

In the jungle you do a lot of navigation, and we usually use ridge lines, not cross-graining or going only by compass. This means that you have to drop way down to get water, so two of you wait up on the ridge with the Bergens and another two go to get water. In one instance I and Jockie went down to get water, and we reached the stream, by which there was an old stump. Jockie was covering me, and I leaned slightly forward to ease my way down the bank with all the water cans. Just as I was doing so, I felt a sharp pain, like a red-hot poker, in the small of my back, and because you have to be silent I couldn't cry out.

Then I felt another, and another, and another, and finally realized I had disturbed a hornets' nest. So I dropped everything, the bottles and the weapons, and started shouting, 'Jockie! Come and help me!'

He had run halfway back up the hill and shouted back down, 'No fucking way!'

So I simply dived into the water, swam across to the other side and got out. I was in terrible pain. But then it occurred to me that I had left an unattended rifle and all the water bottles on the other side and had been screaming at the top of my lungs. I wondered if the RSMs had heard. There was nothing for it but to find the courage to cross the water again, fill the bottles and collect the gun. I was in so much pain anyway I just gritted my teeth and went for it. I filled the bottles up a way down the river, and all the time we were making our way back to the patrol Jock laughed and laughed at all my bumps and stings. I was in agony. The DS had heard the screams, thought it was a snake and came to meet us, and I immediately thought of the trouble I would be in. When they asked if it was a snake and I said, 'Hornets,' they just laughed too.

We had to continue. I was patrol commander, with another two or so hours of the patrol to go. Jockie was behind me and every now and again I could hear a little titter. He told me later that with all the pain he was in with his Bergen and his feet, when he saw the lumps and bumps on the back of my neck and, every now and again, my hand going to them to touch them, he didn't feel so bad about himself. He said all that he saw was like a cartoon, with all those black dots around me and my arms waving around, and all of a sudden I just flew off into the water. He never stops laughing about it. Even now.

The blokes played a trick on me once when we went off to retrieve a cache on a navigation exercise. One of the fellows had dropped his *golok* [jungle knife used by the SAS] and we were told upon return to base that next day we would have to go and retrieve it. However, I had to do a helicopter reconnaissance, so I couldn't go with them, which from all accounts sounds a good thing because apparently it was a nightmare, and they didn't find the *golok*. When they got back that night, they decided to shit in a bag and put it under my A-frame, where I slept, just for a laugh. Next morning I swung my legs over the side and all of a sudden there were millions of little needle pricks up and down my feet and legs. The bag of shit had attracted red ants. All I could see out of the corner of my eye was the other three, laughing and smiling and thinking: We got you!

I just thought, You bastards – but they were going to get it next . . .

•

Pete Scholey I went for medical training before going to the jungle, and it was excellent. We would start with a four-week course at camp. This progressed into various courses at specialist hospitals, doing things like tropical diseases and so on, and then finally we would get an attachment at the casualty department of a large general hospital. Four of us went to St Mary's, Paddington. We did minor operations and helped with the stitching, working alongside the medical students. We also did a dentistry course and learned how to do fillings – everything. I even gave my wife a filling one time, and her dentist was very impressed, apparently.

I subsequently used my medical training many times. And

not just me. Some of our people have had occasion to be midwives.

After I completed the course at St Mary's, it was off to Brunei for jungle training. I was part of the newly formed B Squadron. We were taught by the very best: Malayan veterans who I was completely in awe of. What I didn't learn from them, I learned later from Don (Lofty) Large.

My first day we had an hour's walk into the jungle. It's like being on another planet. You don't know how to make head or tail of it. All the things you have been taught come to you slowly. It all begins to make sense to you once you're there. Even really simple things like always removing the lapels from your shirt to stop them getting caught in the foliage.

Two weeks of patrolling were followed by a five-day march. It was just as hard work as anything we had done on Selection. Once there, we had to cut a heli-pad out of the jungle using our *parangs* [machetes].

You learn the principles of survival. Assuming you get cut off from the rest of your patrol, your priority is twofold. First, of course, you have to ensure your survival. Secondly, you have to get back to being operational as soon as possible. The survival kit the lads carry now was developed over the years. It is designed to ensure that you can escape the enemy and success-fully make your way back to your own side without relying on anyone else, assuming that you are unable to get to an emergency RV where stores are usually hidden.

My survival kit was all fixed on to my belt. A *parang* plus a Swiss army knife. A poncho – you want to get out of the rain and under cover. An everlasting match. A magnifying glass: it starts fires very easily (and was excellent in Aden for burning a tiny hole in an officer's neck at 20 yards). A small saw. A whistle. A signal mirror and a waterproof printed list of the emergency signals codes. An Oxo cube and some salt. Sugar. Pencil torch. A sleeping-bag. Tin opener-cum-spoon. A wire snare. A little bit of para cord. Fishing hooks. A candle. Needle and thread. Razor blade. A mess tin. A printed list of survival-operation procedures and priorities. A suture kit. A bandage. A sling. Sterilizing tablets. Potassium permanganate powder used for lighting, when mixed with sugar, or for sterilizing water. (You know if it's all right to drink if it goes pale pink in colour. Put a bit more in and it's an antiseptic. Make it into a thick paste and you can put that on fungi infections.)

All this was essential, of course, when it came to the real thing in Borneo.

•

Mack At the end of Continuation Training in the jungle, you go to an estate about 11 miles from Hereford for three weeks of combat and survival training, followed by a week of interrogation. This is what I call the old Up Against the Wall syndrome. Shit or bust. Get through this and you've more or less made it.

We had all sorts of lectures about survival and then were sent out on the run, the practical part of escape and evasion training. You are given nothing except some terrible old clothes and a button compass. You are supposed to live off the land but, of course, we were sly: if you were clever, you could sneak out some money with you. Many of us, including me, sewed various things into our shirts and the seams of our clothes. Things like a larger compass than the one they give you, some money, a couple of fishhooks, a small bit of candle, wax-headed matches, a flint wheel off a lighter.

But when you arrive for the actual escape and evasion exercise they strip you bollock-naked. Nasty Neal, one of the instructors, would go over you with a metal detector, check your hair to make sure you hadn't secreted anything and even look in some guys' arses. I had a fiver stuck up my arsehole. He didn't spot it. (It took three whole days before it came out. I was hardly eating, so there was nothing to force it out.) I was given a pair of old boots and laces, no skiddies, a pair of old trousers and part of a greatcoat.

There was one rupert, a right toffee-nose, who turned up at the counter to collect his escape clothes. He was handed his bundle. He looked like a miserable tramp in his old boots and jacket and coat. Just as he was walking out of the door, one of the instructors called him back. 'That's too good for you.' By the time the instructor had finished with him, he had one trouser leg cut off at the groin, the other at the knee, a jacket with just one sleeve and big hole cut in the back of his greatcoat.

Outside we were being given our brief when one of the instructors appeared holding a boot. Without hesitation he launched it over the roof of the nearby cookhouse. The stupid rupert had left his boots inside. So he had to do the whole week with just one boot. I remember us all sitting in the back of the truck as we headed of. He tore off the other sleeve of what remained of his coat and tied it around his bare foot. He was in a shit state when he finished, but to give him his due he did pass.

We were dropped somewhere in the Black Mountains. I still don't know where to this day. It was dark. We were challenged while walking up a firebreak in the woods on the first night by the hunter force who were out looking for us. We took off and managed to escape. On the third day of the exercise my partner Bob and I had met up with another pair. We were sitting on the edge of this wood absolutely soaking wet. I remember suddenly saying, 'Ah, boys, I can feel a shit coming on.' I went and had my shit and the money appeared. I was so pleased. I washed it in a puddle.

But, of course, you know you're going to get caught. It's part of the deal. You start off being dropped in a corridor 40 to 50 kilometres wide and it narrows to half a kilometre. If you go over the line – across the border, so to speak – you're out of bounds and you've failed. If they catch you before the end of the week, they hold you prisoner for about seven or eight hours and then put you back into the exercise. If you get caught two or three times, you fail. I know of only one guy who never got caught. He was a Dutch marine, and he went missing for two weeks. He was spotted in Hereford. He was nicking milk off doorsteps. There was a notice in the papers about him, but he wouldn't come in. As far as I'm concerned, he did well. They eventually gave him a pass, but he still had to do interrogation.

Beforehand we had had lots of lectures from various experts, including psychologists, who taught us interrogation techniques used by us and the enemy. We had lectures by a guy who had been held prisoner by the Viet Cong and another by someone from the regiment who had been a prisoner in Korea.

Once captured, you are deprived of sleep and also subjected to sensory deprivation. You are blindfolded and disorientated from the moment of capture. They also subject you to stress pain. For example, they make you stand spreadeagled against a wall, holding yourself up with your fingertips. It tends to hurt after a few hours. And then they make you kneel with your legs crossed and your hands on your head. After several hours it really aches. It is not acute pain. It is like cramp that never stops.

While I was there I was interrogated five times. I found that I could get by. I kept track of time because I knew that I only had to survive about one and a half days. I reckoned they interrogated me about every six hours, so each time I kept the mental clock ticking and said to myself, 'OK, that's only another twenty-four to go,' or whatever it was. And also thinking, When I get out of here I am going for a beer and to get something to eat. I was bloody starving. We were given a little water but nothing else. Quite a few blokes keeled over and fainted. They'd be carted off to see the doctor and then put back into the system.

Two guards come and escort you to the interrogation cell. They walk you this way and that in order to disorient you and also to make you think you are being taken to different parts of the building. I maintain that I was actually always taken to the same room. There were certain sounds that I recognized that were very distinctive. Of course, in a real-life situation you are always trying to work out the layout of where you are being held so that you can plan a mental map for your escape.

In the interrogation room you are stripped off. There are two questioners. The old Mutt and Jeff routine. You know, the good guy and the bad guy. One is gentle and persuasive and supportive, while the other is bawling and shouting and swearing at you and using fear tactics to get you to talk. All in all I think I was interrogated by four different guys. It was quite confusing because Mutt and Jeff swapped roles sometimes. And some people crack right enough. The nice guy will ask about the bloke's mum or his sister and off he'll go chatting and fail because you can only respond with name, rank, number and date of birth.

The interrogators were all provided by the military security department [Joint Services Interrogation Wing]. Basically they were all green slime. I mean, anybody who wants that job has got to be sick, right? Deskbound warriors. But I suppose someone has got to do it. Of course, a lot of fear, maybe all fear, is in the mind. I mean, not the kind of physical fear you get when you are being physically attacked but rather the kind of fear that cracks you up under stress.

And all the time you are being put under physical stress as well. It's more of the same, really: what sorts out the guys who make it through Selection from those who don't is a combination of physical and mental strength. The regiment does not want super-strong robots. It wants people who can work off their own merits and use their intelligence as well. Anybody fit and strong can run over a couple of hills to reach a destination. But what the regiment wants is people who can get to the other end, sit down, get out a map and work out a plan of action that is going to succeed.

Also, getting there is one thing, but getting back is quite another. That was a problem that caused a lot of blokes to fail. Nasty Neal, a senior instructor, was a specialist at throwing in a little surprise to catch you out. One time we had just finished a long walk in the Forest of Dean. There was a bank of shale nearby about 20 feet high. So Nasty Neal had everyone going up the shale bank, which is hard. Nice man. We had to keep doing this, for about forty minutes, until the last blokes had got in and we were ready to get on the truck.

I had only been a couple of times when I said to myself, 'He doesn't know who's here and who's not,' so I took my Bergen off at the top and slipped into the trees to have a break and a fag. I'd only been sitting there a few minutes when I got caught. Bergen back on. Press-ups followed.

However, I have to say that no matter how much people tell you about interrogation and torture and so on, you can never really tell how you are going to react. The drills they put you through are a good test, but I guess they can never actually fully indicate how you will react when it comes to the real thing.

•

Johnny Two-Combs Out of about 200 starters we were left with ten people. We moved straight on to combat survival in the freezing cold, at times −14 degrees. It was so cold that occasionally we got frostnip, but there was no time for recovery because straight after that you went on to the next phase, which was CQB work and CQB shooting. Range work and shooting.

We would sit in lectures or stand on the range with our feet throbbing. The blood coursing through them was seriously painful – so much so that at night we would elevate our feet in bed with books and boxes.

Once, on survival training, when we approached a checkpoint we were ambushed by the hunter force, Parachute Regiment, which had been chasing us. We immediately headed off, but one fellow was captured. I legged off and got quite a way away because at this stage it is every man for himself in these things. You have a predesignated RV point to meet up at later, but initially you just get out of there.

It was pitch-black night, and I was being chased. I slowed down to let this guy catch up with me, then stopped and, as I did so, brought my elbow and arm back and dropped the guy like a stone. I thought that would buy me some time, and I ran off as fast as I could. There was a fast-flowing stream by the side of the road, and I went down the bank. It was quite steep and I ran and then jumped into the water to get to the other side. I could see the lights of the searchers and hear the dogs, and I thought to myself, I have to get out of here.

I saw a barn but decided the searchers would look there for certain. There was a copse not far off, so I headed there and lay watching the path I had come by. I was freezing, soaked to the bone, shivering. Then I saw a lot of lights and cars. In tailing me, they had gone past the barn, but inside the barn was Jock's patrol, hiding. They took them in and questioned them, and it was only afterwards, when I was telling Jock about it, that he told me I had effectively led them straight to him, which made me smile. The rest of the night, I figured, I wouldn't have any more trouble, and in the morning I reached the designated point. No one else was there.

I went to another, and another, but I only linked up with someone a couple of days later, at the final checkpoint.

I was never so proud as when I was badged.

It takes such a great deal to get to that point, when you parade in front of the colonel and he congratulates you and tells you that you have achieved what thousands have tried and failed to achieve. And what thousands dream of. Then he gives you your beret. I just couldn't wait to hide away in my room and put it on.

Such a fine achievement that you feel like shouting out to the world, 'Look what I have done!' But you don't because now you play by the rules and you have to be very secretive about it all. About what you do. Even keeping it secret from my mother and father and brothers and sisters. But then to see their pride when I told them – that was great.

•

Mack After a bit of parachute training at Brize Norton, it was time to be assigned to one of the four squadrons. I went to Mobility, and whatever we did we always had a laugh and took things to the extreme. One time we were motorbike training in Canada. The bikes were these special all-terrain models that had been specially adapted. On the first day a very serious Canadian appeared wearing a crash helmet with 'INSTRUCTOR' printed in large letters on the front. Of course, as soon as we got our hands on that we changed it to read 'HEAD STUDENT', and he had a total sense of humour failure, which was a pity because I don't think he had ever had any dealings with the regiment before.

We were all lined up on our bikes at the bottom of a hill with a gentle slope. Very carefully and slowly he made his way up to the top of the hill on his bike. When he got to the top he intoned, really patronizingly, 'Now, students, try and make your way up to the top where I am.'

I had already spotted an almost sheer cliff of rock about 50 yards off to the left-hand side. I caught a couple of the lads' eyes, which were twinkling, and with a couple of nods and knowing looks we moved off at some speed away from the instructor at the top of the little hill. We built up more and more speed as we arched in a great circle and then came full tilt at the rock face. Everyone made it to the top, just. It was pure aggression and energy. The instructor was ashen faced. The bikes had taken a bit of a bashing as well, but he got the message.

A few days later one of the ruperts was sick and missed the river-crossing lesson. When you cross a river on a bike, you use a low gear, high revs and slow speed. Well, of course, the chance of another wind-up was too good to miss. A couple of days afterwards the rupert asked some of us about river crossing. We took him to a river, and one of the lads says to him, 'Right, sir, the secret is speed. You know, it's like skimming a pebble. The faster the better.' The rupert must have hit the water at 60 mph. He took off through the air and was catapulted on to the opposite bank. It was hilarious.

But that was small beer compared to what we got up to on specialist courses. Some of these operational tasks are still too sensitive and secret to talk about, but we do regular exercises in conjunction with our colleagues in Military Intelligence and the Home Office.

This is the real James Bond stuff. For example, we would be given a scenario set in Europe, often in the Eastern Bloc. The operation would consist of covert entry with a view to snatching or killing somebody. It really was the full business: false passports, fake names, disguises, everything.

On one occasion we had to rescue an imaginary European royal family. The scenario was that their country had been overthrown. The skills we developed on these exercises, like covert insertion, are applicable in many different scenarios, including full war. In order to make the exercise realistic, on the first day we would go into isolation in the camp. We would be kept in what they call the war room. It was here that the operation would be planned. Just like in a real situation, we would start off with just a trickle of information. Over the next few hours and days we would be given more and more information and therefore had to update our plan constantly. We would eventually come up with a final plan and submit it to the hierarchy for approval. Once approval was given, we could basically get whatever we asked for, within reason – helicopters, agents waiting for us on the ground with equipment of our choice, vehicles of every description you can imagine. The exercise would be run very realistically. No one apart from the group directly involved in the exercise would know what was happening.

Sometimes we were used to test the defences of military establishments. I remember one RAF base near St Andrew's that we were briefed to destroy with a full squadron attack. Four of us went ahead to do a week's recce. We went up by train, got ourselves some digs and, using a couple of hire cars, gathered information about the layout of the base and its defences through careful observation. All this information was passed back to Hereford.

On the day of the attack we located a suitable landing site, and the rest of the squadron arrived in two Chinooks. We had hired three large furniture-removal vans, and the squadron, armed to the teeth, together with eight motorbikes, piled into the lorries. The RAF base knew it was going to be attacked but didn't know exactly how, when or who by.

I was driving one of the lorries. I calmly drove up to, and then straight through, the main barrier, which was chained and padlocked. A large group of people were resting in the garden. Flashbangs and some gas soon sorted them out. We handcuffed a guy to what remained of the main gate, using his own cuffs. At the same time one of the other lorries had drawn up alongside the fence at the far side of the base. Two of the lads jumped off with chainsaws and cut a neat slice through the fence. The bikes rolled straight off the back of the lorry, roared into life, charged through the gap in the fence and dispersed at high speed. Those poor bastards didn't know what had hit them.

I was running around firing a Schermuly [a flare gun] from the hip. These are normally used to light up an operation. I mean, you're not supposed to fire these things at people, but the RAF blokes were shooting at me, so I had to return fire. They were a little bit upset because a flare will take your head off, but it's all good fun.

Within five minutes we had placed all our dummy charges on the various target buildings and were off. We piled back into the lorries and took off down the road at some speed. Unbeknown to us, the local CID had been keeping an eye on the exercise. As we were driving away, Big Joe, who was driving, turned to me and Nasty Neal and said, 'We're being followed. It's trying to get past. He's flashing his headlights too.'

Without hesitation, because you do everything like it's for real in these exercises, Joe swung our lorry so that it knocked the chasing car. Despite the knocks it managed to get in front of us. It stopped dead in front of us and we had to break hard. We hit it as we came to a halt, but Joe was out of the cab and dragging the driver out in just seconds. He hit him a couple of times. The bloke tried to get something out of the inside of his jacket, so Joe hit him a couple more times for good measure. Eventually the bloke managed to get his warrant card out. All he had wanted to do was tell us the exercise was over and to ask us not to speed. Poor bloke had lumps and bumps all over him. We explained we were on a tight schedule and had to get the squadron back to the helicopters. He was good as gold and never complained about what had happened.

We often used to do exercises in Germany. Mostly we would be part of a larger operation, involving US and British troops, in our classic role as behind-the-lines information gatherers, and we also did demolition and sabotage jobs on bridges and so on.

Once six of us did a special exercise within an exercise. We were to operate from several safe houses provided by the US. We were in civvies and given unmarked cars. A US Army colonel had volunteered to be 'lifted' by us. He knew that we were coming to get him, but no one else on his staff knew. He did not know when or how we were going to make the snatch.

Meanwhile, unbeknown to us – we discovered this later – someone in US Intelligence gave our car registration numbers to German Intelligence, warning them that we were members of the Baader-Meinhof terrorist group. This was part of the exercise that we had no knowledge of. It was extremely serious because German Intelligence did not know that this was an exercise. They genuinely thought we were terrorists and began looking for us in earnest.

Minky had a very lucky escape. On the third night into the exercise he went out to get us some supplies. He noticed, of course, that he was being followed. He immediately put his foot down, and for the next three hours he was chased at high speed by German Intelligence officers. He eventually managed to lose them and ditch the car. If they had caught up with him, he would have been shot, no questions asked. Only the previous day German Intelligence officers had blown away three Baader-Meinhof terrorists who were standing in and around a public telephone box.

We carried out typical covert operational procedures, noting the distance and identifying the routes that our American colonel took to and from work. There was one long, straight stretch of road that he always travelled along, and we realized that this was the place to make the 'lift'. We cleared the operation with the major, and he liked the plan so much he came out on the ground with us.

We borrowed several road-work-in-progress signs and some diversion signs too. One of the lads could speak German. So in the early morning of the day of the snatch, while we were pretending to be doing road works, the German speaker dealt with enquiries from passing motorists and even the local police.

We had a couple of cars in place about a mile up the road. Their job was to trigger the colonel. At about 8 a.m. his car appeared. Our target had decided to drive that morning. His sergeant was in the passenger seat beside him. The target clocked one of our cars behind him, and he put his foot down. As he reached about 90 mph, he came over a rise in the road. On the other side was where we had laid our ambush. Right across the road were two telegraph poles we had chopped. He slammed on his brakes but he still crashed into the poles and pushed them down the road.

I jumped out from the bushes, dressed in civvies and a black balaclava, together with the other guys, all brandishing blank-loaded weapons, thunder-flashes, gas and so on. I was carrying a sledge hammer. As I took a swing for the wind-screen, our chasing car screamed over the rise in the road and rammed into the back of the staff car. It completely stove in both cars.

At that moment I swung the sledge hammer and it ended up going through the passenger window. That gave a bit more than I expected and I nearly took the guy's head off. Someone else chucked in CR gas, the stuff that really nips – we had just got it then, so we thought we'd try it out – and all hell broke loose. The sergeant thought the attack was real, of course, and he flipped. He was rolling around on the ground screaming, 'My eyes! My eyes! I can't see! I can't see!', moaning and carrying on, plus he had had a bit of a knock on the side of the head. (He later received a medical discharge from the Army.) We left him there, rolling about in the middle of the road.

We had a bit of a fight with the target. To give him his due, he put up a good fight. He wasn't coming out without a struggle even though he knew it was an exercise. We cuffed him, blindfolded him, threw him in the back of our escape car, with its smashed-in front, and made our getaway. Meanwhile some of the other guys were clearing the road.

We drove for three hours at over 100 miles an hour. We used back roads to avoid police blocks. He was trussed up on the back seat like a chicken, whinging and whining the whole way. Of course, two of us were sitting on him. We eventually reached our rendezvous, where we were met by our boss. He took one look at the poor man, whose hands were blue by now, and said, 'I think the colonel has probably had enough of this exercise.'

The look of relief on the man's face was a sight. He was a bit knackered but the exercise was a complete success.

•

Johnny Two-Combs About six years after I passed Selection, our training was unexpectedly useful in a civilian situation.

It was in January 1989, early evening, and eight of us from Boat Troop were heading up the M1 in an Army Bedford towards Ripon to do a canoe-instructor's course. I was in a bad way because my girlfriend Karen had called off our engagement. It was the old story of the Army. A year's tour of Northern Ireland had turned into fifteen months, and she couldn't take the separation – fifteen months across the water and back to a bleak Christmas alone.

I was in the back when suddenly there was a sharp jolt and the sound of brakes screaming, with the truck skidding all over the road before coming to a halt. All the traffic had stopped.

We asked the fellows in the front what they could see, but all they could tell us was that something was going on up ahead. A few minutes later we heard a siren in the distance, so a couple of us got out of the truck to have a look. There were so many cars slewed across the road that even the hard shoulder was partly blocked. As a police car appeared alongside us we waved it down and asked what was going on. The very worried-looking driver said, 'There's been a report of a plane crash on the road up ahead, close by, perhaps as close as only about 300 metres in front of our position.'

Without hesitation our troop sergeant, Stu, in the front, without explaining that we were SAS, jumped down from the cab and said, 'We are experienced military paramedics. Do you require us to help?' Four of us were regimentally qualified paramedics.

The policeman looked both surprised and relieved. 'Yes, please. Follow us. We'll give you an escort.'

So without further ado, and not really knowing what we were heading for, we all jumped back in the lorry and, with sirens blaring, the police car led us through the traffic chaos to the scene of the accident. We followed the police car up the hard shoulder to the site of the crash and drew up at a scene of total mayhem. We had all been expecting a light-aircraft crash or something of the sort, so when we saw the size of the plane we were staggered. It was a Boeing. The sheer scale of the disaster in front of us was totally unbelievable.

All around the road cars and lorries were stationed at strange angles. Crowds of people were standing in various states of shock with looks of complete incomprehension. The passenger liner had crashed into the bank right next to the road. The plane had broken into three bits, and as I ran up the bank towards the side of the plane people were starting to emerge.

The first woman I met came through the rubble and mess cradling an arm which was obviously broken, and despite her pale, shocked face, she was smiling, saying, 'I'm alive! I'm alive!'

I headed over to the nose section, which was embedded in some trees, and when I got there first there was a woman, lying down outside the cabin. I don't know whether she had been thrown free or if she had crawled free, but aside, lying there in a daze, she seemed all right. Right next to her, in the fuselage, I saw this foot, just hanging there, obviously broken and needing support, so I took her scarf and tied it around the limb and asked her if she was well enough to support the leg.

While I was doing that, the first fire-fighters, ambulance crews and airport emergency services were arriving on the scene, having been warned in advance that a plane was coming in to crash-land. I was dressed in a blue jacket, and a fireman asked if I was a doctor. I told him I was a paramedic, and he showed me a gap so I could get inside the smashed hull.

I was the first man into that front section, followed by another SAS medic called Elvis, who came up just behind me. I took one look around the inside, exchanged glances with him as if to say, 'Jesus Christ, this is bad,' and then the adrenaline clicked in. I took a deep breath and said to him, 'Let's get to work.'

What was immediately visible was a mangled body that looked as though it had been chopped in half by a cheese grater and squashed into the floor. I could see ribs and parts of body. We couldn't even tell if it was a man or woman. Next to it was a fat woman who had been quite literally chopped in two. Her torso was to one side and her hips and legs were to another. She was in the way, so we had to move her to one side. We tried as best we could to cover her body with an airline blanket.

The seats, with everyone strapped in, had concertinaed, one row of three seats on top of the row in front, and another on top of that. Everyone I could see was still. One by one we looked for vital signs. Nothing. No moans. No breathing. No pulse. Every one of them was dead. There was an eerie silence inside. It was a terrible feeling.

We started to fling away the debris and try to find people who were alive and to get them off the aircraft. One of the firemen said that there was a severe danger of fire, but we didn't really have time to think about the consequences of that. After more searching we found some less seriously injured casualties. A chain had formed outside the craft, and we passed them out and over to people who passed them back down the hill. Elvis and I were joined pretty quickly by our troop sergeant Stu and Ken, another qualified medic.

Checking for live people and cutting away the wreckage to get them free took a long time, but quite early on Elvis trod on something, and we heard a noise.

A teenager was buried under an older man's body. The older man was clearly dead, but the boy's head had become embedded in the fuselage, with his body outside under the dead weight of the older man, who had become wedged between the seats. He was in a great deal of pain, and it was very difficult to get to him. We tried to stop his blood loss but parts of his body were inaccessible because of all the other wreckage as well as the body. I asked Ken to keep an eye on the fellow. I didn't know it was going to take so long. For the next four or five hours we were in there. We kept talking to him to let him know we hadn't forgotten him, but he was just too difficult to get to while there were other people around him who were accessible. One by one they were cut free and removed.

At one stage, a young woman appeared near me, wearing a

black cocktail dress. She looked down at the 'grated' remains of several people. It turned out that she was a medic, but it was obvious that the shock of the carnage was immense, and only when we had covered them and helped her get past did she come round. After that she was excellent. In particular, she really helped one young girl who had her lower leg all mangled. At the same time I was trying to get to the boy who had his head stuck in the fuselage.

A doctor in white appeared. This man, older and rather portly, was having difficulty dealing with the horror as well. I couldn't get to the boy because the dead man on top of him was jammed between the seats. The only expedient I could think of was to cut off the foot of the dead man and manoeuvre him out that way. So I said to this doctor, 'I'm going to have to cut this man's foot off in order to make some room. I need some cutting equipment. Can you organize that for me, please?'

He shouted out to someone, 'We need a traumatic amputation kit up here now. A traumatic amputation kit!'

The girl with the badly mangled limb started screaming and saying, 'No, don't cut off my leg! Don't do it!' and I shouted over to her, 'No, it's okay. It's not you, it's somebody else,' to reassure her.

The rest of us got on as best we could. The amputation equipment arrived and the portly man removed the dead man's foot, but he was obviously suffering, and I spoke to one of his colleagues, explained the situation and said, 'This man should leave the hull.' He did as he was asked.

Then we went back inside to work on the others. The worst of all was the children. I am a father and, at the time, had a young daughter. In the back of the wreck I saw a young blonde girl who had been pushed into the back of the seat in front, and I recall checking her, trying to see her face. She had no face because it was smashed into the back of the chair. This was really hard because she was the same age as my daughter.

Throughout the whole thing we could hear a baby crying. Eventually we found it on the lap of a dead woman, and we passed it back and outside, and everyone cheered.

We continued to do what we could to get everyone out, including the pilot, who was seriously injured and had to be winched out. Percy, one of our lads, used his climbing gear to scale up the tail and help pull people out. In the news footage of the incident you can see him up there, clearly visible to the left of the motorway. It even shows our truck. The others from the truck were all in different parts of the plane, getting people out, but most of the dead were in the front, where the plane had gone into the hill.

Once we knew that the living casualties had all been extricated and it was clear the numerous emergency services could handle the situation, we helped lay some of the dead out at the top of the hill and then decided to leave. One of the last things we did as a group was to carry the young fellow we had spent so long trying to rescue up the hill to lay him out.

That was quite hard.

We trooped down the hill, keeping away from the news crews, and spoke to the police who had given us an escort to the nearest exit. The first thing we did was to stop at a service station for a cup of tea. Driving away, no one in the back of the Bedford said a word. Total silence. We didn't even look at each other.

As we went into the service station to get our tea, and to pay, the woman at the cash register just gaped at us. It was then I looked at Elvis and at the others, and saw the blood and gore which covered us head to foot: we looked pretty dazed. We rushed off to the bathroom to clean up, and afterwards I was struck by how calm and composed we had been throughout the whole incident. It was amazing, really, that we were all so disciplined and methodical about it despite the horror. We had to ignore that and just get on with the task at hand.

We got back into the Bedford and arrived at Ripon in the early hours of the morning. At 8.15 a.m. we were in the canoes doing our training and still none of us had bothered to talk about it. It occurred to me that we shouldn't be doing this, that I needed the morning off. Later that day Shaw Taylor appeared on the *Police Five* television programme and made an appeal for the military personnel involved in the rescue of passengers from the crashed plane to make themselves known to the police authorities.

That morning Stu phoned the adjutant at Hereford to inform him of what we had done the night before. I have always thought that it would have been good PR for the regiment to have released the fact that we had assisted at the plane crash because we were getting such a bad press at the time about the Gibraltar terrorist shootings and it might have shown the regiment in a different light. But, as usual, the regiment decided to keep silent.

Six months later I was giving a personal-protection demonstration to an MP and was introduced as one of the chaps who assisted at the M1 plane crash. The MP turned to me and said, 'Oh, yes! We heard about that. That was excellent. I heard you chaps were the ones who more or less coordinated the operation from inside. Why were you so composed?'

I explained that the team we had all knew each other, and that the training we do is for an emergency, and that in executing your task nothing shocks you, and that you are trained to act without any emotion.

That is the whole point of Selection.

3
BORNEO

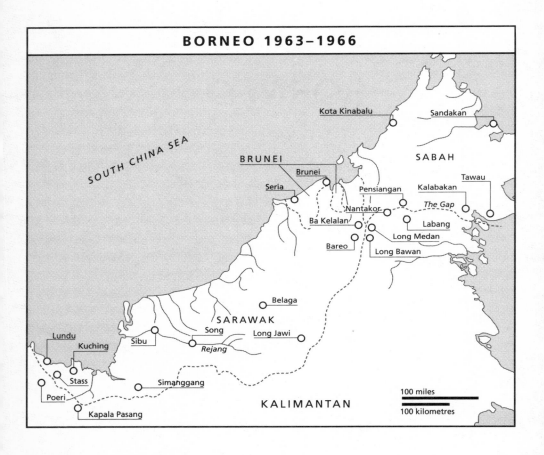

BORNEO 1963–1966

SOUTH CHINA SEA

Kota Kinabalu

Sandakan

SABAH

BRUNEI

Brunei

Seria

Pensiangan

Kalabakan

Tawau

Nantakor

The Gap

Ba Kelalan

Labang

Bareo

Long Medan

Long Bawan

Belaga

SARAWAK

Song

Long Jawi

Lundu

Kuching

Sibu

Rejang

Stass

Simanggang

Poeri

KALIMANTAN

Kapala Pasang

100 miles

100 kilometres

Death doesn't worry me in the slightest ... As far as I'm concerned, I should have died on 28 February 1965.

Jock Thompson

Three years after the Malayan Emergency, in 1963, the SAS turned its attention to the island of Borneo. At that time Britain had two colonies on the island, Sarawak and Sabah, and gave protection to the Sultanate of Brunei. Malaya, the former British colony, was lobbying hard for the formation of a new political entity in the region, to comprise Sabah, Sarawak, Brunei, Malaya and Singapore. It was to be titled the Federation of Malaysia, and it was fully supported by the British.

However, President Sukarno of Indonesia was opposed to the proposal, as it threatened his own territorial ambitions in the region. So too was the predominantly Chinese guerrilla group, the Clandestine Communist Organization (CCO). Largely based in the Sarawak region, it had cells in many of the towns. Sukarno supplied it with weapons and allowed its members to train in Indonesian Kalimantan on Borneo, after which they infiltrated into Sabah and Sarawak.

On 8 December 1962 a revolt erupted in Brunei engineered by a young sheikh named Azahari. The rebels attacked police stations, government offices and a power station. A force of Gurkhas, Royal Marines and the Queen's Own Highlanders was despatched from Singapore and crushed the revolt, which was a purely local affair, with ease. However, many of the rebels fled into the jungle and joined the CCO. In January 1963 A Squadron, 22 SAS, arrived in Brunei, prior to their campaign in Sabah and Sarawak.

Their task was to patrol a 700-mile jungle border between the British dependencies and Indonesian territory. Another 'hearts-and-minds' campaign was initiated to win over the local tribesmen and, as with Malaya, the SAS fought an undeclared war. No ID discs were taken on patrol. Where Malaya had been an Emergency, Borneo was a 'Confrontation' – a confrontation during which Jock Thompson was Mentioned in Despatches, or as he prefers to call it, Mentioned in Disgust.

•

Jock Thompson When the Brunei rebellion started, the other squadron, A, were sent out. We relieved them and I found myself straight into the jungle without even doing a jungle course. I didn't find it difficult because I've always been a countryman and I settled in straight away. My other three patrol members were Malayan veterans, so I watched what they did and learned as I went along. It was a non-shooting war at this time.

The first action that we came up against was the Tentara Nasional Kalimanatan Utara (TNKU: Freedom Fighters of North Borneo). They were a bandit group, like terrorists. They used to come over the border and started things off by shooting a couple of tribal chiefs. They stayed well clear of British forces. When we began actually fighting them, the SAS's role was intelligence gathering. As Major-General Walker put it, 'The SAS are my eyes and ears. I rely on them.'

It bloody worked. We were very good at our job. We would enter the jungle, identify an enemy position, pull back 5,000 yards, get on the radio – it was all Morse then – to whoever was our step-up (our word for 'back-up'), usually the Gurkhas, or the Queen's Own Highlanders or the Leicesters. When the platoon or company was ready, we would lead them in and let them go to it. So once a week we would provide the Gurkhas with an opportunity to give the enemy a bloody nose. We would have meanwhile vanished again.

We had plenty to do because one squadron of SAS covered the full length of the border between Indonesian territory and our own. If you were lucky, you had a four-man patrol, but once just two of us had to go in for three months. The four-man patrol was ideal: the patrol commander, the linguist, the signaller and the medic, although, of course, we were all inter-trained. I was the linguist in our patrol – I speak very good Malay. Once we'd got rid of the TNKU we then had to deal with the Indonesian regular army and their special forces, like the Resemen Para Kommando Angaton Darat (RPKAD).

The first serious incursion took place in the fifth division of Sarawak. We had just relieved the newly formed B Squadron. As usual on relief, we were briefed on all their latest intelligence. Our squadron commander, Punchy Williams from 1 Para, got eight of us into his office. He said: 'We know for a fact there is a whole company of CCO and RPKAD at this place on the Sugy [river] Sekayan, which is about 5,000 yards over the border. We want you to hit the river and do OPs [observation posts] on it.' (Unlike the British, the Indos had no helicopters, and so they had to supply their forces using the rivers. The Sekayan was over the border, in Indonesian Borneo.)

The briefing finished, we got aboard a Belvedere helicopter and landed at a place called Tebedu, which was about 3,000 yards from the border. We were then given another, even more up-to-date briefing from the intelligence group of the 6th Gurkha Rifles. We stayed with the Gurkhas that night and at first light we set off up the Gunong Rawan, which means 'Melancholy Mountain'. We marched all day, and at about five we stopped as usual and just listened. We didn't unpack. Just listened. About ten to six, just before it got dark, we rolled up in our ponchos. We couldn't do any chopping, so we didn't even put up any sleeping platforms.

There was no smoking either. Smoke is a dead give-away in the jungle, assuming the wind is blowing the right way. I could smell cigarette smoke half a mile away. And curry too. In fact, anything that is not jungle. Toothpaste, soap. Once there, we wouldn't even wash except if there was a chance to jump into a stream, so that you could give yourself a rub-down. We became part of the jungle. That's why we were so successful. In the four years the SAS was in the Borneo jungle, we lost only three men to enemy action and only two were wounded: me and Sergeant Geordie Lillico.

The sun came up at six in the morning, so we would get up at five thirty. Because we were in enemy territory, there was no cooking, so there was no morning tea. Just a drink of water and some biscuits. It took us to the end of the second day to get to the top of the Gunong Rawan, which was the actual border. We didn't stop on the top. We crossed down on to the other side. It was beautiful primary jungle there, just like walking through a beech wood. There were no shrubs, just great big beautiful trees and loads of wildlife. There were *paya* (a small breed of deer), and a big deer similar to the ones we get in Scotland, and wild pig, and stacks of life up in the trees: long-armed gibbons, masses of birds – screeching hornbills and parrots – and hundreds of enormous fluorescent butterflies. Sometimes it was so noisy, it was like standing in a machine house.

That night Geordie Lillico and I decided to do a 2-mile recce. We left the others, took a bearing and headed out for 200 yards. From there we would do a circuit just to see if there were any signs. You do your best to avoid tracks – whether made by humans or animals – but sometimes a swamp or other obstacle would force you to use one. We spent most of our time contouring back and forth over the tracks. I was always lead scout. I liked that position. I like to know what's in front of me. I was the only one of the eight of us to be carrying an Armalite and it was always set on automatic. I had two magazines taped to the weapon and one actually in the rifle. I had six magazines on my belt. So I had 180 rounds in total. If you were carrying an SLR [self-loading rifle], you normally carried two magazines on your belt and one in the rifle plus two belts of fifty rounds in your Bergen, making a total of 150 rounds.

We hit some bamboo and I led us around it so as not to leave any sign. Suddenly we happened upon a clearing about 20 feet square. There were three lean-tos in it, a lean-to being three sticks arranged at an angle with a large tropical leaf rested against them. In the high ground of Borneo you are virtually guaranteed rain every single night and these little lean-tos are surprisingly effective. We watched it for a while then moved in. We found rusting tin cans left behind by the Indonesian army, which confirmed our suspicions, but we could tell by the length of the new growth around the cuttings that it hadn't been used for at least three months. We returned to the other boys and Geordie gave us a briefing.

'First thing in the morning, lads, I want you to split into two four-man patrols. Four of us will go down the watershed in light order [just weapons and belt kits, no Bergens]. We will leave our Bergens with the other four. This point will become our emergency RV.'

The SOP [Standing Operating Procedure] was that in the event of getting bumped and split up, the emergency RV is the place you stayed the night before, and that stays open for twenty-four hours. After that it moves to the place you stayed the previous night, which lasts for the next twenty-four hours and so on.

So the following morning, 28 February 1965, we had our usual drink of water, and some cheese and biscuits, and set off, myself as lead scout, Geordie and two others. We were wearing our belt kits, which had survival rations, escape and evasion kit, water bottle, personal medical kit and ammunition.

We stopped at a clearing and sat there for a good ten minutes, just listening. Nothing apart from the usual jungle sounds. Geordie motioned to me to move on. I stood up and moved forwards. Geordie was about 5 yards behind me. Unbeknown to us, the CCO had heard us moving through the bamboo. It is impossible to move through bamboo silently. Standing on a piece of dead bamboo is like a shot-gun going off. Luckily for us, they only had time to do a head-on contact. They were very close to us when they heard us and had to take an immediate ambush position. They must have frozen where they were the moment they heard us, because when we were listening out for them in the clearing, we heard no sound whatsoever. Had they managed to get into a linear ambush position, from the side, they would have got the lot of us.

As I moved forward through the clearing, all hell broke loose.

Bullets everywhere. Our SOP was to shoot and scoot, so the two guys behind Geordie bugged out. I immediately returned fire. I couldn't see anybody. I just let go a full magazine, twenty rounds side to side in front of me.

The next thing, I felt an almighty kick and I was flying through the air. I didn't know what was happening. I hit the ground on the side of this bloody great rock and propped myself up a bit. A second later a fucking Indo popped up about 6 feet in front of me. He was so close I could see his tiger's-head shoulder flash, and if I'd had a bayonet I would have used it on him. I thought, I've got to get this bastard quick. He was obviously petrified. It could have been because I was covered in blood and yelling fit to bust. His eyes were sticking out of his head and he had a carbine in his hand. I retrieved my Armalite, which had been knocked out of my hands, and turned it on him and gave him a burst. That was him.

Then I realized that I had been hit. There was blood coming into my face in great bursts from my femoral artery, shooting up at me out of a great big hole in my groin. The bullet had gone in through my left crutch and come out through my buttock. I was watching my life pumping out of me. I instantly remembered Lofty Large telling me in training, 'When you're hit, move. You won't feel like it, but if you don't, you'll be hit again.' There were bullets flying everywhere, so I forced myself to move a few yards into some cover. As I crawled, the shattered bones of my femur were grinding against each other. I turned myself round and went on to autopilot. Face veil off. Tie a knot in it. Get the knot right into my crotch, tie it off, commando dagger out, put it underneath the veil and twist it round and stick the end into my trousers. That stopped the bleeding. I put a field dressing on the exit wound, which is easier said than done. And I thought, Fuck me!

I looked around and saw Geordie lying flat on his back, white as a sheet. I thought he was dead. I was busy swearing at those bastards while I put a new magazine on. I shouted as loud as I could, 'Geordie! Geordie!' After a few moments he came to – he

still doesn't remember being unconscious. The first thing he said
was: 'I'm hit.'

'So am I.'

There had only been a total of about ten seconds' firing, but
a lot of bullets can move in ten seconds. The RPD light-machine
gun that hit me can fire 2,700 rounds a minute and it makes
your eyes water when it hits you.

I lay there quietly listening to what was going on. I heard
some orders being given in Indonesian, which is similar to
Malay, and I could make out the odd word like *samati*, which is
'there's one dead'. Well, they meant either me or Geordie. All of
a sudden the bloke who'd shot me came out from behind a tree
and started walking up towards the clearing. I thought to myself,
Right, you bastard. I let him get to about 5 yards from me and I
fucking blew him away.

There was a platoon of them, about twenty men. They opened
fire again. There was such an exchange of fire that branches
from the trees above us were being torn away and falling down
on top of us. They still couldn't see us and we still couldn't see
them. I just kept putting automatic fire into the jungle below
me. I was obviously hitting people because I could hear screams.
And by now Geordie was banging away as well.

At last I was able to drag myself to where he was. I could feel
something stinging in my thigh as I was crawling along. I
thought it was a thorn and I pulled at it. It was a splinter of
bone about 3 inches long. I've still got it somewhere. The bone
in my thigh was sticking out at a horrible angle, protruding from
the flesh, all splintered at the end. As I reached Geordie, I took
a syrette of morphine that was hanging around my neck.
'Geordie, I'm hit through the leg.'

'I don't know where I'm hit.'

There was blood on his chest. 'You've been hit in the chest,
mate.' But on closer inspection I found that the bullet had hit
him near the hip, ricocheted off his pelvis, gone up through his
stomach and come out between his shoulder blades. He was
lucky to be alive.

He said to me, between bursts of fire: 'Do you think you can make the RV?'

'Och aye.'

'OK, make your way up the ridge, see if you can get to the top and I'll RV with you up there.'

'But, how are you going to get up there?'

'Och, I'll be all right. I'll make it.'

'All right, then,' I said and set off.

I crawled on my elbows with a bit of help from one knee, the Armalite in the crook of my elbows. I'd gone about 20 yards when there was another burst of fire from below. By this time I was vertically 20 feet above Geordie's position, so I managed to get up on my arse and started pouring fire above Geordie's head, even though I couldn't see him. The enemy firing stopped almost immediately. There was a long silence, then I moved off again. I got to the top of the ridge and lay there for about two or three hours. Everything was quiet. I thought, They must have got Geordie.

I crawled into a pig hole under a tree. I covered myself and the rifle with shit and mud. I just lay there. Then I heard movement. The next moment a patrol of Indonesians went past. They were so close I could have reached out and touched their ankles. I thought, If they do spot me, I'll take as many of them with me as I can before I go. They didn't see me. I lay motionless, listening all the time. About twenty minutes later they came back. Again they didn't see me. I got out my map and a pen and wrote an intelligence report about the contact, so that if my body was found by our side, I would be of some use. Soon after I passed out.

The next morning the first thing I did was take another syrette of morphine. I released the tourniquet for a couple of seconds to stop gangrene setting in. I said to myself, 'I've got to make a move.' I fired three shots in the air and continued to do so every hour. Then I started crawling through all the shit. My Highland upbringing stood me in good stead as I went up the hill and then cut down again. Then, up ahead, I saw something that was not quite jungle: my and Geordie's Bergens. I had hit the actual

RV smack-on. Instinct. The homing instinct I had developed as a child running and crawling about in the Scottish woods. I opened my Bergen and tried to eat a biscuit and take a drink of water but I simply couldn't. I vomited them straight back up. My system wouldn't accept anything. Despairingly, I thought, Oh for fuck's sake. Sain – the company base – is 7,000 yards away. How the fuck am I going to make it to there?

I started crawling down the slopes of Rawan on to our side of the border. I got over the stream, and that was it. I stopped there. I couldn't go any further. I had run out of steam. I thought, This is it. Endex. Again I tried to drink some water but I couldn't. I kept throwing it up. Mind you, if it had been Famous Grouse whisky, I wouldn't have thrown it up.

Suddenly I saw that I was covered in thousands of maggots. They were all over me, from my knees up to my chest. I rolled into the stream to try to get rid of them. The fish must have had a field day. I just thought to myself, Ah well, here we go. End of the road. I started worrying about my mum because she was getting married again and I was supposed to give her away ...

I realized I was going to die, so I thought I might as well make it quick. I took some more morphine. And then some more. And some more. Normally we carried two syrettes each, but for some reason I had a pocket full of them. In the end I took twelve. It's funny stuff, morphine. You don't feel a thing, like you're floating, but your brain stays alert. I knew what was going on but I just didn't give a fuck. I heard the sound of a chopper but I couldn't see it because the tree canopy was so thick. I got it into my mind that it was Indonesian – although they didn't have any. I emptied a full magazine into the air. I missed. Luckily. It was one of ours, looking for me.

I can remember everything that happened next as if I was there now. I started talking to my father, who died when I was twelve, and then I talked to my grandma. 'There's nae point in asking God to intervene,' I told her. 'He's got Vietnam on his hands and all the rest. I'm just one.' Then I talked to St Andrew. I says, 'Right, St Andrew, get off your fucking arse. You're supposed to be my patron saint. I've got a problem here. And,

Dad, if you're there, get a hold of my Gran and get moving.'
Then I went out like a light.

When I came to, there were these great big butterflies filling
the air all round me. I thought I'd died. I thought, Fucking hell,
this is all right. Gradually I realized I was still alive, although I
still couldn't feel a thing.

Then there was the crack of a twig breaking close by. Here we
go again, I thought to myself. I managed to roll over on to my
stomach and got my Armalite ready. I put one magazine to the
side and said, 'OK, I'm going to take as many as I can and then
I'm going to blow my own head off, rather than get captured.'

I saw a tiny twig movement with a rustle of leaves about 30
yards away. I took aim. I saw a brown face come out from
behind a tree and I put my finger on the trigger. 'Right, here
you go for a start,' I promised him silently as I was about to
pull. As I squinted to take perfect aim, my brain suddenly
registered the red band around the man's hat. He was a Gurkha.
I let out my breath and released the pressure from the trigger.
Unbeknown to me, the Gurkhas had heard my hourly shots but,
professional soldiers as they are, had not returned the fire. They
had just kept moving towards my shots. I tried to shout but
nothing came out. I grabbed this little sapling next to me and
shook it. The Gurkha vanished instantly. Nothing happened for
ages. Next thing I knew Trooper Kevin Walsh, one of our patrol,
was leaning over me. 'You all right, Jock?'

'Yeah, I'm all right except I'm shot to fuck.'

Anyway, the Gurkhas had assumed that the Indo Paras had
been using me as a bait for a trap, so after first spotting me they
formed a circle around my position. Even then, after they had
secured the area, they only sent a section of six men to get me
while the rest set up defensive ambush positions. Ginge
appeared. He was a medic. There was no way I could talk, so
the first thing he did was give me another bloody morphine shot
in my leg. That made it thirteen. The first twelve should have
killed me. Then he banged some streptomycin in my arm.

Jock, another of the SAS lads, got on the radio and called in a
chopper. When it arrived they put the winch down but the trees

were too high and it swung hopelessly out of reach. It began to
rain again and the sun started going down. I lay down with
Kevin close beside me. He took his poncho and rolled us both
up in it to keep me warm through the night.

The following morning the Gurkhas made an improvised
stretcher using two saplings and a poncho. We set off. It took
six of them to carry me. The rest of their platoon stayed 100
yards behind us, ambushing, in case we were followed. We
reached a clearing on a steep slope. The chopper came in but
the ground was so steep he could only get one wheel down. His
blades were whipping the leaves just above the ground on one
side. Flying Officer David Collinson was the pilot. Rescuing me
got him the DFC, the only one issued during the Borneo war.
Having got me loaded, we took off into a tropical electrical
storm. I thought we were never going to make it.

Next thing I remember was being carried into the hospital at
Kuching and lying on a table where this little Malay nurse
started cutting off my clothes with a pair of garden shears. I was
covered in maggots and shit, stinking to high heaven and very
definitely on my way out.

Suddenly someone was saying to me, 'Jock, we're going to
take your leg off.'

I tried to object but I was speaking gibberish. Then the SAS
regimental colonel, Mike Wingate-Gray, spoke to me: 'Take it
easy, Jock.'

'If you let them take my leg off, I'll never speak to you again.'

'Jock, if you don't want your leg off, they won't take it off.'

And it was as simple as that.

The surgeon who operated on me was a Major McNair, from
Glasgow, and now a full general. He spoke to me as I came
round: 'Are you awake, laddie?'

'I don't feel all that bright, sir.' I could only manage a whisper.

'You shouldn't. Apart from the fact you overdosed on
morphine, we had to restart you twice on the operating theatre
with the old jump leads.'

When I was recovering, Major McNair told me that when he
had opened up my wound, the maggots had eaten right through

my leg, lining every inch of the tunnel created by the bullet, having a right old feast. That's what stopped the gangrene. He said the wound was as clean as a whistle.

Lying there, I suddenly remembered something really strange from my boyhood. My Aunty Agnes was fey. I was thirteen and had been out walking in the hills, studying the wildlife and the fauna. I got home in time for tea and came in all red-faced from the sun.

'Where've you been, laddie?'

'Up on the hills, Aunty Agnes.'

'Well, my laddie, you'll be glad of it because one day it's going to help you out of a wee bit of bother in the jungle.'

Geordie Lillico survived the wee bit of bother too. The firing that I heard when I left him was Geordie shooting at three Indos who had wandered into the clearing. He got two of them, which gave him the chance to move, though his left leg was paralysed and 3 inches of his arse was missing. At least the bullet had missed the artery.

He lay still for four or five hours, then in the afternoon he made his way back up the hill, 500 yards through the thickets, moving on his elbows only.

He spent the night in a pig hole and woke up smelling coffee; a group of Indos were brewing up a few yards from him. Then one of them climbed a durian tree for a look around. Geordie saw him looking straight at him but the Indo didn't see him because of the foliage and the fact that Geordie was covered in dried blood and mud – perfect camouflage. While the guy was up there, a helicopter flew by but Geordie didn't switch on his Sarbe – radio search and rescue beacon. His piece of inaction won him the Military Medal. In the citation, Major W. wrote: 'He showed superb presence of mind and courage in not switching on his Sarbe and therefore probably preventing the loss of his helicopter and its crew.'

Geordie, of course, will have none of that. He says it was just a little Whirlwind helicopter and the Indos could have easily shot it down and what good would that have done anybody?

When the Indos had gone, Geordie lay there for a long time

On Continuation Training you have to find lunch as well as cook it.

Johnny Two-Combs, river-crossing drill in Belize.

A 'brew-stop' on navigation training, Malaya.

Johnny Two-Combs, squadron training in Malaya.

The Iban taught us jungle skills.

With two local youths during a 'hearts and minds' operation in Borneo.

Snapper: 'In front of the Batt House in Mirbat, a week before the battle.'

Laba in full fighting mode: 'He deserved a VC for what he did.'

**Roger and Bob in the .5 Browning *sangar* at the top of the Batt House.
The DG fort is in the background.**

The young *firqa* troops relaxing in Mirbat between operations.

Snapper: a few weeks after the battle, back on hearts and minds ops, having tea with one of the locals.

and then began crawling up the hill again, 200 yards to the top of the ridge. It was almost dusk by then, and it seemed as if he would have to spend another night in the jungle, but he heard the sound of a chopper and this time he did use the Sarbe. The chopper came down and hovered above him. A crewman threw him a strop. He fitted it under his armpit and he was pulled up, but he lost his rifle and all he could think of was how awful it was going to be having to report back to the regiment without it.

Later we found out that we had killed five of the twenty who attacked us and wounded two. So we didn't do too badly.

Eventually I was moved to the British military hospital in Singapore for three months and then flown to the Royal Albert Hospital in Woolwich (now the Queen Elizabeth Military Hospital). I was in hospital for another year. It took that long for them to wean me off morphine. I finally managed to get out to Borneo for the last tour. I must have been the only British soldier in Borneo charging through the jungle with an Armalite in one hand and a walking stick in the other. My left leg was an inch and a half shorter than my right so I was nicknamed the Clog. I was static, manning the radio – I was the squadron commander's signaller. But we would get air-lifted into the jungle and set up a base. Static or not, I loved it.

I've had plenty of close shaves since, but Death doesn't worry me in the slightest. I couldn't give a fuck. As far as I'm concerned I should have died on 28 February 1965. I just live for every day, even now. And every morning, when I open my eyes, I say, 'Thanks, God.' I like life. I'm not in a rush to go. But there again when the Big Boy says, 'Right, it's your turn,' that's that.

•

Lofty Large The jungle didn't come as such a shock to me as to some of the others. Right from the start, during Continuation Training, I always viewed it as an extension of the woods back home in the Cotswolds.

So when I went into the jungle for the first time, it was just the woods to me. It was all a hell of a challenge, and that's why we did it. Of course, I had some apprehension because you hear tales of snakes and *sladang* (a wild water-buffalo), bears and tigers and, worst of all, hornets. But it was also a mixture of anticipation and familiarity. I thought to myself: The leaves are a bit different and I don't know the names of all these trees and plants, but it's still the sticks for me.

And I used to get a prickly feeling when there was something wrong in the jungle, almost like a sixth sense. You didn't always know whether to trust it or not because sometimes it didn't mean anything. But I always trusted it, being a bloody good coward, you see. You don't get to be an old man like me if you are brave.

I went out to Borneo and was in a four-man patrol with Pete Scholey, Paddy M. and Kevin W. A mate of mine used to say he wouldn't go into the jungle with any one of them, let alone all three. They were known as the three clowns, and on occasions things did get out of hand, especially when we really were in trouble. When things were dodgy, these three would be fit to busting with laughter – but what a team!

Paddy was in the Royal Signals before he came to the regiment. He'd joined up as a boy like me. He was a very good signaller. Someone once told me: 'If you're in the shit, get a good signaller.'

I said: 'If you're in the shit, it's too bloody late.' So I got the best signaller I could right from the start.

Pete was my cover man and I relied on him completely to get me out of trouble.

On one occasion, while on patrol looking for an enemy Special Forces base, Kevin fell down a river bank, caught his feet in the roots of a tree and lay head down in the river. The other two were killing themselves laughing and I had to kick their backsides to pull him clear before he drowned.

From then on I realized that if we were all killed on operations, we'd probably all die laughing. But I knew I could rely on them all to be in the right place, looking in the right directions, and that they all knew what to do. That meant I could get on with my job. We all knew each other so well, I had only to look at them with a certain expression or make a hand gesture, and they would spring into the appropriate action.

Due to the dense jungle in Borneo, no movement could be seen from the air and so 'confrontation' was man-to-man – rifles and bayonets at close quarters, sudden savage encounters. By the time I got there, the regiment was committed to cross-border operations as well as patrolling our side of the border.

Movement could be quiet if you followed animal or old hunting tracks; otherwise it was much slower and unavoidably noisy. These tracks could never be found or followed by the untrained eye. You can rarely see more than 30 metres, after which the greenery is like the solid wall of a room. There are places where it may not be possible to see further than 3 or 4 metres. Movement can be severely impeded but there is no such thing as impenetrable jungle. In order not to leave marks, knives were never used to cut back the undergrowth. The forest floor was covered in leaves and twigs that could make loud noises when you stepped on them but there was almost always somewhere quiet to step. Hanging vines had to be avoided, as a knock could wave the high branches like a warning flag to the enemy. These hazards were at most 5 or 6 metres apart, and you could never grasp trees or branches for support in case the enemy noticed.

If we found an enemy track, the options were either to ambush it or follow it. We couldn't walk on it. It was necessary to walk parallel and loop round where you thought it was running. The problem was that the enemy wouldn't make any noise on a track but the patrol couldn't help but make noise moving through the bushes.

On one patrol we crossed the border back into Malayan Borneo and were told to proceed openly, on tracks, to a forward infantry position. We walked down an open track and when we arrived the officer couldn't believe it. 'No one uses that track,' he said. 'It's a death trap. We ambush it. The Indos ambush it. And on top of that, it's mined.'

We knew that the Americans had been advisers for the

Indonesian special forces and had taught them the latest booby-trap techniques, including laying down tripwires attached to Claymore mines. Another problem was pig traps, which consisted of very sharp bamboo spears attached to springy saplings, triggered by a hidden tripwire. These could also be set up to trap humans. Another booby trap fired a bullet from the ground. It was practically invisible and could be hidden under a single leaf. And one patrol found a grenade necklace with the inscription: 'No further, winged men of England.'

Another time the Indonesians were rumoured to be preparing for an attack and we were sent out as a screen for the battalion front. We crossed a river and started to transmit back to base. As we were kneeling in the bushes, an Indonesian patrol passed only 15 feet in front of us. I was panicking because I couldn't see Pete. It turned out that he was right behind me.

'Well,' he said, when the danger had passed, 'you always told me: if there's going to be any shit flying, get behind something thick.'

•

Pete Scholey's flippancy hides the enormous admiration he feels for his patrol leader. Lofty himself may joke about his cowardice having kept him alive, but his remarkable recovery from the injuries he received in Korea are a testament to his determination and courage. Let Pete take up the story.

•

Pete Scholey No one can imagine how much respect I had for this man. To survive Korea and then come back was amazing. At the battle of the Imjin River in 1951 the Glosters were hugely outnumbered – some figures put it at 1,000 against 27,000 Chinese. Lofty would have been almost twenty-one then. The battle lasted for four days and they were shot to bits.

He was shot up and taken prisoner. His left arm was useless, but he worked on it for a year until he got some movement back. He was two years in the camp and they only took one bullet out of him the night before he was released. He had two entry holes and no exits. The other bullet was never found. It took him four years to get fit enough to go for Selection. And he passed. Amazing.

On patrol I used to stick close behind Lofty's shoulder. Always looking ahead. Looking through the undergrowth. As Lofty used to say to us, what matters is whoever gets the first shot off. The minute they hear your fire, they will go down. That gives you a few seconds' advantage.

If you're going behind enemy lines, a four-man patrol is ideal for a number of reasons. First, if one is injured, you've got two to carry and one still to cover. Second there is a wealth of skills and experience – patrol commander, medic, signaller, linguist (who doubled as the demolition man). If it took you two weeks to get in, it was going to take you just the same to get back out, as you had to be just as tactical on withdrawal.

One of the best things about working as a four-man patrol was that you got to know each of the other blokes so well that you could recognize them instantly, even in very low light or just from a silhouette. You know the back of a man's neck, his hair line, the angle he wears his helmet or cap . . .

A typical patrol started with an ops warning. You'd go to the stores and draw all your kit, weapons and ammunition. The clothing we wore would fall to pieces after being in the jungle if we were in for any length of time. Then we would test-fire our weapons and rehearse contact drills.

Once all our kit was packed we would go for the briefing. The map on the wall would be covered by a curtain. The officer would pull back a bit of the curtain just enough to reveal the sector relating to our forthcoming operation.

On one occasion he told us that information had been received that an enemy troop had been reported in a four-square area of map. We all gathered around and peered at the map and then at the aerial recon. photographs. The trouble was our maps were taken by a Canberra at 30,000 feet, so it was all guesswork.

Lofty's system for beginning to search four map squares was as follows: from the moment you are heading towards the target area, you are looking out all the time for cut signs – that is, any scuff marks or broken foliage, or the tell-tale sign of even one leaf hanging loose where you wouldn't expect it to be. You head in a straight line – which is easier said than done – towards the target area. Information concerning enemy positions, concentrations, bases, etc., was invariably very vague so the thing to look for was well-used tracks leading to them. This was done by circling the whole area but of course there was always the possibility of wandering into the defences before any track was found.

On this particular occasion we had got to the last square and were beginning to relax because there had been no sign at all. We sat on top of this ridge. Lofty whispered, 'Get the brew on, lads. I'm just going down a few yards to have a look around.'

A minute later he was back with us, slightly out of breath and whispering with more urgency, 'Get that fire out. Double quick. Get your kit together. There's a bloody great troop track just beyond that clearing.' He pointed to where he had just come from. We took up an OP, gathered the necessary information on the enemy and we bugged out. Paddy got the information to base, which then organized infantry to come in and take them out. It wasn't that simple when it came to the Koemba River.

•

In May 1965 Lofty was called in to discuss a last-ditch attempt to find out if the enemy were using the Koemba River to bring in more troops and supplies. B and D Squadrons had tried more than once – and failed.

•

Lofty Large The problem was that the parts of the river that were accessible were patrolled by the Indonesians and other parts were hard to reach because of swamps. It seemed, from past experience, that if the swamps didn't get you, the Indos would. But the squadron commander thought we might just do it.

Our job was to see and hear but not to be seen or heard.

We'd been pretty lucky so far. As usual, Pete had the answer. Coming back in the chopper from a fourteen-day patrol he was on a real high. He cut up some four-by-two weapons-cleaning material and handed strips round to the rest of us as armbands. When we landed, the commander wanted to know what they were.

Pete piped up: 'That's how we've been getting away with it, sir. We've been going in as umpires.'

So, it was one last job. The squadron commander asked if I was up to it after so many ops and gave Pete the option of dropping out. I had to ask him. His reply turned the air blue.

It was the same patrol. The two of us, Paddy and Kevin. Our first task, as ever, was to get as much information as possible. The secondary task was to disrupt any military traffic we found on the river.

I studied the maps, aerial photos and previous patrol reports and decided to go for a spur of high ground that looked as though it might be a way through the swamps, which were high because of the rain. It vanished on the map but there was a corresponding bend in the river and so that was the place to head for. I reckoned it as a two- or three-day slog from the spot where the chopper would drop us.

The first problem was Pete. When the weapons turned up, he'd been issued with the wrong rifle.

•

Pete Scholey I knew immediately it wasn't mine. I knew, liked and trusted my particular gun. It never got a stoppage. I had it set for just the right pressure. I knew if I had it set on gas regulator 4, it would work. I cleaned it and looked after it.

I asked Paddy and Kevin if they had my weapon. No. I started honking. I was Lofty's cover man. If I saw anything I was the first one to fire. Even though I was a young SAS soldier, I knew the training I had been given by the Malayan vets was good. There was no way I was going to let that patrol down. Lofty gave me a bollocking for honking so much.

As soon as we were airborne, I started stripping the weapon

down. It took me twenty minutes in total to strip it right down, check and reassemble it, and that wants some doing when your hands are shaking and you're bouncing around in a Pioneer flown by two old World War Two pilots. I remember glancing out of the window and thinking, Oh, God, anything, please, but not a plane crash in the jungle.

Lofty tried to console me. 'Don't worry, Pete. We might get a chance for you to test-fire it when we arrive.'

Did we hell. When we landed the chopper blades were turning and we went straight into it and off to the border. And the moment I was in the jungle, my honking stopped. It has to. You've got to get on with the job.

•

Lofty Large On the first two days we moved west, away from our target, because, no matter how good you are, you leave tracks and we didn't want the enemy, if they found them, to know our destination; then we hit swamps and had no more choice. We headed for our target.

On the second day I heard a sound up ahead and moved forward to find an enemy patrol in the way, and so we detoured and pushed on, Kevin keeping an extra sharp look-out to the rear.

Then we were into swampland. Not a nice place. Under the black water you can jam your feet in roots or you can disappear into holes, and this swamp had green scum with leaves on the surface which crackled and made a hell of a noise. I could imagine the enemy waiting and grinning in ambush. When the water rose above my waist, I stopped and we went back. I wasn't going to fight a war more than waist deep in that lot unless we absolutely had to.

We turned back and tried another route, kept going, getting knackered. At one point Pete, about 20 metres behind me, whispered: 'I hope we're the goodies.'

'What?'

'I hope we're the goodies.'

'What?'

'Well, if we're the baddies, we'll just as likely finish up with our hats floating on top of this lot.'

It's hard to laugh silently. But I managed it and a lot of the tension was released.

•

Pete Scholey Probing into the swamps was bloody hard work. We were sometimes in it literally right up to our necks. When you meet a dragonfly at eye level in the water it looks like a Twin Pin (light aircraft) coming straight towards you.

I remember once Lofty went for two weeks without a crap. When eventually the time came, I went along as his escort man. When he came out from behind the tree, he said: 'I've laid a magnificent egg. I don't know whether to register it as a birth or a death.'

We carried all our other rubbish with us. If you buried cans or whatever, the pigs would dig them up. We tried not to leave signs but you always do. It's impossible not to. That's why we avoided tracks and tried wherever possible to penetrate parts of the jungle that even the Abos and the most determined Indos would avoid.

At noon one day, Lofty told us to make the midday brew while Paddy got the radio set up. He would send two reports per day, morning and evening. If you missed the first one, okay. If you missed the second one, the crash team would come in and try to find you. We were completely knackered. It was really hard work and we weren't getting anywhere. It was time for a Chinese parliament, an informal meeting where anyone is free to suggest ideas.

After Lofty gave the sit rep, Paddy shrugged and said: 'Well, Lofty, we should all have been out of here two days ago. We'll never get out of here alive. We're all doomed.' And then he gave a big daft grin.

'You might be doomed,' Kevin said. 'I've got a few rations left.'

I went along with them, saying, 'Lofty, when I joined the SAS, nobody said it was going to be easy. If they had done I wouldn't have wanted to come in. I volunteered for it. Nobody dragged me screaming from the recruiting office. I'm paid to do the job. If we go out now, old Matt the cha wallah will be waiting for us with a nice brew and a big cheese-and-onion sarnie and we'd all get a good pat on the back for what we've achieved so far.'

But it was just banter. No one considered going back. Our objective was clear.

•

Lofty Large I would use Chinese parliaments to get confirmation of my assessments. For example, when working out tactics or questions relating to navigation or distance travelled, I would ask each member of the patrol for his opinion.

A lot of troopers in the SAS had previously been NCOs in their own units and therefore had a lot of experience that could be very valuable. Their opinion was always worth listening to. The commander makes the final decision, but by that time it is an informed decision and the other blokes in the patrol know what you are talking about. If you have asked one of your blokes for his opinion and you decide not to do it his way, he knows why you have made the decision you have because you tell him so. And there's no question of muttering under the breath, 'Why are we doing this?' or 'We should be doing this my way.' Each bloke knows why you are doing what you are doing and knows exactly what is expected of him in order to achieve it.

And so we pushed on and probed for two or three days and then we cracked it. Around midday we came across the river, muddy and swirling, about 35–40 metres wide and about 70 metres away down a steep slope through an abandoned rubber plantation. It was a perfect spot for an observation/ambush position – there was an old ditch, 10 feet by 3 deep, hidden by bushes and only a few feet from the river bank.

We knew from air photos that we were only a few hundred metres from an enemy base but we reckoned they wouldn't be looking for us in a ditch in a rubber plantation – not with all that jungle around.

Later that day there was almost a disaster. Kevin was fishing for water, his water bottle on a cord dangling 7 or 8 feet down the steep bank, the cord in full view of the river, when a canoe with two men approached upstream. I watched them closely. The others turned and stared up the hill in case the two men were a distraction and we were about to be hit from behind. But they were only fishing, so we let them go.

Several diesel launches passed by that day, then three men in an open boat arrived and beached nearby to bale and refuel the boat. I thought of taking them prisoner but they might not have been military and it would have been hard to get them back over the border. Also, until the primary task was achieved, I didn't have authority from base to take offensive action.

Morale was high and I decided to break the rules of ambush. You are not supposed to cook, smoke or fart; no hot drinks; complete silence for days on end, sometimes even a week. That night we had a curry. We smoked – even Pete the non-smoker. We had a brew every couple of hours. I wanted fitness and morale at its peak for the bug-out which we all knew would come. I wanted a cock-a-hoop patrol which would take on the world with a grin.

As the days passed we reported back to base everything that moved on the river. A raft came downstream one day, on it four men singing lustily. I glanced back at the others. They were waving their arms as if conducting an orchestra.

After several days, I decided we had collected enough information as to whether the Indos were using the River Koemba to build up their troops and supply them, and so I got Paddy to make the request for permission to carry out our secondary task. We had a special code of figures for words which was handy for short signals. So, as the James Bond films were then at their height, our signal read: *Request 00 licence*. Everyone in the base understood except the clown responsible. We had to send a long, hammered-out message, hoping against hope that it wasn't intercepted, that no enemy signaller was getting Morse interfering with his pop music. Eventually we got permission to shoot and scoot. Now to select the target.

The others wanted to hit the first floating object we saw and get the hell out. But we waited. The ambush wasn't a problem. Getting away without encountering the enemy patrols, who would have heard the noise, was. There was a right and a wrong time, a right and a wrong route back.

•

Pete Scholey Lofty briefed us. 'We hit the boat when it goes arse-end to us. That way we don't get a broadside back from them. Fire about one mag at it. That should mean about eighty rounds, hit it up the arse and with any luck that will ignite the fuel tanks they carry on the back. As soon as we've hit it, get out, Paddy and Kevin to the top of the ridge first, covered by us. As soon as they are up there, they will cover our withdrawal.'

Paddy carried a particular grenade all through his five months on ops. When Lofty said that we were going to attack a large boat, Paddy said: 'I'll get it with this, Lofty.'

Quick as a flash, Kevin said: 'Paddy, you'll need arms like an anthropoid to reach it from here.'

The most important thing was to start firing at just the right moment. Too soon and they'd get a chance to fire back. Too late and they were going to get away. I kept looking at the time. I knew that if we waited long into the afternoon before we even commenced the attack, we might not be able to get out because of the dark.

Next morning we lay in wait. The boats normally started coming past about one thirty, two o'clock. It started to rain, which is good for cover but not so good for the swamp levels. Just after two we heard the chug, chug, chug of a diesel. It wasn't a very big one and it was pulling two canoes behind it.

Lofty shook his head. It wasn't big enough for him.

Three o'clock came and went.

Half past three, chug, chug, chug.

I tapped my watch, indicating that it was time to start thinking of going, but Lofty held up his hand, telling us that we had to wait. Kevin grimaced. He was thinking, he told us later, What's he waiting for? The fucking *Ark Royal*?

A couple of minutes later we heard another boat coming. It

was a good 'un. About 40 foot and gleaming white. Lofty gave the ready signal, then he noticed a woman on the bridge between an army officer and a naval officer. She was wearing a long white chiffon dress. He signalled for us to hold our fire. In that situation, where there is one woman, there is likely to be others, and maybe children, and the British Army does not make war on women and children.

Time was moving on and there was a storm brewing, when all of a sudden an even larger boat appeared. We could see two soldiers in the stern.

This was it.

Lofty took out the two soldiers at the stern, the only ones visible because the drapes were down along the sides of the boat. The boat got arse-end and I opened up. Bang, bang, bang, click. Stoppage. I cocked it double quick and then it fired again. It was the weapon I'd been honking about on the way in. It was lucky all four of us were lined up, firing at once, and that we hadn't been caught short in a head-on contact.

The boat took sixty-nine rounds in only a few seconds. The odd nine came from me. Next moment there was a great flash, then a jet of flame and smoke and the boat began to list.

Time to bug out.

Kevin and Paddy went off at a fair pace away from the river. We turned to follow. Next moment I saw Lofty charging back towards me and I nearly fell through my own arse. I thought, Oh, my God, they're coming from that direction. He pushed past me and grabbed his water bag.

'It took me three months to get another one after Paddy holed the last one. They ain't getting that.' And with that he stuffed it in his shirt and took off again.

I yelled after him, 'You long streak of piss! You frightened the living daylights out of me.'

•

Lofty Large Now we had to get out, and potentially it was the nastiest trap I'd ever been in.

If the Indos at base had heard the shooting, they would have been out of their bunks and up the tracks to cut us off or ambush us double quick. The noise of the heavy rainstorm certainly must have helped cover the gunfire and also helped us make our rapid escape. As it is, they probably only just missed us.

We had to move as fast and as carefully as possible and we were in luck. The pouring rain covered the sounds of our movements, but we still expected to see the enemy. The ambushers can easily become the ambushed, and trying to move up silently on someone waiting for you is one thing to avoid in the jungle.

Just when I estimated we were about forty or fifty metres from the first enemy cut-off track, going up a short slope, a movement ahead stopped me. It was a snake on flat ground at the top of the slope coming fast towards me. I immediately brought up my rifle sight, and it reared up 4 or 5 feet so that, with the slope, we were eye to eye. It was a king cobra, ready to strike. I aimed at the centre of its hood but I didn't dare shoot. The Indos might have been just ahead. It felt like for ever as I stood there, both of us poised to strike, the snake about 7 feet away. I stood wishing I'd learned more about the bloody things. Did they give any warning? How far could a cobra strike? I must have stood still for ten of the longest seconds, then it just dropped down and buggered off behind a log. I loved that snake then. I would have stroked it if I could. Beautiful, sensible snake. But there was now the worry of what it had been in such a hurry to get away from that it nearly ran into me? What did it know that I didn't?

When we reached the first track, we all lined up and crossed as one. You never cross a track in single file. When we got into the cover of the jungle, we checked our weapons. Pete was savage. It would be bad news if we had a contact with the enemy and his rifle wasn't working properly, and especially bad for me, as I relied on him completely to get me out of trouble.

When we stopped later for a break, Kevin asked what had happened. I told him. For some reason Paddy had forgotten to pass on the message down the line.

'You bloody Irish bastard,' he said. 'I could have been bloody scoffed.'

Bunch of comedians.

We made it through till nightfall and settled down to ambush our backtrack. Then we heard mortars from the enemy camp.

Kevin wasn't bothered. He was a good mortar man. As Pete says, he could hit a bean can at 4,600 yards using a steel helmet as a base plate.

'It's okay,' he said. 'They're mortaring downriver. That's where they think we are.'

And I said: 'Why do you think they aren't shelling this area?'

The penny dropped. They had their own men where we were.

There was silence and then someone whispered: 'Shit.'

•

Pete Scholey Next morning we made our way out. The last thing we felt like was another detour across country, but we had to avoid the patrol we had encountered on the way in. We managed it and eventually found our way to the border. Paddy sent a message asking for a chopper to hover over the LZ for thirty seconds. We pressed on and about ten minutes later we heard the lovely sound of a chopper just above the trees. We had no voice radios, so they dropped a message tied to a tin can. It came down through the canopy and the message read: 'We will winch you out from here.' They lowered the winch, but it wasn't long enough, so they added an extra 60-foot length of paradrop webbing.

Down it came. Lofty told me to go first as I had the dodgy rifle. There were two slings, so I put one around me and attached three Bergens to the other. About 40 feet off the ground, the bloody Bergens came loose and fell back to the ground. I wasn't quite high enough and suddenly realized that they weren't going to pull me into the helicopter. I was left swinging underneath. All the time I was thinking: I'm sure some bastard Indo's going to start firing up at me. Lofty reckoned my eyes looked like chapel hat-pegs.

To indicate how magnificent his navigation was, the chopper's pilot landed me on the LZ just three hundred yards further along the exact line we had been following. There was a Jock platoon on the spot and the officer came up to me and said: 'I understand you are being followed up by two platoons.'

I looked around me at all these Jocks in bare buff and said: 'Well, I don't know about that, sir, but with respect, if you're right, I think you'd do well to get the men kitted up and into an all-round defence.'

He did it without another word being said.

Meanwhile the other three had found a winching spot and had all got aboard the chopper. They picked me up and the four of us went to Lundu, where we got back in the Pioneer which flew us to Kuching.

When we finally came back off all our ops and handed in the equipment we had left Paddy found out that his grenade was defective and would have been useless in action. Cradling it in his hands, he said, 'This grenade has been of great comfort to me . . .'

•

Lofty Large Looking back now, the river job was the cushiest I ever did. It was the only time in my Army career when I was shooting to kill and not being shot at, but it was probably the worst tactical position I've ever been in. While we were waiting there I thought to myself, Any chance I get, we are going to do the ambush. I knew that if we were successful in carrying out a hit on the river, it would mean that the Indos would have to divert troops in order to guard their supply routes. It worked. They simply could not continue attacking along the border front and guard the river route at the same time. They never carried out another attack along that front following our ambush. They had to redeploy 700 front-line troops. And twelve years later this was confirmed by the officer on the boat, Colonel Moerdani of the Indonesian Parachute Regiment.

•

Pete Scholey Kevin and I were flown by helicopter from Hereford to the London base of the regiment, and during the trip on the way down the colonel explained to us that Moerdani had been talking with various people in the corridors of Whitehall, including a senior officer from the regiment, and they had started discussing various incidents relating to the Indonesian campaign. Particular reference was made to the time when the boat just behind his was destroyed in an ambush on the Koemba River. The officer informed him that at least two members of that original patrol were still serving in the regiment, and Moerdani said that he would like to meet us.

We went in to meet him. He shook hands. During our conversation, which lasted about three-quarters of an hour, he said, 'Your ambush was the pinprick that burst open the bag of water.'

And at the end he said, 'I want to thank you for letting me live.'

•

The Koemba raid was but one SAS action that took place in 1965. The SAS war continued into 1966, including secret cross-border raids, which helped convince the Indonesians that Britain would continue to support Malaysia. The Indonesian military leadership began to lose faith in their president, and in March 1966 he was overthrown in a coup. Five months later Indonesia made peace with Malaysia.

4
OMAN

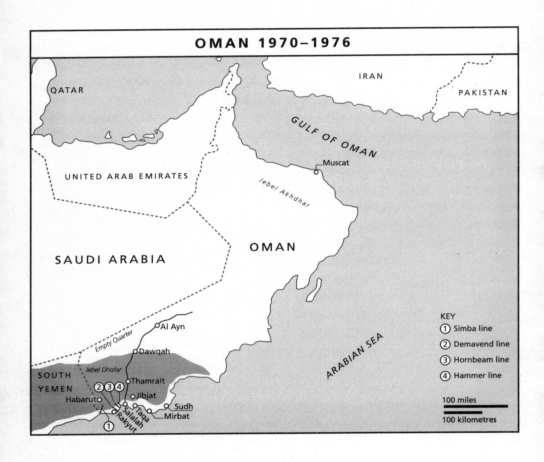

OMAN 1970-1976

QATAR

IRAN

PAKISTAN

GULF OF OMAN

UNITED ARAB EMIRATES

Muscat

Jebel Akhdhar

SAUDI ARABIA

OMAN

Al Ayn

Empty Quarter

Dawqah

ARABIAN SEA

Jebel Dhofar

SOUTH
YEMEN

Thamrait

Habaruto

② ③ ④

Jibjat

Salalah

Taqa

Sudh

Mirbat

① Rakyut

KEY

① Simba line

② Demavend line

③ Hornbeam line

④ Hammer line

100 miles

100 kilometres

Laba deserved a VC for what he did at the battle of Mirbat in
1972. To keep the war secret, all they gave him was a Mention
in Despatches. You can get that for walking the Falls Road.

Snapper

Oman is an independent sultanate in the south-eastern part of
the Arabian peninsula. Bounded on the west by the Yemen
Republic, it is bounded on the south and east by the Arabian
Sea. To the north, separated from the rest of the country by the
United Arab Emirates, is a small mountainous area at the tip of
the Musandam Peninsula known as Ru'us al-Jibal (the 'Moun-
taintops'). Its people are poor and the land is barren, with a
particularly unforgiving climate: summers are stifling, and in the
mountains in winter it is cold enough to freeze a hot-water
bottle.

In 1954 the Sultan, Sa'id bin Taimur, ruled over a populace
which one British Embassy official described as the most
poverty-stricken and debilitated by disease he had ever seen.
Encouraged by their imam, Ghalib bin Ali, the people of the
Jebel Akhdar ('Green Mountain') region rose up against Sa'id's
autocratic regime three years later. A fertile 350-square-kilo-
metre plateau high above sea level, it is bounded by sheer cliffs,
and the only access is via narrow mountain passes. It had never
been conquered.

By the end of 1957 the rebel force was comfortably ensconced
and well armed with .5 Browning machine guns and land mines.
The Sultan's forces, led by British officers, consisted of only a
few hundred men. Britain, which had treaty ties with the Sultan,
sent in the RAF and a battalion of infantry to help the Sultan

crush the rebellion. The Jebel was bombed, but to no avail. Two attempts to seize it by the infantry also failed. Between March and November 1958, 150 vehicles, including eighteen British Ferret scout cars, were blown up by mines. It was time for a new approach.

Major Frank Kitson, serving in the Directorate of Military Operations, thought of the idea of using the SAS. Both the British and the Omani forces desperately needed climbing experts and specialized assault teams, but there was another reason too. It would have been politically unacceptable for the British government to deploy larger forces, with the risk of incurring heavy casualties. Lieutenant-Colonel Anthony Deane-Drummond, the commanding officer of 22 SAS, brought the forty-two soldiers of D Squadron from Malaya under the command of Major John Watts.

One of those soldiers was Lofty Large.

•

Lofty Large I had just passed my education course in Malaya when we were told we were off to a different theatre of operations. Our destination was top-secret and none of us knew where we were going. We were not allowed to disclose that we were SAS and were given blue berets to wear. We flew to Singapore, then Ceylon. It was so secret we then changed planes again. This time we were in a Hastings, the old four-engined jump aircraft, flying to Masirah, a small island off the south coast of Oman. At the RAF base in Masirah we boarded a Beverley – an aircraft which could land and take off on very short, rough airstrips – and flew on to Muscat. Some of the blokes tried to work out where we were heading by looking at the stars. There was no airport, so we landed in the desert. We went straight into a tent the engineers had put up for a briefing at Bait El Falage. Everyone was saying, 'Where the hell is this?' It was rumoured that even Johnny Watts, the squadron commander, didn't know our destination until he was sent a coded message during one of the flights. He unveiled the ever-present map and announced: 'You are in Muscat. You must have heard of it?'

Nobody had.

'They've got a bit of a problem,' he told us and outlined it. Friendly forces: a battalion of the Sultan's infantry (about 200 men), a few artillery bods and the forty-two of us. Then he told us about the enemy.

'A bit vague, really,' he said, 'but as far as is known, about 500 well-trained and -armed troops [having been trained by the US in Saudi], and an unknown quantity of local tribesmen who are very well armed. The total force we are up against is somewhere between 2,000 and 5,000 and they are sitting on a bloody great *jebel* 10,000 feet high with precipitous cliffs all around. It hasn't been taken for 2,000 years since the Persians did it and lost half their army. There is a small problem as well: all the roads are mined.'

I thought: Oh, God. I've been here before. It's the Imjin River all over again. Plus, because of the education course, I hadn't trained for five weeks.

But nobody batted an eyelid. Someone said: 'No shit. We'll do them.'

The Jebel Akhdar was something else: about 80 miles in total circumference and rising to 12,000 feet in places. It is big and like something from the lost world. They decided to split us in half. Two troops (16 and 17) to the north side, the other two troops (18 and 19) to the south. I was in 16 troop. We had no helicopters, no back-up, no support except a couple of trucks. As soon as we got down off the trucks, we began climbing. It was pitch-dark. They never saw us coming. No one in their right mind would have expected us to get straight off the trucks and rush up the mountainside.

We were in light order (just belts and personal weapons) on the recce, but when we reached the top unopposed, we realized we were going to be able to hold the position. So, 17 troop, went back down to collect their Bergens; when they came back, we did the same. It was so cold at the top that the water in our water bottles began to freeze. I'm not a cold weather soldier, but having got up there by sheer luck we weren't going to let it go. When we got to the top, the guy who had been our guide was down on his knees giving it, *thump*, to Mohammed because he couldn't believe we had made it.

On the second night there were only thirteen of us at the top when we were stumbled upon by some donkey herders. We had camped in a hollow around the embers of the fire. I was on sentry duty when I heard this mass of noise. I thought there was a load of blokes heading towards us, so I kicked the guy next to me. At the same time I lined them up in the sights of my Bren gun and I remember saying to myself, 'Jesus Christ, there's a lot of them!' In the moonlight, with the glint of rifle barrels in this mass of dark figures, it all looked quite promising. I was just about to fire when Rory, our troop commander, said, 'Hang on. Hold fire.' Luckily I did, because what I had thought was a group of dozens of men was only donkeys and four farmers who had taken a short cut over the top of the mountain. Because I didn't shoot them that night they were well and truly on our side after that, bringing up water and supplies for us. In fact I can honestly say that not having shot them saved the situation.

Our brief was to thwart the rebel army. The first week they were frightened of us. After a month they were terrified. We took a hill, which we named Casino, about 3,000 yards short of the enemy main defence line at a place called Aqbat al Zhufar. This is where they really lost their bottle and they realized that we knew they had lost it, so it was quite a time.

They were based in a great fortification in a gorge which ran through sheer cliffs about 50 to 100 feet high right across the mountain. It effectively stopped us getting to the main villages. You could walk through this gorge and out on to the plateau, but in the cliffs and in the gorge itself there were caves full of men with machine guns – .50-calibres, .30-calibres and Bren guns – plus a lot of men with rifles. We had watched for a day from about 400 yards away before having a go at it. Then Rory came up with the best way to crack it: 'The best thing to do is climb the cliff, go around the back and take them from behind.' So off he went to find a route for us.

The rock was really difficult, just crumbling in Rory's hands. And it was the middle of the night. Even Rory, who was a mountaineer, wasn't able to make it. Climbing the Eiger is all very easy for Mountain Troop, but give them a piece of crumbling Oman cliff face and they're scuppered. He got about 15 feet up before he got stuck. He had to be roped down and then he set off to find somewhere easier for us non-climbers to climb. All by starlight. Meanwhile I was tidying up the rope we used to rescue him, and by the time I had finished looping it all up and putting it around me, I looked around and everyone had gone. We were attacking this fortification, and they had left me behind! I headed off after them, at a gentle trot. I didn't run because it was too bloody rough to run and anyway I don't like running into trouble.

After a bit I found Miley, the patrol commander, at the side of the track, and asked him where Rory was. He told me and I raced off to give him the rope in case he needed it to scale the rock. Suddenly, I heard a grenade lever clatter out. I hit the deck, not knowing what was going on or who was throwing the grenades. After the grenade blew I heard Rory saying, 'Give them a phosphorous,' which is a really nasty piece of kit. Sets fire to everything as well as people. Next minute this phosphorous grenade goes off, lighting up the lot, including us. There was lots of screaming and then all hell broke loose. I thought, Shit, we've got no chance.

Instead of going up the cliff and around, what we had actually done was bottled in through the front door of the fortification. It was like standing in the middle of a street with big tall buildings 100 feet high stretching away either side of you and where – if you can imagine – everyone in every window was sticking a gun out at you and firing. There were four of us in there – the others were waiting outside to cover us. For us inside it was unbelievable. There was shit flying like you've never seen. Rory and the troop sergeant were tangling with the defenders in the caves they had set on fire, while the other two of us were letting rip with everything we had in every direction. I only had a rifle, but my mate Scouse had a Bren. They had all sorts of machine guns and it was all coming our way.

I was expecting to be dead at any minute or at least badly

chewed up. I kept thinking, Shit, I've been here before. Here we go again. Really, none of us should be here now to talk about it. Some of them were only about 15 to 20 feet away from us. As they shot at us, there were spurts of fire which we fired back at as fast as possible. The phosphorous also lit up their ammunition belts. They had the beautiful and very handy habit of wearing them across their chests, like markers. Scouse was just ploughing it all as fast as he could. Suddenly I saw out of the corner of my eye that there were rounds spilling all over the ground and that Scouse had stopped firing. I thought: Oh, no, that's all we need. No bloody Bren gun. They had shot the magazine off. He had another magazine on there so bloody fast. Then, suddenly, it all stopped.

After the firing ended, there was the usual moaning and babbling to be heard. I thought I recognized the voice of one of my mates, so I headed back in, but Herbie Hawkins, the troop sergeant, grabbed my arm, shouting, 'Get the hell out of it.' He told me all of ours were out.

We all pulled out, walking back across this weird moonscape. I thought we might be approaching another of their caves. Not wanting to be surprised from behind, I threw a phosphorous grenade into what I thought was the cave mouth, but the whole thing turned out to be a huge pile of brushwood, which, of course, went up in flames. After that, we had to walk the length of a football pitch back to safety, lit up by the blaze, with our backs to this great fortification, but not a shot was fired. I knew then that they had all bugged, none of them knowing what they were up against. They never knew there were only four of us. There were at least fifty of them. It all came down to a question of morale, and in the end we defeated them, no problem.

•

By December 1958, forty rebels had been killed, but more men were needed to take the plateau and the main rebel base of Saiq. On 9 January 1959 A Squadron arrived. On 26 January, together with D Squadron, they climbed 8,000 feet in nine hours, each man carrying approximately 100 pounds. On the way up the track leading to the plateau they found a machine-gun position at the top. Fortunately, it was unmanned. Had it been manned in daylight, they could have been wiped out.

Just before dawn the two squadrons reached the top and consolidated their position. An air drop supplied them with ammunition and food, and the rebels – including the imam – seeing the parachutes and thinking a full-scale airborne assault was taking place, fled over the Saudi Arabian border. The SAS marched into Saiq unopposed and the rebellion was effectively ended.

Six years later, in 1965, oil was discovered in commercial quantities and, with peace seemingly assured, it might have been assumed that the country was about to stabilize and prosper, but Western visitors reported problems. There were no schools. Omanis were prohibited from adopting the ways of the West, such as dancing or wearing Western clothes, on penalty of flogging or imprisonment. John Townsend, a British economist, remembered meeting the Sultan: 'a strange, small old man with a splendid set of Father Christmas whiskers, tended and guarded by burly young men of undoubted African origin who were known as slaves'.

Townsend wasn't permitted to meet Omanis because the people were not ready for development. 'There was great poverty and disease ... yet nothing was done because the Sultan would not permit it.' No one could leave his village to seek work or even repair his house without permission of the Sultan. The old man never left his palace in Salalah and ruled the country via radio telephone.

Throughout the 1960s there were sporadic and often savage rebellions, which were equally savagely repressed. The Sultan survived two assassination attempts, in 1965 and 1966, the latter by his bodyguard, but his days in power were to be numbered. For the first time an Omani sultan could not consider himself the feudal master of all he surveyed. There was oil beneath the sand. There was oil passing by his coastline. His country was strategically important. Outsiders had vital interests in his activities, and those activities were causing turmoil. He had to go.

Since 1962 there had been a rebellion in Dhofar province in the south-west of Oman. It was led by the conservative Dhofar Liberation Front (DLF), which demanded improvements in the quality of life of the Dhofaris. The Sultan's Armed Forces (SAF) were initially able to contain the revolt, but then the DLF was subsumed into the Communist and better-armed People's Front for the Liberation of the Occupied Arabian Gulf (PFLOAG), which was backed by neighbouring Yemen, as well as by the Soviet Union and China. The SAF began to lose ground to the rebels, and the Sultan's regime started to fall apart. The British could only watch helpless, though salvation came from inside the Sultan's family.

On 23 July 1970 a member of the Omani aristocracy, encouraged by British officers, went to the palace and demanded the Sultan's resignation. Sa'id drew a pistol and began firing. In the mayhem the aristocrat was wounded, a servant was killed and the Sultan shot himself in the foot and the stomach but not fatally. That evening he abdicated and was flown to hospital and then, by the RAF, on to London, where he lived out his last two years in exile. His son Qaboos succeeded him.

Within hours of the coup an SAS team was on its way to Salalah to act as bodyguard for Qaboos and to initiate a 'hearts-and-minds' campaign called Operation Storm to provide basic medical care for the 500,000 or so people in Dhofar, plus veterinary help and water preservation. An intelligence cell was to be established to collect and analyse information, and leaflets were prepared to be dropped in the mountains, explaining the policies of the new Sultan and amnesty terms for those who surrendered.

It was quickly successful. Salim Mubarak, one of the most important rebel leaders and a former soldier for the old Sultan, accepted the terms and came over to work with the SAS. Those who followed him were retrained into units known as *firqas*, from the Arabic *firqat*, meaning 'party of men'. Meanwhile back in Beaconsfield, SAS soldiers were doing intensive ten-week courses in colloquial Arabic. Once in Dhofar they were attached to *firqa* units and, in the early stages, they were not authorized to patrol enemy territory.

Then, in September, the odds changed significantly when the PFLOAG and the DLF split. Communist ideology, it seemed, did not readily mix with Islamic tradition. Fighting broke out, which led to mass defections of the DLF tribesmen to the government side. Between September and the following March, encouraged by amnesty terms and hard cash – £50 for a rifle – 201 rebels changed sides.

By the middle of 1971, unknown to the British public, there were eighty SAS men in Oman, working under the innocuous title of BATT – British Army Training Teams.

And in the autumn Snapper joined the fray.

•

Snapper Three of us out of the 135 had made it through Selection and Continuation Training, and one day in August we were told to report to Major Pirie, the CO of B Squadron. Ten feet tall, the three of us, off to the office behind the sergeant-major. We were ushered in and the first thing I noticed about him were his eyes, piercing blue eyes, sizing us up. There was nothing personal about his room, just a desk and a couple of chairs. The walls were covered with blue curtains. There were maintenance men working on the building and there were lists and maps everywhere so that they couldn't see through the windows.

I thought it was just going to be an introductory meeting and then we'd be told to go back to the *basha* and stow our kit. Instead he pulled back one of the curtains to reveal a map of the Sultanate of Muscat and Oman with the word SECRET top-right like a postage stamp. I knew the place. I'd worked there in 1968 building roads and helipads not long after the Aden débâcle.

Major Pirie briefed us for a while. He told us about Dhofar, which was remote even by Omani standards. The Dhofar Liberation Front, which had earlier rebelled against the Sultan, was now allied to a Communist group from Aden, now called South Yemen. They were named the People's Front for the Liberation of the Occupied Arabian Gulf, but we would soon get to know the lot of them simply as the *adoo*, which is Arabic for 'enemy'.

The *adoo* controlled the Jebel Massif, the plateau which dominated the area. With its terrain of 4,000-foot peaks and deep ravines, the Jebel was ideal guerrilla country. The *adoo* were secure. The Sultan's army couldn't get near them.

The assignment was simplicity itself. The SAS task was to bolster the Sultan's army, save Dhofar and – by extension – the Straits of Hormuz, thereby keeping the lifeline open for essential oil for the Free World.

It was to be a private business, 'deniable' by the Foreign and Commonwealth Office. Once victory was achieved, in the tradition of the regiment, there would be no glorious march-past or ostentatious gong-worship. They'd learnt from Vietnam. There was to be no press around stirring things up. No fuss about body bags returning. We knew we could win it militarily. The danger came from publicity.

We were dismissed and I went out of there full of myself. This is it, I thought. I'm going back. I'm going to get my pride back.

•

As the sun went down on 1 October, a force of 250 of us sat around in a *wadi* [a dried-up river bed] at the foot of the Jebel Massif, ready to set Operation Jaguar in motion. There was B and G Squadrons of the regiment plus members of the Sultan's army, five *firqas* of Jebeli tribesmen and a platoon from Baluchistan. We were tasked to climb the Jebel that night in full battle order and seize an abandoned airstrip on the plateau. The monsoon was over. It was a hot, humid, moonless evening and there was the rumour of maybe 2,000 *adoo* as a welcoming party, complete with AK47s, Simonev semi-automatics, anti-tank weapons and mortars.

I had been designated number two on the general-purpose machine-gun sustained-fire team, which gave me the privilege of carrying the GPMG tripod weighing over 30 pounds with 1,000 rounds of 7.62-mm link ammunition – half in the Bergen, half wrapped around my body; add rations, water, belt kit and self-load rifle and there was some 130 pounds to heave up the mountains before daybreak.

The journey had begun two weeks earlier at RAF Lyneham, by C130 Hercules to RAF Salalah in Dhofar via Cyprus, then after a period of acclimatization, by Skyvan to a staging post 55 miles to the north of the Jebel, followed by a jolting, vomitous journey across the Negd desert in Bedford trucks, keeping off the road for fear of mines.

Close by were three new friends from Fiji: Valdez, one of the SAS men I'd met after Aden, Sek and Labalaba, whom I'd met at Otterburn in Northumbria on preparation exercises for the operation. Sek was to fight with me like a brother throughout my career, which was rare, as team members were regularly changed. Labalaba, shortened to Laba, was a colossus of a man. He was Rambo before Sylvester Stallone appeared on the screen.

The word came to move. I heaved on the Bergen and lifted the tripod on to my shoulder. The guy who helped me said I looked as though I was being strangled by an octopus.

Within seconds of moving off, I was soaked in sweat. A signaller collapsed under the weight of his radio equipment. Another of the lads spewed up. I began to think of my grandfather and his father and all their strong-man exploits and reckoned that I had a tradition to live up to.

It took two hours or so, onwards and upwards for 5 kilometres, to reach a pool which was our staging post and the first stop. Thank fuck, I thought, as I got the Bergen off. I'd drunk all the water. As I refilled the bottles I felt like someone had taken me apart and reassembled me in the wrong order. Now for a bit of a rest, then up the mountain.

The *firqas* wailed in prayer as we cleaned our weapons and filled ourselves up with tea, like camels, then we were off again. I checked my equipment and the two syrettes of morphine round my neck and wondered if I'd need them; then off we went up the Jebel with a five-minute break every hour. The guides had told us that there was a good four-hour march up. It was hot. It was humid. The four hours came and went and I was down to my last half bottle. Then came an unscheduled stop. I looked at my watch: 0115. Must be the well. It wasn't. I saw Jim the Jock running upwards, then the radio crackled and one of the lads said that our mate Ginge had had a heart attack. I went across to see if I could help, and there he was, poor old Ginge, on his back over a rock. He had rested his Bergen on the top of the rock and it had slipped over with three large radio sets inside and wedged itself under the rock, leaving Ginge spreadeagled, pinioned and breathless.

Jim couldn't find a pulse. Come on, Ginge, I thought, for fuck's sake. If he died, a casevac chopper would have to come in and our position would be known to the *adoo*. Jim splashed valuable water on his face, then forced his last half pint down Ginge's throat. Ginge had been 'dead' for five minutes, then he spluttered into life again, looking bewildered. He received the best sympathy an SAS team could provide. His kit was split up among his mates before we set off again.

As for Jim, his action nearly did for him. He had picked up a bug back at the pool and had been vomiting all the way up. He began to fall back, suffering from heat exhaustion and dehydration, but he wouldn't ask for water; that went against the training and the grain, plus he was carrying the GPMG, spare barrels and 600 rounds. Arthur Hornby went back to remotivate him and did more than that. He swapped his rifle for the GPMG. (Arthur later died attempting to row the Pacific Ocean single-handed.)

On and up, up and on. I began to see rocks as phantom *adoo*. Everything in me was so parched that I wished the monsoon would come back, and for the first time I could properly imagine the horror stories of the Korean war when men, crazy with thirst, would open up the radiators of trucks and drink the contents, a cocktail of rust and anti-freeze. Then I began to spot things on the track: hexamine blocks (used for cooking), rations, a tube of condensed milk, but this was no hallucination; this was the *firqas* unloading, on the point of jacking in and giving up. It was the best sight of the night, that condensed milk. It gave me strength. I'm fucked if I'm jacking.

It was about half an hour to first light, 5 a.m., and we were supposed to be on the plateau. I could see the first of the crocodile on the skyline and vanishing, and I figured we had made it, but it was a false crest. I got there and discovered that we were going down into a *wadi*. Going down was worse than climbing up, due to the weight on my knees and ankles, and it took us another half-hour to reach the bottom. It seemed that the local guides couldn't find the way up and so two of the mountain troop did a recce and eventually found a track. Up we went again.

At 6.30 in the morning and an hour over schedule we moved on to the plateau and across to the airstrip. I was tensed up for battle, pumped with adrenaline, waiting for my first experience of coming under enemy fire: rifle, mortar, shell – whatever. It didn't happen. There wasn't an *adoo* to be seen. Later we discovered that a diversionary attack to the south had been successful in drawing the *adoo* away from the airstrip.

We had grouped into our teams by now. There was Sean, the trigger man, an ex-para, a seasoned soldier who had been in Aden taking shit. Jimmy from Wigan, another ex-para who'd seen service in the Middle East and Cyprus. Lou, the spotter, a South African previously with Intelligence but who'd been converted to the real thing. Lou had a violent scar running from his left eye to the corner of his mouth, a legacy of being bottled in Aldershot. And there was me, the new boy, the one who fed the gun and did the shit job of humping the equipment.

Jimmy was about to decide where to build the *sangar* when Major Pirie turned up with the colonel and told us to move to high ground on the left another hour away, so off we went again.

A thought crossed my mind as we trudged east. Most of us had nick-names. The Honk was so-called because he honked [moaned] all the time. Like most British soldiers, he is prone to honking. It's a good sign; beware when he stops. Clutch-plate was a corruption of another man's real name, Catchpole. I wasn't Snapper then. That came later after I'd been RTUd. I'd done a diver's course and a snapper was a big fish and somehow the name stuck. But why was Major Pirie known as the Duke?

'Because,' Lou said in his South African grunt, 'he keeps marching us up these fucking hills and marching us back down again.' Fair enough.

At 8.15, we reached our position. There was no time for 'bodily functions'. First priority was to get the *sangar* built, 3 feet by 8 of stone dyke, and then the GPMG to be placed in position. As we finished, we heard the first helicopters arriving with the back-up force. Then came another lift of choppers, then the Skyvans bringing in reinforcements from the Sultan's army and more *firqas*. Then came salvation in the shape of Laba, bounding up the hill towards us. He had about 500 rounds across his chest, a GPMG in one hand and two 5-gallon cans of water, one in the other hand, the other on his shoulder.

'Come on, Laba, we're pissing fresh air here,' I yelled.

He dropped the two cans and was off again with just four words. 'Here's your water, lads.' Like he was on a stroll before breakfast.

We spent the day consolidating our position and fighting off sleep. It was a beautiful day with maximum visibility. The GPMG with 200 rounds coiled on the ground and ready to fire was a reassuring sight because we knew the *adoo* would be back eventually.

There was just Sean and me in the *sangar* late in the afternoon – the other two had moved position – when the world erupted, green tracer reaching out over our position and cracking close by. I grabbed my rifle and tucked myself down by the wall, then looked across at Sean. He was stirring the tea, totally uncon-cerned. 'They were only "overs",' he said. I wasn't to worry.

Sean was a seasoned soldier. This was nothing to him. There

was nothing we could do anyway. The fire was coming from the west and the lads over there were returning fire. This went on for about twenty minutes, then there was silence. I looked out and saw Jimmy and Lou coming back towards us. Apparently there had been twenty or thirty *adoo* over there. Testing our strength before bugging off. Jimmy told us that next day we would be on the move again. The airstrip had broken up under all the traffic of the airlift and we were to move across the plateau and build a new one.

And that was that. My first time under enemy fire. A guard list was drawn up and I shut my eyes. We'd all been awake for twenty-four hours. Peaceful oblivion.

•

Over the next few days we consolidated our new position with the force split into two groups, and it was the others who were attacked as they probed deeper into enemy territory. From where we were, 8 kilometres away, we could only watch the eerie display of tracer fire. The battle lasted for six days. The *adoo* got to within grenade-throwing range, and a guy called Steve Moors was the first SAS man to be killed in action by direct gunfire. He wasn't the first fatality. A soldier had been killed on an operational freefall jump in the Musandam Peninsula. His 'chute failed to open and he whistled in from 10,000 feet.

It was 9 October when I had my first close call. We were to take an *adoo* water-hole known as Ain. We arrived in the early morning and then put the plan into operation. Sean and I set up the machine gun on high ground overlooking the water-hole 600 metres away. Jim sat by the radio while Lou scanned the area through binoculars. The water-hole was at the far end of a horseshoe of high ground covered with thorn bushes, which was ideal for the enemy if they were lying in wait. Three action groups and the Firqa Khalid bin Waalid (FKW) were to advance to the water-hole while the rest of us gave cover. It was a tense time. No one knew if the *adoo* were waiting. We had to make a fast move before every *adoo* in the area turned up.

I watched through the spare binoculars as the FKW skirmished forward. They were half way to their objective when they dropped prone and motioned our guys forward. That wasn't right. It was their tribal area. It was up to them to take the water-hole. As I was wondering about this, a high-velocity round cracked overhead and zipped past my ears. Then, a second later, the high ground erupted as the *adoo* opened up with rifle fire, RPD (Russian 7.62 millimetre) light machine guns and, somewhere, a heavy machine gun. Jimmy and Lou saw its position in the tree line. The *adoo* had made a mistake. The HMG must have been newly taken out of the arms cache because its preservation grease and oil was burning. It was like a little fire. A perfect target.

Jimmy yelled, 'Rapid fire!' and Sean let go a burst of thirty rounds that overshot the target. The line was right but too high. 'Fire another long burst,' I shouted, 'and I'll turn it down on the elevation drum.'

I unlocked the drum and tweaked it downwards. Sean fired again. I made another minor adjustment and then watched happily as the tracer found its target. I locked off the drum. Jimmy yelled, 'On!' and I clipped on a fresh 200-round belt and began to feed the beast. Streams of tracer hurtled towards our target, then mortars opened up all around, starting fires on the tree-line and what we call a mixed-fruit pudding was cooking up – being HE [high explosive] to get the enemy running, white phosphorous to fry-and-frag-'em, then more HE to finish them off.

It went on and on and on. Then we heard that Valdez had been hit by an ambush party on the high ground to the right. Jimmy fired off a dozen tracer rounds from his SLR to show Sean the position. Sean swung the machine gun round, following Jimmy's tracer, and disposed of the ambushers.

In the end we had too much fire power for them, and after about two hours they were gone and we had the water-hole. I felt strangely elated, on an adrenaline high. That first bullet had caught me cold, before the adrenaline locked on. Someone with an AK must have seen us setting up and taken a pot shot. The first thing they go for is the machine gun and the radio aerials, but he probably didn't zero his weapon or gauge the distance properly. If he'd been a sniper, I'd have been dead. I'd escaped by inches. I'd been looking at death very closely. I had indeed become a seasoned soldier.

We were dug in on the Jebel for Christmas and New Year, then I went back to the UK on a signals course, then back to Dhofar again in May, to a place called Tawi Atair. We were defending an airstrip in a perfect position on a hilltop. We just sat there for six weeks, soaking up incoming fire, but there was no real danger. The *adoo* would never have attempted a frontal assault. We had far too much fire power. Then down came the monsoon. The airstrip was no longer operational. The Skyvans couldn't land in that weather. The *firqas* dispersed and went home, and we headed for the coast, to a little town of mud houses called Mirbat.

•

The battle of Mirbat in July 1972 is one of the proudest moments in SAS history. It is also an extraordinary testament to the fighting skills of those involved. Following the implementation of the SAS 'hearts and minds' campaign and the recruiting of *firqa* units, the *adoo* were losing ground. The rebels therefore decided a victory was needed to persuade the wavering Dhofaris that their cause would eventually triumph. They chose to attack Mirbat, which was occupied by a nine-man SAS team commanded by twenty-three-year-old Captain Mike Kealy, plus a handful of Arab soldiers and some gendarmes. The rebels thought they would win an easy victory. They were wrong.

For two and a half months Snapper, Sek and Laba had lived by the sea, training the local *firqas* and going out on patrols on the Jebel.

•

Snapper We lived in a small mud-and-brick building called the Batt House [British Army Training Team HQ], and from its roof we could see the town behind us. It was like a small Cornish fishing village, only made of mud-and-brick buildings with a *wadi* in between. To the front and slightly to the left on the beach was the governor's [*wali*'s] fort and to the right up the hill another fort manned by the Dhofar gendarmerie with a 25-pound field gun in a gun pit beside it. A perimeter fence had been built some 500 yards from the Batt House, snaking from the beach behind and close to the DG fort, over the *wadi*, down behind the town and back to the beach.

●

Sek We worked with the surrenderees: people who came from the guerrilla side to surrender themselves and their weapons. They were willing to take salaries from the government so that they could be re-educated and given medical facilities and a lot more freedom than they were used to on the other side.

●

Snapper and Sek got on well with the young *firqas*, of whom Snapper says: 'Armed with an FN or a Bren gun, these were the guys who helped us win the war. But no shoes. They'd run over bare ground, stubbing their toes. They could stand on nails. God knows how they did it. They fought a war in bare feet. They helped us win the war. Without them we couldn't have done it. Brave lads.'

The problem was that, at the crucial moment, the young men were on patrol on the Jebel.

●

Sek I was running the *firqas* at the time. We had about 200 sur-renderees and local volunteers, and some of the surrenderees still had brothers and cousins in the guerrilla forces on the other side of the fence. Four or five days earlier I spoke to the *firqa* leader, who told me that they were going to do some recce and look at the areas the guerrillas were going to use. So they went out, well armed and well supplied, to search for and destroy the enemy before returning to base. We kept in contact through radios.

After a while I began to get worried. There was no information coming back from them. Then we heard they had been ambushed on their way up by a large guerrilla force. They had lost about four or five men, a few others were wounded and some had disappeared. I told my boss, Captain Kealy, that something was going on. It was quite normal to get this sort of information daily from the local people. We trained them. If they had any problems, we tried to advise them, and if they needed any further support, we went with them and made sure they did the job properly.

Once we knew that something was happening, we passed the information back to headquarters at Salalah. There was also a lot of information coming from other locations, which told us that there was a large force mustered about two days' walk from Mirbat. But, according to base, these local forces could never have mounted big enough numbers to attack. We were worried, but next day we were due to hand over to G Squadron.

Morale was very high that day. We'd just about completed our four-month tour. The other squad, part of the advance party, had arrived the day before, and we spent the day going through what we'd been doing and showing them all the various personalities in the town. Then they went back to base at Um al Gwarif, 40 miles away.

We'd done quite a hard four months. We had had so many battles. Many of the people had seen action almost every day in the mountains. Now we were all looking forward to going home. Everybody was relaxed. Nobody expected anything to happen, especially on the last day.

•

Eight men and the officer settled down that night in the Batt House. There were Snapper, Sek and Laba. Fuzz from Lancashire, described by Sek as 'very small, about 5 foot, but very strong: he could carry the same weight as Laba and me. Long hair and beads and he liked rock and roll – and a few pints from time to time.' Tommy Tobin, who was stocky, younger than the others, the medic. He was quiet, shy and friendly, the type who wouldn't hurt a fly. Bob Bennett from Devon, the command post orderly, again, according to Sek, very shy. Tall. One of the married ones. Very cheerful. Roger from Bristol: 'all ribs and dick,' says Snapper, 'like a gypsy's dog'. Jeff from G Squadron – 'He was from the advance party,' says Snapper, 'and only stayed over to do a two-day inventory. An Irish Guardsman from Southern Ireland.' And, in command, a young officer whom the men called a 'baby rupert' because of his lack of experience, Captain Mike Kealy.

In addition there were thirty Askars in the *wali*'s fort, old boys who used to be the bodyguard, and twenty-five Dhofar gendarmes, and an Omani gunner in the other fort. The monsoon had just about finished, leaving the Jebel misty and obscured by low cloud. The forecast for next day was like that for a drizzly English summer's day.

They all turned in on the top floor, but Sek, Laba and Fuzz didn't sleep. There were songs to be sung and rum to be drunk. Laba was in a particularly good mood.

•

Snapper Nothing ever bothered him. Just after a firefight during Operation Jaguar I saw him drilling a group of young *firqas*. He had a mortar-aiming post tucked under his arm in place of a guardsman's pace stick, and he went through a full mock drill. 'Squad shun, stand at ease, open order, march,' and the firks lapped it up. When he dismissed them, all the *firqas* in their *sangars* broke into wild applause. Laba had relieved the tension.

It was the sort of thing we came to expect from him. He was the leading chorister for the rugby songs, knew all the words. When he came to a zebra crossing, he would bound over like a cartoon character, saying, 'Now you see me, now you don't.' His party piece was eating cigarette sandwiches, half a pack between two slices. And one night, fuelled by alcohol, he claimed a blood link with the British missionary fraternity, as his great-great-grandfather said he had roasted and eaten John Wesley and followed up with the man's boots, marinated in coconut juice.

That night when we heard the first mortars, Laba wasn't bothered. 'It's just the dawn chorus,' he said. 'Regular as clockwork.'

Sek agreed with him. 'Just the *adoo* coughing themselves awake.'

•

Sek It happened all the time. After six at night they used to mortar us from a long distance away, fire twenty or thirty rounds, then they would pack up and go away. Same thing at first light. When the first mortar landed we would go and take up standard positions: the machine-gun people to the GMPG, others on the .5 Browning, the mortar team got ready and the radio operator started sending back to base. When it got light we normally sent mortars or the jets to strafe them. Just another tedious day in Dhofar.

•

Snapper I didn't take it so easy as the other three. They were lying there in their olive-green shirts and shorts without a care in the world. I always slept in my shorts. We all had our morphine syrettes round our necks, just in case – never took them off. I dragged on my shirt and belt kit, pushed past the other three and up the ammo boxes that served as a ladder on to the roof.

When I got there, the first mortars were impacting just outside the perimeter wire. I went to my stand-to position behind the Browning in the command-post *sangar* on the north-east corner of the roof. I could clearly see the flashes of the mortar tubes 2,000 metres away in the foothills of the Jebel. And from the Jebel Ali – a 300-foot hill 1.5 kilometres away – came the white flashes of machine-gun and rifle fire, while green tracer from an RPD light machine gun zipped into the walls of the DG fort.

As I wondered what had happened to the DG picket – I learnt later that they had been silently taken out by the *adoo* – the others took up position. I was on the north-east corner of the *sangar*. To my right Bob checked the mortar plotter board. Below and 10 feet from the house, Fuzz, Sek and Tommy were in the mortar pit, getting ready to do battle. Fuzz was bent over the illuminated dial of the mortar. Sek was holding a bomb as if it were no more dangerous than a rugby ball. Tommy was preparing them, unscrewing the plastic container tops, checking that the charge cartridges were in position, removing the safety pins, replacing them, fins first, in their containers and stacking them so that there could be as many as four dozen at hand when required. Roger and Jeff took their position by the GPMG on the far corner of the roof, and Laba started legging it to his position in the gun pit up by the DG fort.

And that was it – an 81-millimetre mortar, the Browning GPMG and the 25-pound World War Two gun against God knows how many. The Browning in front of me was a fearsome weapon with a rate of fire of between 450 and 500 rounds at an effective range of 1,800 metres, but the sum total of our defences didn't seem much compared to what was coming in. I began to have a bad feeling about this one. This wasn't the *adoo* showing off, flexing their muscles like before. This was something different; and at that time I'd no idea that there were anything between 250 and 400 of them out there.

A mortar salvo blew away part of the perimeter wire and a round exploded on the edge of town. Shrapnel flew over our heads. Then I turned to see Mike Kealy clambering over the *sangar* wall. As he was telling me to go down to the radio and contact base, an artillery round went overhead and into the centre of town. This was much worse. That was no mere mortar. It turned out to be a 75-millimetre RCL [anti-tank weapon].

I went down the *sangar* steps and across the radio room. It was already tuned in. I tapped out the call sign in Morse: 'OA, OA. This is 82. Radio check. Over.' It was a nervous moment, waiting, and then a gush of relief as the signaller at Um al Gwarif responded. As I went for the code book, an explosion nearby shook the building. Plaster fell from the ceiling. There was dust everywhere. To hell with the code book. I decided to send all messages in plain Morse. I was about to breach security and deviate from regulations, but what did it matter? The enemy were at the gates. There was no need for secrecy.

'Contact. Under heavy fire. Wait. Out.'

Another explosion. More plaster and dust. Now that they knew the situation back at base, I had to get back to my position. As I got there and eased off the safety catch on the Browning, a massive explosion took a great chunk out of the DG tower, and in the flash I could see Laba kneeling behind the shield of the 25-pounder. Bob shouted across that he reckoned it was a 75-millimetre RCL and then I was momentarily deafened as our mortars opened up.

It was beginning to get light. I checked my watch: 0600 hours. Across in the *wali*'s fort I could see the Askaris with their old weapons, bolt-action .303s, but we all held our fire, not wanting to give flashes for the enemy to aim at. We could make out the noise of a heavy machine gun and a GPMG. They were stepping up the bombardment, not slinking away as per usual with the dawn.

Then, maybe an hour and a half to two hours since the bombardment began, I saw the first assault troop. They must have formed up just below Jebel Ali, having despatched the night picket, and they used that as their final assault position. A group of about fifty got in extended line and advanced across the plain towards us about 200 to 300 yards away. I started to sweat. I fingered the trigger of the Browning, knowing that this was it.

This is the worst moment, just before a contact. It's the fear of the unknown. You welcome the fear; without it you can't have the concentration that means the difference between life and death. You go through every move and then on to automatic pilot. As I watched the men advance, I realized what all the training, all the discipline, all those years on the range, fire discipline, counting your rounds, was all about ... because no one was opening up. No one had made the decision to fire. You had to be sure that it's the enemy, that you're not going to waste some civilians.

Mike still hadn't seen them. When I pointed them out, he put his specs on, stared at them, took his specs off again and wiped them on his shirt tail. I waited for the order to fire, but he didn't give it. He kept saying, 'Don't fire. It must be the *firqas* returning.' Then the decision was taken out of our hands. Some old guy with a Bren gun in the Askari force must have said, 'Sod this,' and opened fire. The general order to open fire was given and the battle was on.

I felt the adrenaline begin to flow. It's a warm, physical feeling as it kicks in. The emotional shutters come down and all feelings of humanity are locked out. It's a kind of exhilarating insanity. It's me or it's him. Kill or be killed. It has been said that the most exhilarating feeling of all is to be fired on with no effect, and I can vouch for that. All fear disappears. You feel as if you are unbeatable, or at least I do. I felt then that there was nobody out there who was going to take me out personally. I'd take them out before they took me out. It's this adrenaline rush that carries you through, that and the discipline and the training. But it's the adrenaline that gives you the feeling that you can't be beaten.

The only concern when battle is joined is not to let the others down. And so we set about taking them out, eliminating them. The group in front were hit by the Browning .50-calibre bullets and the GPMG. The line faltered and collapsed, then we turned towards the plain, where wave upon wave of them were advancing on the perimeter wire, spread out in groups of ten, grabbing at the barbed wire with bare hands, while in the gun-pit Laba traversed the 25-pounder into direct-fire and was blasting them into oblivion. But still they managed to cut the wire, and we concentrated our fire on the groups assaulting the DG fort. If the gun was taken, they would use it on the Batt House and the town, and we'd have big problems.

•

Sek (manning the mortar) Things settled down a bit. We'd stopped firing because we couldn't see the targets. Then, about an hour later, Laba called on the radio, saying that he had been chinned. That was enough for me. I had to join him, so I picked up my SLR and started to run.

I ran up the hill, dodging as much as I could, taking cover when I had to. They were advancing, and the firing was getting heavier all the time, but I had to get there because Laba was on his own with the Omani artillery, and I didn't know how many of them were with him at the time. I got to the top and crawled in to where Laba was and he was alone. Normally it takes three men to fire the gun and he was doing it all by himself. When he said he'd been chinned he meant he'd been grazed by a bullet, either a ricochet or a direct hit.

I started banging on the door of the fort, trying to get the DG to come out. Only one emerged, the gunner Khalid. I got back to the *sangar* wall but Khalid was hit. From then on it was just the two of us.

By then it was getting light. We could see figures or bodies everywhere, some still a long distance away towards the coast, along Jebel Ali, and some on the plain due north of us. There were people advancing with machine guns, some running, some firing heavy machine guns, mortars and rocket launchers. All Laba and I did was fire close to Jebel Ali. We couldn't fire at the Jebel because the Omani soldiers were protecting one of our high grounds.

At the same time some of the *firqas* were coming back into Mirbat, and we were worried about firing on them. So we fired towards the plain. That's where most of the guerrillas were coming from, doing a frontal attack.

It was just like watching a movie. It was about 6 a.m. and it was very, very cloudy and misty too, so they were lucky they had lots of cover and lots of time to make their way in. When Laba and I were firing, we were really under heavy attack. As soon as you put your head up, you could hear the bullets whistling by. It was so close. We literally had to crawl to be able to do anything. We'd crawl and load the gun, fire it and then crawl down and do it again.

It was ridiculous. They were almost on top of us, shooting from all directions. At least we could hear on the radio that our comrades back in the house were still okay. It was getting very, very fierce, and Laba and I were joking in Fijian. All the fear seemed to go away.

We knew the gun was their main target and we were still

firing at point-blank range. We had no time to aim. All we could
do was pick up a round, load it in and fire as quickly as we
could. But the guerrillas were coming closer and closer towards
us, and at the end we had to abandon it. You can't fire a 25-
pounder at 50 metres. You'd just get metal fragments in your
face. And we had to cover ourselves.

I heard the crack of a gun. Something hit my shoulder and
the shock knocked me out for a few seconds. I really didn't
know where I was. I totally curled up. The clearest way of
describing it is like an elephant charging at you at 120 miles an
hour with a sharp, pointed trunk.

Laba, still bleeding from the graze on his chin, crawled across
to give me a shell dressing to cover the wound which was on my
left side. After that I had to fire my rifle single-handed with my
right hand. I still wasn't frightened. It was us or them. I always
had a feeling we would survive in the end. So we just fought on.

We were pretty short of ammunition by now, and the battle
was getting fiercer. They were still advancing towards the fort.
They were close. Maybe 100 yards at the most and moving
slowly from all directions. Laba and I knew we were almost
surrounded. Then he told me that there was a 66-millimetre
mortar outside the gate of the fort.

Again we were joking in Fijian and I said: 'Laba, keep your
head down.' And Laba did the same to me. He crawled away
from the gun pit towards the mortar. I was covering him. I
looked at him, and he looked back at me as if he knew something
was going to happen. Then I heard a crack. I turned. All I could
see was blood. A bullet had hit Laba's neck and blood was
pouring out. He died instantly, within seconds.

I was very sad when it happened and very alone.

•

Back at the Batt House Mike Kealy was worried. The 25-pounder
had gone silent and there was no reply from the walkie-talkie at
the gun pit.

•

Snapper He called a Chinese parliament in the radio room. I'd just called for an air strike and a casevac chopper, and I joined in the discussion as to what to do next. Mike decided to take Tommy with him to the gun pit. He was the medic, after all. Bob would take over command and control the air strikes. I was to give covering fire and man the radio. I felt both guilt and disappointment. I wanted to help Laba and Sek, but I had no choice but to accept the decision. We were surrounded now.

Then came a lull. The *adoo* had fallen back. Bob reminded Mike to get out of his flip-flops and into his 'desert wellies'. You can't run in flip-flops. Tommy waited, patting his belt kit, checking he had chambered a round in his SLR, then they were off and out and running.

Back up at my post, I flipped off the safety catch on the Browning once more and watched Mike and Tommy run the first 90 metres towards the *wadi*, which gave them cover some of the way from the machine guns. They were pepper-potting forward, one running a few yards while the other covered him and vice versa. They got about half way when they were spotted. A heavy machine gun to the east of the fort sent tracer across their path. I lined up the Browning on the spitting flames and squeezed the trigger. The HMG vanished under tracer and incendiary rounds. That was one major obstacle out of the way. The two guys went on again, closer and closer.

•

Sek I had been alone with Laba for around fifteen minutes. I'd propped myself up against the *sangar* wall and was potting away at the enemy with my SLR. There was no time to grieve for Laba.

I had to think of how to survive. There was hardly any ammunition. I could hear the radio going but I was too far away to call for help. Then I saw Mike Kealy and Tommy Tobin coming towards me, dodging bullets. As they approached, the *adoo* were getting nearer the fort, advancing. They were so close you could almost reach out and touch them.

Tommy was the first to reach the *sangar* and as he climbed

over, he got shot in the jaw. I heard machine-gun fire and all I could see was his face being totally torn apart. He fell, and Mike Kealy dragged him to a safe area. Then Mike spoke to me. He decided we'd be better off if he got himself into the ammunition pit a few metres away. It was 4 feet deep. He ran to it and jumped in and landed on the body of a DG soldier, a 'powder monkey', one of those who had been detailed to carry the ammo to the gun pit. There was another soldier cowering in the corner. Kealy told him to move the body and checked our situation.

Mike and I were now about 3 or 4 metres away from each other. We couldn't see each other but we could talk. I was shouting at him to tell him that I was running out of ammunition. Luckily, he was with one of the local Omani artillery who still had loaded magazines, so he started throwing them to me At last I could reload my magazine and keep on firing. The battle was really getting heavy. Mike and I could see two or three people on the corner of the fort throwing grenades only about 4 or 5 metres away from us. Mike said, 'Look, we'll take one each on each corner.' When he was firing I was covering; likewise when I was firing he was covering me. We managed to kill a few.

All I could hear was Mike trying to get across on the radio, trying to get some support, although our guys were giving all they could with mortars, firing to the side and on top of the fort itself to protect us.

•

On the roof of the Batt House Snapper was stunned at the news from Kealy of his friend's death.

•

Snapper It lasted just for a moment, then the shutters came down again and humanity was locked out. It was beginning to look desperate over there from the moment the *adoo* cut through the inner perimeter wire only 15 metres from the gun. They were also using the fort's dead ground. From where we were we couldn't see the dead ground behind the fort. Because the fort was in a raised position, they were able to work their way round the back and move along the side of the wall to grenade-throwing distance.

'Get on the set and call for reinforcements,' Bob said, amazingly calm. My resolve stiffened even more, if possible, by the death of Laba, I ran back down to the radio room, keyed my call sign again, got the acknowledgement and sent the bad news: 'Laba dead. Sekonia VIS. Tobin VIS. Situation desperate. Send reinforcements. Over.'

A hesitation, then I was asked to send a wet rep [weather report]. I yelled in frustration, jumped up and looked out of the door, saw the limp flags and the low cloud and reported back. No sooner had I got back on the roof than we saw two Strikemaster jets breaking through the cloud. They streaked at about 80 feet over the town. Roger appeared at the wall. He had been controlling them. He thought a casevac chopper was arriving and he was directing it with his small air-to-ground radio. Instead the jets had appeared.

'The seventh cavalry has arrived,' he yelled, and disappeared.

Bob grabbed the radio. 'Hello, Red Leader,' he said. 'This is Batt House. Enemy left and right of the fort. Over.'

The voice of the pilot crackled back a 'roger'. 'How long have they been going at you?'

'Since dawn.' It was now 0815 hours.

'Roger, Batt House. They're like ants down there. I can see hundreds of them.'

The *adoo* now turned their attention to the jets as the first strafing runs were made. The first jet went into a vertical dive, spraying the left perimeter fence; the other put two rockets into the *wadi* to the right. Then they came back again with bullets, rockets and a 500-kilogram bomb loosed into the *wadi* to the east of the fort. One of the jets was hit in the tail section and limped away. The other made one final run and then it too was off.

The jubilation was short-lived, however, because now we could hear firing behind us to the east. The *adoo* had regrouped and were counter-attacking.

Mike Kealy came on the walkie-talkie again, asking for more mortar support, this time in the *wadi*, at a precise spot. Bob did his sums, then shouted instructions to Fuzz, who was now firing it on his own. Fuzz pulled the bipod legs back to get the angle and let one go. It exploded just past the fort. Another adjustment, then another, until Fuzz had reached maximum elevation and still he was off target. With a shrug, Fuzz lifted the mortar barrel to his chest so that the legs were gangling, hugged the barrel close as if it were a dancing partner and slid a bomb down the barrel. This time he got it right and he continued to send bomb after bomb right where Mike wanted them.

By now I was having trouble with the Browning. It is fine for two people, with one feeding the belt through, but the breech-block and the slide had become jammed with brass shavings, and I could fire only single shots and recock the firing mechanism each time. There should have been someone to feed the belt through, but we were stretched thin – lack of manpower. This was war on a shoestring. Maximum stakes with minimum back-up. After a few hours feeding the belts across my palm I was getting tired.

Then came two more Strikemasters on strafing runs. Bob directed them to Jebel Ali and the back of the fort.

'It looks hot down there,' said one pilot.

'Roger, Red Leader,' said Bob. 'Sheets of lead.'

The jets disposed of the *sangars* on the top of the hill, then rocketed the top of the hill until it disintegrated, then they came back to the fort and strafed the *adoo* with rockets and tracer.

•

Sek In the gun pit I thought the screaming of the jets was the best sound I had ever heard.

I looked at the sky and I could hear the roar of the jets coming in and I think that's the only thing that saved us at the time. I overheard Bob Bennett telling the pilot on the radio : 'I say, look, just fire whenever you can or hit the fort.'

They came more or less right on top of us. The pilots were briefed to fire willy-nilly, just to hit the side of the fort. Anything to the other side of the fort towards the plain was enemy; anything on this side towards the coast was friendly forces. They came in very low, I'd say about 50, 100 feet and I'm sure the pilots could have seen everything.

It wasn't over, though. I could see figures on the eastern skyline about 2,000 metres away, a disciplined-looking bunch. I lined the front sight blade on the leader. Okay, maybe I was down to single shots, but a single shot was all I needed to get rid of the officer leading them. Bob was following my gaze. We waited, then he told me to go down again and get a sit rep from base.

It was the best news I'd heard. The little black dots on the skyline were G Squadron. When I got back to Bob, he'd already guessed and had sent Fuzz with the other medical pack to the gun pit. Then he picked up his SLR and began sniping at the retreating enemy. And I followed suit with the Browning.

I began to wonder how it had happened, why we had not been warned by the green slime, then I turned to see a Huey chopper take off from the gun pit and come towards us. It landed a few feet away from the building, but before I could take a look I was ordered downstairs to help with the casevac. The ground floor was like an abattoir, littered with the wounded, stinking of piss, sweat and blood; flies were all over the place. There were plenty of the old Askaris from the *wali*'s fort and they all had the same skin wounds on the scalps where rounds had grazed them as they popped their heads over the wall. Some had more than one wound. Another centimetre and they would have been dead. Amazing wounds.

Then there was an *adoo* with a dreadful throat wound. He was making a terrible sucking sound. Even now in my front room in Hereford I can still hear that horrible sound. He died later.

I looked out and saw the chopper pilot gesturing me to come over. He wanted me to check the bodies in the back to find out which one was ours. There were six on stretcher racks. I pulled the blanket off the nearest and saw an Arab with his head caved in; then a young one, maybe seventeen – I couldn't see the wound, just the dead, open eyes. The third was face down, lying on the crook of his arm. I attempted to roll the body over but rigor mortis had set in. It was solid. I then had to lever the whole body up, using the elbow, and as I did so I could just see Laba's features.

The jaw line had been shot away but I could tell it was Laba by his eyes. They were still open. It was like a sledgehammer blow to the morale. I was still hyped up after the battle but all feelings of exhilaration disappeared in a flash. Here was a man I'd drunk with, fought with, laughed with . . . and here he was, laid out on a stretcher, stiff as a board. It was just too much. I was engulfed with sorrow at the loss of such a comrade.

The first to be taken out were Labalaba and Tommy Tobin, who was badly wounded. I went out on the last helicopter. They wanted me on a stretcher but I could walk, slightly off balance but I was okay. It was just a bit of pride, but I walked down to the helipad which was about 20 yards from the fort.

The bullet had entered my left shoulder and been deflected by my shoulder blade past my spine and was finally stopped about an inch away from my heart. But also I had a graze on my forehead which I didn't know about until I got back. I'd lost a lot of blood. I got shot roughly about six or seven o'clock in the morning and didn't get casevac until about eleven.

•

Tommy Tobin died of his wound. Mike Kealy took a patrol to the Jebel Ali to look for the *firqas*. He came back later in the day with four bodies and three wounded and learnt the fate of the eight-man DG picket on the hill. The guerrillas had hoped to dispose of them silently but they had been spotted. A firefight had developed and four DG had been killed, the others escaping. The final tally of the attack was two SAS, six DG and the Omani gunner dead plus one DG wounded. The guerrillas left behind thirty bodies and ten wounded, although sources later indicated that the casualties had been much higher, probably half the force having been killed or wounded.

Mirbat was the beginning of the end of the rebellion, the *adoo* having received a loss of credibility along with their casualties, and they never again deployed such a large attacking force. Gallantry awards were later made public in Britain although the war itself received no publicity. Kealy got the DSO, Sek the DCM, Bradshaw the MM and Laba received a posthumous Mention in Despatches.

•

Sek I believe we achieved quite a lot by denying the coastal town to the guerrillas, although we were outnumbered. I think everybody did very well: us – the British Army Training Team – and the local force, the Omani forces and also the local *firqas* and the Askaris. The enemy did not achieve their aims. They were totally destroyed, morally, physically and psychologically, as a result of being defeated at Mirbat. I believe one of their aims was to capture the main gun, kill all the British Army Training Team and then use the victory as propaganda to warn the Omani forces who were calling the shots.

I don't think it was heroism. We were given a task and we did it. There was nothing special to it. I'm sure that any of my comrades would have done the same. But it was very sad to see Laba and Tobin die. I do feel let down that all the men who were involved in the battle were not recognized. I think all the people involved should have been given a medal. But it didn't happen. Blokes who served in places like Northern Ireland or the Falklands got medals for nothing compared to what my lot went through.

•

Snapper Nobody ever tackled Laba. He was a bear of a man. Just to see him walk down the street was enough for most people, but when he was fully tooled up he was the original Rambo. He would never surrender. He just didn't know the word surrender. He would give his life for his comrades. Same with Sek.

They wanted to give Laba the VC for his actions at Mirbat, but because the war was a secret in 1972 they said a VC awarded

to a Fijian would be headlines in every newspaper in the UK. So
to keep the war secret, all they gave him was MID. You can get
that for walking up the Falls Road. The guy deserved a VC for
what he did.

•

In 1984 Snapper found himself under observation in the British
Army Psychiatric Unit of the Royal Hospital, Woolwich. The
colonel of the regiment thought that he was 'a time bomb
waiting to explode'.

•

Snapper I was playing games with the psychiatrists and I wasn't
getting anywhere. I was stuck in the place like Jack Nicholson in
One Flew Over the Cuckoo's Nest. I was idly flipping through one
of those publications of World War II when I saw an old photo
of a 25-pounder in action and I remembered seeing the sign to
the Woolwich Artillery Museum as I was driven into this place.

I got out via the fire escape and crossed the road into the
museum. And there it was. The Mirbat gun with a gleaming new
barrel and protective shield. Show-piece condition. The last of
its type to be used by British troops in action.

I went back, refreshed, hoping to climb in unnoticed, but I
was spotted by a nurse who asked where the hell I'd been. When
I told him, he didn't believe me. He breathalysed me – twice.
Negative, of course. So he sent me to the major. I explained
again where I'd been. Mirbat? What Mirbat? He'd never heard
of the battle. He thought I'd been having delusions. He didn't
even have my war records. To him I was just an ex-drunk, liable
at any minute to explode.

•

The secret war was finally won by the gradual penetration of
Dhofari society, with *firqas* trained by the SAS, using water as
the most powerful bargaining chip. The main military objective
was to cut the guerrillas' supply lines from South Yemen. In
1973 the SAS cleared the area between Salalah and Thamrait,

and the next year the whole of central Dhofar was cleared. Though some of the fighting was heavy, the *adoo* were in retreat and disarray. Towards the end of 1974 the new commander of the Dhofar area, Brigadier John Akehurst, aimed to end the campaign by pressing the *adoo* back towards the Yemen border.

In January 1975, as the rebels were being pushed back to the border, a *firqa* unit, supported by the SAS, attacked a number of heavily defended caves. The advance was ambushed and the leading Sultan's Armed Forces company lost thirteen killed and twenty-two wounded in less than an hour. The battle raged for two days and nights. At dusk on the third day, the SAS unit moved forward to make withdrawal possible. The SAS officer in charge was awarded an MC and one of his troop commanders later went on to command the SAS Regiment during the Gulf War. As a result of the battle, the strategically important caves were never used by the rebels again.

The Dhofar rebellion was finally beaten in October 1975, when a sweep was undertaken in the mountains near the border with South Yemen, resulting in the rebels' supply routes being blocked for good. The original object was to seize high ground about a 2,000-foot-deep *wadi* while an armoured car column advanced from the plain to control the foothills. It was a diversion, though, that became the main pivot of the attack.

The diversion was from a mountaintop government-held position at Sarfait. Breaking out of this position was considered suicidal, as it included climbing down a 600-foot sheer drop. The SAS units and their allies found the route unopposed, however, and on 14 and 15 October two more companies were flown in. The troops went forward to occupy a 3-mile corridor to the sea which finally cut the guerrillas' last supply line. As a result they were forced to cross over into South Yemen.

The war ended formally a few months later, in 1976, with a cease-fire between South Yemen and Oman. In the six-year war the SAS had lost twelve men.

5
THE IRANIAN
EMBASSY SIEGE

> The baddie with the grenade. He got four magazines emptied
> into him. He was pretty well dead. The coroner stopped counting
> at seventy-eight bullets.
>
> *Mack*

At 11.25 in the morning on Wednesday, 30 April 1980, six men walked up to a five-storey, white-fronted terraced house opposite Hyde Park. They wore chequered *shamags* and anoraks and carried holdalls which contained three Browning self-loading pistols with thirteen-round magazines, one .38 Astra revolver and five Russian RGD5 hand grenades. Two of them had Polish Skorpion W263 sub-machine guns concealed in their anoraks. The house was the Iranian Embassy, and the men were terrorists of the Democratic Revolutionary Front for the Liberation of Arabistan, a small province of Iran peopled by ethnic Arabs.

Ascending the three steps up to the front door, the armed men first confronted PC Trevor Lock of the Diplomatic Protection Group, who was standing in the lobby between the main doors, which were open, and a pair of security doors. One of the terrorists grabbed Lock, who managed to kick the outer door shut, but another fired three shots from his Browning through the glass panel and the men forced their way in, one of them firing a burst from his automatic into the ceiling.

Inside the Embassy only a handful were quick enough to escape. Two men got out of a back window; another climbed through a fourth-floor window into the adjoining building. The chargé d'affaires, Dr Ali Afrouz, jumped from a first-floor window but injured himself and was dragged back inside. The doors were slammed shut and twenty-six people were now hostages – sixteen members of staff, including six women, eight visitors, including Sim Harris and Chris Cramer from the BBC, plus Lock and the Embassy chauffeur, Ron Morris. The Iraqi-backed terrorists began issuing demands: the immediate release of ninety-two Arabs held in Iran and safe passage for themselves. Provided their demands were met, no one would be hurt. If they were not met, then the hostages would die.

Immediately, police negotiators set about trying to negotiate with the terrorists, while at the same time the entire area was sealed off by specialist units. Soon Prince's Gate was surrounded by police marksmen, anti-terrorist officers, men from the Special Patrol Group and Scotland Yard's Technical Support Branch. And the SAS had been called in as back-up.

It was not the first time the regiment had been involved in counter-terrorism. It had begun in Aden with the *keeni meeni* undercover operations – *keeni meeni* being Swahili for the unseen movement of a snake in long grass, which, translated into regimental English, became close-quarter battle training. This continued throughout the 1960s with the aim of providing a pool of expert marksmen to act as bodyguards for the government and top brass in the forces. SAS men were also hired out to friendly powers, which had the combined effect of yielding goodwill and intelligence.

Then, in 1972, the Palestinian Black September terrorist group kidnapped eleven Israeli athletes at the Munich Olympics. The rescue attempt at the airport failed. All the hostages were killed, and European governments realized they had no forces capable of dealing with such atrocities. The SAS was given the task of preparing an anti-terrorist force and the Counter-Revolutionary Warfare wing was expanded to include a counter-terrorist team.

As a direct result of this, the regiment built the Killing House. Initially it was just a room full of paper targets where the men were taught to differentiate immediately between hostages and terrorists. They were shown how to gain entry and kill the enemy without injuring the hostages in just four seconds. By 1980 the 'House' had grown to six rooms, including a mock-up of the interior of an airliner. The men were now trained to attack not only buildings and aircraft but also ships, oil rigs and nuclear power stations.

Live hostages were, and still are, used despite fatalities like the one in 1986, when a sergeant was killed accidentally. Dummies are used as the 'bad guys', and each exercise is recorded for subsequent appraisal. When the call came that April morning, the SAS counter-terrorist team had been in action only three times.

Snapper and Sek were shooting at targets in the Killing House that day and Snapper wasn't in the best of moods. 'I had a hangover. I'd ripped a nail opening an ammo box. My lungs were bad from breathing in lead fumes. The day before I'd spat out something black and horrible. And I was fed up with fucking and farting around, fitting targets of sinister-looking Russians to wooden veneers. Then our bleepers went and we were summoned to a meeting in the hangar. It was 11.48. The Kremlin [the nickname of the SAS Operations Planning and Intelligence cell located at Stirling Lines] had got an early tip-off that something was going on from a former member of the regiment, Dusty Grey, who was with the guard-dogs section at Heathrow Airport.'

Mack was also in the camp, preparing to go out on exercise. 'The Toad [an assault team leader] told me about it and I thought it was just another exercise. When he said it was for real, I didn't believe him. I thought it was a wind-up.'

R. F., meanwhile, was at his home in Hereford. 'I was due to play football that weekend for a local team called Westfields, and we were also to go off on a training exercise, but as soon as Dusty rang, everything was put off. The regiment doesn't wait for official approval before getting going. My bleeper went and I was told to come to the camp for a briefing. All we got told at first was that there had been an incident at the Embassy and we'd be moved closer to await further instructions.

'Our kit was already organized within an alarmed compound and we put it all in the back of the team pantechnicon, which would follow us out of the camp. That just left personal kit, and

what you needed immediately, to be thrown into the Range
Rovers.

'We were told to head for the Royal Army Education Corps
barracks at Beaconsfield (where many of the lads had done their
language courses), but by the time we were ready, the TV had
got wind of things and so we had to go out in twos and threes
so as not to attract attention. We got to Beaconsfield about half
past nine and they told us to wait for further orders. Since we'd
been travelling since seven thirty, none of us had eaten. A chef
turned up at about ten. He was drunk and started abusing us
because, of course, no one had told him what was going on.
He'd arrived to find all these vehicles and men there, fifty of us
demanding to be fed.

'A couple of the lads burnt his hands on the hot plates to
make him cook us something. Which he did.'

Snapper remembers: 'By now we knew that if the terrorists
didn't get what they wanted, they were going to blow up the
Embassy at noon the next day. So that was it. The chance of
some action.'

•

Back at Prince's Gate, the police had moved into the Montessori
Nursery School at 24 Prince's Gate and established a link with
the terrorists. Communications were cut and a green field
telephone passed in through a window. A Farsi interpreter was
brought in, as was a psychiatrist with experience of sieges. At
3 p.m. Home Secretary William Whitelaw chaired a committee
meeting known as COBR (Cabinet Office Briefing Room, pro-
nounced 'Cobra'), which was attended by senior members of the
Ministry of Defence, the branches of the secret service and the
Director of the SAS, Brigadier Peter de la Billière. Margaret
Thatcher did not attend, but her views were made clear: namely,
that the terrorists were to remain subject to the laws of the
United Kingdom, that they would not be allowed to leave the
country and that the police were to negotiate for as long as
might be necessary, even if it took months, in order to achieve a
peaceful solution. De la Billière left the meeting certain that the

siege would end in bloodshed, but there was never any suggestion that the SAS would go in for a pre-emptive strike. The terrorists had to act first. Whitelaw decided that an assault on the Embassy would be justified if two or more of the hostages were killed. It was with these instructions in mind that the SAS team, now based at a central London barracks, was briefed.

●

Mack As soon as we arrived, we were briefed on the immediate action plan, known as the IA. This is ultra-violent: breaking down the doors and all hands do what you can. The plan is based on the minimum amount of information from snipers, witnesses and photos. You're ready to go straight away if needs must. The plan was completed within an hour of us arriving. We were going to sledgehammer the door and ground-floor windows and also break in through the upper windows, clearing the place room by room with CS gas. It's risky and bloody. While half the team are on stand-by for IA, the other half go away and start planning the more complicated Deliberate Assault Plan (DAP), which is the better option because we are in charge. The DAP is always launched when we think the time is ripe, when – hopefully – the terrorists are exhausted and we know the exact location of the hostages. After about twelve hours you change over, as you can't stay on IA for too long or you lose your edge. Over the six days of the siege we developed these plans more and more, or rather the hierarchy did, and we practised them again and again.

The basic ground rules are these. Over the years we did endless training on all aspects of anti-terrorism work, including hostage-rescue scenarios. We would regularly practise all the specialist skills employed: close-quarter combat, live shooting practice in the Killing House, abseiling, breaking and entering skills, use of explosives to gain access, sledgehammer drills, working with night-vision goggles, working in the black stuff, getting used to combat and assault drills while wearing a gas mask and to shooting while wearing gloves and so on.

It's called the Killing House because that's exactly what we do with terrorists. There is no way we were training to take prisoners. The weapons we use are the Heckler & Koch MP5 sub-machine gun and a Browning high-power handgun. The Sterling sub-machine gun was the first one preferred, then it was replaced by the Ingram, but the MP5 was used for the first time at the Embassy siege.

Remington pump-action shotguns are sometimes used to open doors by blowing away hinges and locks, and the Browning 9-millimetre pistol is also carried as a back-up weapon. You need weapons that fire rapidly and precisely on target and at low velocity, hitting the intended target without penetrating one body and striking another. The MP5 is perfect for hostage situations. We call the stun grenade a flash-bang. It's filled with a fulminate of mercury and magnesium and the thing can disorientate someone for up to forty-five seconds. Because of the fumes and the CS gas, we have to wear respirators.

There were fifty of us in the barracks, split into two teams – Red and Blue. I was in the Blue Team. The other guys were on IA. In the middle of the night they went off in furniture vans to the Forward Holding Area (FHA) next door to the Embassy, and the rest of us tried to get some kip.

•

Snapper It had been an uncomfortable night. The barracks were derelict and draughty and the toilets were blocked. There was no hot water. There was grey dust everywhere. A right health hazard – but then again we weren't promised duvets and room service when we joined up.

Early next morning, 1 May, we got a green-slime briefing. The leader of the terrorists, code-name Salim, had released a woman but he wasn't happy about the response to his demands. The Iranian government had replied that, as far as they were concerned, the six men were CIA agents and the hostages would consider it an honour to die as martyrs of the revolution.

We lay on our camp beds, wondering what would happen. I was wearing my black overalls, belt kit and lightweight boots. The MP5, body armour, respirator and assault waistcoat loaded with stun grenades were close to hand if the word came to go. I stripped and cleaned my weapons, hoping this wouldn't go on and on. Waiting around was boring. Your mind is active all the time. Will we manage to rescue the hostages? Will we take casualties? Will I get hit? How many of us will get out of this in one piece?

•

R. F. Meanwhile, the Red Team and people from various other intelligence teams were working away in the next-door building, drilling holes in the walls to plant microphones, cameras and stuff. We got the Gas Board to start drilling in the street to cover the noise, and planes were diverted to and from Heathrow to fly low over the Embassy, but despite all this we found out later that the terrorists had heard something and got suspicious and twitchy.

Apparently one of them complained about the noise and said he'd hate to live in London. Well, he certainly didn't in the end. We saw to that.

The deadline came and went and then Salim made a mistake by releasing one of the BBC guys, Chris Cramer, who was sick. He'd picked up dysentery in Ethiopia and, luckily for him, he had a recurrence of it. He was able to tell us the number of terrorists and how well they were armed, but he couldn't say whether their claim to have wired the building with explosives was true. We never knew, right up to the moment of going in.

Then we got a big bonus. The caretaker had been found. It was his luck – and ours – that he'd had the day off when the siege happened. He gave us a great briefing. He knew every nook and cranny of the place, which allowed engineers to begin building a training mock-up of the building in hessian and wood, scaled down for us to work in: all the rooms and positions so we could walk through what each person was going to do in each room as we entered, room by room, floor by floor, getting an idea of what we could expect to see and what it would be like in each room, whether you'd go in by window or door, always bearing in mind that it was just a mock-up. It was worth doing, certainly better than relying on photos.

It was a fortress situation. Six floors, including the basement, fifty rooms and easily defended front and back because of the open spaces; and it was just as well we had the caretaker because he told us that the ground and first-floor windows were armour-plated, and it was he who told us about the security door. If we hadn't known this and gone ahead with the original plan to batter in the front door and windows with sledgehammers, it would have been a disaster. They'd have just bounced off. We had to rethink.

•

At five that afternoon Salim phoned the negotiators with a new idea. He wanted a bus to take himself, his men and the hostages to an airport where Lock, Morris and Harris would be released and the rest, the Iranians, taken home.

•

Mack That was the beginning of the bus option. We got hold of a single-decker, forty-seat bus and started planning what to do in the garage. It was cleared out for us, and Gonzo was chosen to be the driver. They'd asked for a police driver, so one of the lads gave Gonzo a haircut to make him look the part. He was picked because he was small and wiry and most easily able to get out of the driver's sliding window, 18 inches by 9.

The plan was that, at a prearranged spot along the route, Gonzo would stop and we would hit the bus front and rear and from one side; you couldn't attack from both sides because a bus is paper-thin and we'd be shooting at each other. Depending on what state of mind they were in, the baddies would probably start killing the hostages immediately and Gonzo would be the first to be topped. So two of the attack team were briefed to get Gonzo out through the wee window. He got bruised and scratched rehearsing the routine time and again. Still, better than a bullet in the head – he had no body armour, no weapon.

Bare-buff. There's a fantastic camaraderie among the lads, and Gonzo was our first priority. Not that we would be neglecting the hostages, of course, but Gonzo was to be the first out. Eventually we got it down to three seconds from the bus stopping to Gonzo getting out of there.

•

R. F. That night, about three thirty in the morning of 2 May 1980, we relieved the Red Team. The Forward Holding Area was Numbers 14 and 15 Prince's Gate. Number 14, an end-of-terrace building, was the home of the Royal College of General Practitioners. Number 15, next door to the Iranian Embassy, was also ours for the duration of the siege, and in addition we had access to the Ethiopian Embassy at the far side, Number 17.

It was quite an effort getting in. There were vans and rental vehicles pulling up everywhere, and in the middle of it all we got whisked in down side alleys and along walls in little groups and in through the back, which was less exposed to coverage by the world's press, who were all at the front. The risk of being seen by the terrorists was quite small because we went in against the walls. Unless they were leaning out of the windows looking down at us, they weren't going to see anything. Everyone had been evacuated from the surrounding houses before we moved in.

That first time was a bit tricky, but from then on it was easy enough to make the change-over. The police had got furniture vans parked for us at the side alley at the end of the terrace, and everything was blocked off, so we could get in and out without being noticed.

The FHA was luxurious, light years away from the dusty old barracks up the road. But when you're on IA, the last thing on your mind is the quality of the furniture. Mind you, it was better than being banged up in a ditch in Northern Ireland for two nights in a wet February.

I was put in charge of the IA on day four (3 May). Third in command leads the IA if needs be. The IC or the 2IC is always working on the main plan. The stand-to of the IA means you are on line to go should the terrorists start shooting and killing hostages.

•

It was now clear that Salim was becoming more and more frustrated that his negotiations were getting nowhere. By the morning of Friday, 2 May, the terrorists were enraged that their demands had not been fully reported by the BBC radio news and insisted that a request for Arab mediators be broadcast. It was, immediately. It was at this point that Salim showed himself for the first time, at a first-floor window. It was not an encouraging sight for those outside the Embassy. He was holding a gun to the head of Dr Abdul Fazi Ezzatti, the cultural attaché. PC Lock leant out and shouted that there was a man about to be killed unless Salim could talk to the media. A police negotiator yelled back that this was impossible, and Salim pressed the gun hard against Ezzatti's skull, then pushed the man away from him.

Meanwhile the orders from COBR were consistent. There was to be no giving in to the demands, and the SAS were not to go in unless a hostage was murdered.

•

R. F. We studied photographs and plans and everything that came in to the FHA, including the snipers' reports. I'd been in the snipers and the roofs were bristling with them. Snipers are required to find opportunity targets and to provide cover for those going in. They'll be the ones passing information to those in and next to the building through the Command Centre. You build up your best information from them. They are your eyes and ears because, from outside the building, they will tell you what lights have been switched on, what movements are being made, who has passed in front of windows. All of a sudden, when an assaulter can see only a piece of the picture, they will fill in the whole picture, like what is going on on the other side of the building, so the assaulter knows where all the activity is on the inside of the building. Then you know where, how and when to attack.

We waited and waited, just like Tommy's team before us, all that day and throughout the night.

•

By Saturday, 3 May, the siege had reached stalemate. The British government talked to the Arab ambassadors Salim asked for and tried to persuade them to tell him to give in. The ambassadors took a different view and suggested that the six men should be given safe conduct out of the country. William Whitelaw asked Brigadier de la Billière what he thought. He was still convinced that they would never give up peacefully.

•

R. F. Salim had been complaining that the BBC had buggered up the broadcast of his demands and so the police negotiator said that if more hostages were released, he would take down Salim's statement personally over the phone and guarantee to have it broadcast that evening on the nine o'clock news. A pregnant woman and a man who snored and kept them awake were chosen as possibilities. Then came a stalemate. Which came first – the broadcast due at nine that night or the release of the hostages? The answer was a compromise. The woman was released, the broadcast was made, then the man whose snoring had made him lucky stepped out of the Embassy.

In those first few days everybody was quite excited. You think that your team is best and so in any training you do the other team is always the 'anthill mob'. We trained and trained in case it went ahead but even by Saturday no one thought it would. Looking at other historical examples, we didn't really believe we would be going in. We imagined them coming out with their arms above their heads. Still, it was exciting enough just getting into the building next to them and coming so close to going in.

•

That night Snapper got even closer.

•

Snapper It was decided to do a roof recce. Roy T. was the leader. The third one was Pete. It was about eleven when we climbed through the skylight of Number 16 and on to the roof. It was a fine night. The stars were out. It was Bank Holiday weekend, so the streets were empty, which made it really eerie. We made our way as quietly as possible about 30 yards across the slates, between thickets of aerials, like cat burglars. There was silence except for the creaking of our leather belt kit, the rustle of our clothing and the scuffling sound of our running shoes.

Suddenly there was a crack like a pistol going off. We froze. Roy pointed his foot. He'd broken a slate. We looked across at the sniper hidden on the roof of Number 14, gave him the thumbs-up and carried on. Then Roy stopped and I went up to him. He was pulling at a skylight, but it was locked solid. Pete suggested peeling back the lead waterproofing. Fifteen minutes later he'd done it. He lifted out a glass panel, unlocked it and opened the skylight.

We could see in the moonlight that we were above a small bathroom and I got a dose of adrenaline; through the bathroom door and we would be at the terrorists' throats. Adrenaline is such a powerful stimulant that I almost got carried away. I wanted to get down there, get at them. I wanted to be the first SAS man into the Embassy. Fortunately, Roy was more realistic. We'd found what we were looking for – a guaranteed entry point. That was enough for now.

•

It was now Sunday, 4 May, and the men had been on stand-by for four days.

•

R. F. And so we went on, day and night, alternating between IA at Prince's Gate and the DAP at the barracks. We couldn't have a bath or a shower, just a splash and a shave at a basin. By Sunday the news bulletins were more optimistic. Arab ambassadors were attending COBR meetings, and that evening Salim had released another hostage, a Syrian journalist called Karkouti, who had a fever. He was the fifth to be released (Ali-Ghazan-Far, a Pakistani educationalist, and Haideh Kanji, a pregnant woman, had been released on 2 April), and he said that the terrorists were beginning to grumble at Salim. They were young men in their twenties, uneducated guys who had been told the siege would last only twenty-four hours and they would be heroes, and now it was five days later and the siege was apparently going nowhere. Salim was losing control over them. At least he'd now agreed that only one Arab ambassador would be required to negotiate their safe passage where before he had insisted on a whole team of them. If anything was on, it looked like the bus option. We spent the day at Prince's Gate while the others were practising abseiling from the roof of a police residential block, Peel House in Pimlico.

•

Snapper Back in the barracks that evening, the clerk was working on the squadron ration requisition. Malcolm was from the Royal Army Ordnance Corps, a nice, nervous lad, pale and thin, the squadron scribe. I think being involved in the siege, even on the sidelines, was a big thing for him and we decided to rope him in, make him even more involved. He was standing beside the model of the Embassy in full assault kit and Del, one of the assault-team leaders, and I went up to him and told him the good news and the bad news. The bad news was that one of the guys had gone sick. We were on stand-by and had no time to get a replacement. The good news for Malcolm was that he was going to take the guy's place.

He looked briefly shocked, then, fair play to him, he nodded, picked up his respirator and began adjusting the straps. His fingers were shaking as Del told him that he was going to be number two on the team, that he would follow Del in and take out specific targets.

'Remember,' Del said, 'if you get hit, I'll have to leave you, but the medics should find you within half an hour.' And, with a pointer, he indicated the spot on the model.

The respirator was shaking, but Malcolm nodded and squared his shoulders: gung-ho, ready for action. Five minutes later he was sitting between us in the main briefing area. It was a badged-personnel-only briefing by the colonel, and as he spoke about the removal of corpses from the Embassy, Malcolm began to fidget. He couldn't look up. He kept staring at the eyepiece of the respirator on his knees and playing with the filtering canister. He went red in the face and his chin dropped on to his chest. I was about to tell him that the plans had changed and he was going to go in by the skylight, when I saw Del making a throat-cutting gesture. Enough was enough. I whispered to Malcolm that he was on *Candid Camera*. He stood up, shaking violently. I said it again. *Candid Camera*. He began to blink.

'You mean it was a stitch?' he said.

'Yes, Malcolm. A stitch. A rubber duck.'

He had the bottle to look briefly disappointed, then he stopped blinking and grinned. For twenty minutes he had been prepared to risk his life. Now he was back to the ration books.

•

R. F. We spent that night, the fifth since the bleepers went off, back at Prince's Gate. As I nodded off, I was more convinced than ever that the terrorists would give themselves up. The longer it went on, the more likely a peaceful conclusion was. The good news was that in the last few days we had had time to get the DAP sorted out to the extent that each man knew exactly what to do if it went off. We would be working on automatic pilot. The preparation was such that Lieutenant-Colonel Rose, the CO, was able to report that we had a 60 per cent chance of saving the hostages' lives. Often the odds aren't so good.

•

At 9 a.m. on Monday, 5 May, William Whitelaw announced that the 'ambassadorial phase' of the siege was over and a firmer line would be taken with the terrorists. The one concession was that an imam from the Regent's Park Mosque would be brought in as a mediator.

An hour later Iran's Foreign Minister sent the hostages a telegram praising them for their steadfastness, adding that he was certain that they were ready for martyrdom.

For the first time the Red and Blue teams got together in Prince's Gate for a morning briefing. Inside the Embassy Salim appeared to be reaching breaking-point. He'd noticed a bulge in the first-floor party wall with the Ethiopian Embassy and demanded to know from PC Lock what the police were up to. Lock fobbed him off but he was clearly very volatile. The police negotiator told him to listen to the lunchtime news on the World Service, but no developments were reported.

Salim had had enough. He telephoned the negotiators to say that there would be no more talking. He wanted the Arab ambassador brought to the phone or a hostage would be killed.

At just after 1.40 p.m. PC Lock phoned through the news that a hostage was being tied to the banister at the bottom of the stairs. Salim grabbed the telephone, promising that someone would die. Then a new voice came on the line: 'I am one of the hostages. My name is Lavasani.' There was a tense silence and then came the sound that everyone had been dreading: gunfire.

•

Snapper The news of the hostage's death caused everyone to move. I thought: This is it. There could be no going back now. Direct action had to be taken. I began to strip and clean the MP5.

I'd been reading Paddy Mayne's autobiography. He was one of Stirling's 'Originals' and he advised: 'When you enter a room full of armed men, shoot the first person who makes a move, hostile or otherwise. He has started to think and is therefore dangerous.'

I knew that final orders to move into assault positions wouldn't be far off.

•

A COBR meeting was called immediately after the shots were fired. William Whitelaw was told that the SAS could not react until there was proof of murder; it might be a bluff. Lieutenant-Colonel Rose did not think so, but proof was required. They had to see a body.

At 4.30 p.m. Brigadier de la Billière visited the Forward Holding Area: 'I talked to the members of the assault team, and found the atmosphere typical of the SAS immediately before an operation: there was no sense of over-excitement or tension; rather an air of professionalism and quiet confidence prevailed ... they knew full well that the terrorists were heavily armed, and that the building could be wired with explosives, and might go up as they broke in. They simply accepted the risks and carried on.'

By 5.00 p.m. the SAS teams were ready to implement their DAP. De la Billière had told COBR that his men would have a better chance of success if an assault took place before nightfall – which would come at 8.30 p.m. It was also important that the terrorists were fed a cover story before the assault took place. It was agreed that the police would hand over control to the SAS if more than one hostage was murdered.

At 5.05 p.m. PC Lock managed to report, via a telephone, frightening snatches of the terrorists' discussions: 'We'll do something before sunset ... kill two, or three, or four ... kill all by 10 p.m.,' and warned that the furniture was being moved to barricade doors and windows.

At 5.30 p.m. Salim phoned the negotiators demanding that the ambassador arrive within the next forty-five minutes or another hostage would be killed and both bodies thrown out on to the street.

Just before 6.00 p.m. the Home Secretary convened a meeting with representatives of the Foreign Office, the Ministry of Defence and the SAS. If there was clear evidence that hostages had been murdered, the DAP would be put into effect. Blue and Red teams were put on a ten-minute stand-by.

At 6.20 p.m. the imam was put on the line and there was a brief argument in Arabic. During this conversation, three more shots rang out. Soon after, the corpse of Abbas Lavasani was thrown out on to the pavement. Salim phoned the negotiators ten minutes later to announce that a further hostage had been shot and gave permission for Mr Lavasani's body to be collected. The authorities now believed that Salim had killed not once but twice. These last shots were shortly shown to have been nothing but a bluff.

Three minutes after the body was collected, Sir David McNee telephoned COBR to say he wanted the SAS committed to action. Whitelaw in turn telephoned the Prime Minister to get her permission to send in the SAS. She gave her consent, reputedly uttering the immortal words, 'The time has come to use the final option.' At 7.07 p.m. Lieutenant-Colonel Rose formally took control. Operation Nimrod was under way.

The plan was simple. Red Team would deal with the top half of the building and Blue Team would go in and clear the basement, ground and first floors. Between them they had to search and clear fifty-odd rooms, over five floors, all in the hope of reaching the hostages before they came to any harm.

•

Mack (Blue Team) We'd all been briefed up. We were stood to, watching the snooker. It was the final of the World Embassy competition. We were lounging about, and several coppers were making tea, and I got out this cardboard frog I'd found lying on a bed. I pulled the strings and its little green legs started leaping. It was as funny as fuck. Snapper and Rusty just looked at me like I was nuts, then they started to laugh as well.

We were all fully kitted up and, of course, our radios were switched on. A couple of minutes later the voice crackled over the radio, 'Right. Stand by. Stand by.' I thought to myself, Fuck me. Then I found myself running up the three flights of stairs. I kept on thinking to myself, Have I got everything? And going through a check list in my head of all my equipment and what I had to do. Is it fucking cocked? Is my pistol still in place? Make sure the fucking thing isn't going to fall out! The holsters were crap and we had all adapted them by using black masking tape to stop our pistols falling out. As usual I had my pistol loaded with one up the spout so, as and when I had to draw it, I could slip the safety off as I brought it up into the aim. That was only a back-up to the old MP5 in case you had a stoppage or ran out of ammunition. You weren't going to stop and change fucking magazines – no time – so the pistol was right there and ready for quick use.

When you use an MP5 while wearing the black stuff you push the weapon out in front of you. There's no lining up of sights or taking aim at the shoulder. Instinctive shooting. Short bursts of three or four rounds at a time. You're going to hit your target within a circle of about 4 inches. You are going to kill them. We called the enemy X-Rays and the hostages Yankees. So your target becomes an X-Ray, not a person. Your job is to extinguish the X-Ray. It was no different from what we had already been doing all the time on exercise in camp except that this time it was real and this time the whole squadron was involved.

Once we were ready in position and about to go out on to the balcony of Number 15, I pulled the mask down over my face and pulled the straps tight on the hood. The charge I was going to use was already set up ready for me. I checked this over and said to Tom who had the clacker, 'Is it all right? Working and that?'

'Yes. All okay.'

The clacker is a little dynamo which produces enough electricity to blow the charge when you press a small handle on it. It is a wooden frame with COC Charge Linear Cut, which is basically a hollowed-out frame which inverts itself in the explosion and punches through, making a nice clean cut. The charge itself was about 3 by 2 with an extra bit to give it some punch in the middle. All in all about 5 or 6 pounds in weight. We had been warned that the glass on the doors was armour-plated, so we had a bit of overkill and no one quite knew what the effect was going to be.

I told Tom, 'Don't fucking press it while I'm carrying it.'

All we were waiting for were the magic words, 'You have control.'

•

Salim was by now threatening to kill all the hostages in the next five minutes. 'It's up to you to decide,' he said. 'If you want to do anything stupid, all would be killed at once.'

The police negotiator calmly and carefully switched the conversation around to the bus option. Salim wanted a 25-foot coach, then one at 29 feet. What difference those 4 feet would make no one could imagine. But at least, for the moment, he had stopped talking about murder.

The SAS teams were at stand-to positions. Red Team's abseilers – two groups of four – were on the roof. Rusty and Snapper were crouching outside the french windows of Number 14. Mack was on the balcony of Number 15.

'Whereabouts can we put the coach?' the negotiator asked.

'Opposite of the door,' Salim said.

'"Opposite of the door" is a very vague phrase. If you look out over the park, you . . .'

'After we have checked it,' Salim said, interrupting. 'Then you will put it outside of the door.'

'Let's talk about it then,' the negotiator said soothingly. 'Can you listen to me and I will talk about the first movement of the coach up to the front door?'

No reply from Salim.

The negotiator continued: 'You look out of the window directly ahead of you, there's the park, and to your right is the end of the wall and that's where the gas men were working on the generators, where the gas men . . .'

Salim butted in, 'I will phone you after three minutes.'

'No, listen, Salim. Let's talk about this.'

'You are asking me . . . three minutes.'

'Listen . . .'

Salim sounded distracted now. 'We are, you know, listening to some suspicious movements.'

'There are no suspicious movements.'

'They're suspicious okay. Just a minute. I will come back again.'

The negotiator called out his name, then there was the sound of an explosion and still the man continued: 'Salim, there are no suspicious movements.'

But in that instant negotiations had become redundant. The negotiator's job was over. Seconds earlier the command signal, 'London Bridge', had sounded in fifty headsets. The explosion was the skylight on the Embassy roof being blown by members of Red Team. It was 7.26 p.m.

Four abseilers launched themselves off the roof, heading for the second-floor balcony at the back of the building and the two windows that led into the main office. Four men went down a ladder to the sub-roof at the rear, known as the lighting area. And Mack went into action.

•

Mack I went out on the first-floor balcony with Mal as my cover while Tom and Derek stayed in the room. I carried the frame charge. Once I found my footing on the target balcony I began to place the charge. There was a fucking *zing* and a puff of dust at my feet and I realized that I had an incoming shot from somewhere. To this day I don't know whether it was a police marksman who let one go accidentally, or a marksman who thought I was a terrorist appearing. Then there was a clunk beside me and I looked down to see a grenade rolling off the balcony. Then it was gone, so it didn't bother me. The terrorist who dropped it on to me had forgotten to take out the pin.

I spotted a white-faced man in the room where we were placing the charge. Miles, one of the team members, waved at him to move away from the window. I didn't know who he was. Tough shit if he got blasted. We had to get in and fast. There were nineteen hostages to rescue.

As soon as I had placed the charge, we took off back across on to the other balcony, shouting, 'FIRE!' as we went. This was the signal to the guys inside to detonate the charge. All this happened in seconds. When the charge blew, half the balcony fucking disappeared. The balustrade was blown clean off. There were clouds of dust from the shattered brickwork.

We stepped through the rubble and smoke into the room and went into our rehearsed routine. Mal went in first and peeled off to the right and I went left. My head kept twitching from side to side because of my gas mask. I had to keep moving in order to be able to see around. I saw this body covered in shit lying on the ground in front of me. Then, still covered in bits of plaster and wood and glass, he began to get up. Later I found out it was Sim Harris, the BBC guy. I sniggered to myself, sort of through relief.

Tom and Derek came in right behind us and went forward down the right-hand side of the corridor. They went into the first room on the right and we took the first on the left. A quick look, flash of the torch, nothing there. Behind us we could hear shooting. It was Derek and Tom killing Salim. We came out of the room and moved on down the corridor. Immediately Derek and Tom also emerged back into the corridor and, pointing to the room we had just cleared, shouted, 'There's one gone in that room.' We heard scuffling and firing, and then Derek yelled, 'I think I hit him,' as we piled into the room. The guy had fired at us and missed, thank fuck. He was lying on the couch and he wasn't going anywhere. He was shot up all one side. He wasn't dead yet, but I could see he was on his way out. Harris was now up on his feet but we ignored him. We finished off the dodo on the couch. He never said a word.

During this action my mask got knocked and I got a lungful of gas. As soon as I pulled it back on, I puked up into it. It was only water but it stank. I forced out as much as I could but later had to take it off.

I put Harris out on the windowsill to get him out of the way before going into the right-hand room where PC Lock was. He was very shocked. Tom was talking to him gently, saying, 'Calm down, mate, you're all right. It's all over.' Stuff like that. We instinctively took up guarding positions, one covering the door, one the corridor. The old flames were starting to lick about the room and somebody said, 'I think we'd better get moving.'

We took Harris back across the balcony into Number 15. He was whimpering and in a right old state of near-total panic. He got slapped a couple of times to bring him down, and apparently he complained afterwards, saying he had been handled too rough. But it's the old thing from the training. You know vaguely who the goodies and the baddies are, but you treat every survivor the same way: firmly and roughly to stop them panicking and to ensure that they do exactly what you want them to do. It keeps you personally in control as well. Panic has to be contained.

While this was all going on I remember thinking to myself, I wish those bastards in the control room would stop fucking talking. We were all linked with radio communications and had pressure pads on our kit with which to transmit messages to each other, but the trouble was the bloody people outside kept on asking ridiculous things like 'What's going on? What's happening?' At one stage there was so much traffic that several of us lifted up our gas masks so that we could shout to each other. The dick-heads on the outside were in a panic because they didn't know what was going on. You couldn't blame them, really. It was easier for us because we knew. You just reacted by instinct.

•

At exactly the same moment that Mack had burst into the Embassy from the first-floor balcony, three of the first group of abseilers had dropped on to the balcony at the back, smashed the windows and thrown in stun grenades. They had expected, from the briefing, to find most of the hostages there, waiting to be rescued, but the room was empty. They moved through the building, searching for them. Their group leader was still outside. He had got caught up in his harness and was swinging helplessly.

•

Snapper In the basement the voice in my earphone said: 'Go, go, go.' I was number one in the crocodile and I thought, What the hell am I doing here? The new boys should be at number one. I've done my time under fire. I should be at the back with Sek. As we went from the back of Number 14 to Number 16 I looked up to the block of flats on the left. Snipers, loads of them, like crows.

We took up position behind a low wall as the demolition call-sign [SAS soldier] ran forward and placed the explosive charge on the Embassy's french windows, then we saw an abseiler swinging on the first floor. It was Tom, one of the Fijians. I could hear bursts of machine-gun fire and women screaming and I thought, Christ, it's all going wrong. We couldn't blow the charge with Tom hanging up there, so the sledge man battered the door and, luckily, it opened. If it had been barricaded, we'd have been in trouble.

'Go, go, go. Get in at the rear.' As we went in I got the best adrenaline rush of my life. I had heavy body-armour on, front and back, which, during training weighs a ton. Now it felt like a T-shirt. In we went, into the library on the ground floor. There were literally thousands of books. If we'd used the charge, we might have set them – and the whole Embassy – on fire. We went through to the head of the cellar stairs which were blocked by step ladders. Maybe they were booby-trapped, but I couldn't see any sign. Mind you, my vision wasn't too good. It was just half-light and there was condensation on the eyepieces of the respirator.

We wrenched the ladders out of the way and, thank God, there was no explosion. Down the stairs to the basement. I tossed in a flash-bang but there was no reaction. In the corridor we drilled the locks of the rooms with 9-milly, booted the doors in and cleared the rooms. It was the fastest clearance I'd ever done. In the last room I saw a shape and I let off a burst of twenty rounds. It was a dustbin.

Up we went again, mouth dry, sweat in my eyes, slimy rubber of the respirator, blood pounding in my temples. All that. Back in the ground-floor reception there was smoke and confusion and a terrible noise from upstairs where the lads were clearing the rooms. The radio told me that the hostages were coming and I joined a line with Sek and Rusty. I counted fifteen hostages coming down the stairs. One woman had her blouse ripped and her tits were partially out. Now all we had to do was feed the hostages out the back through the library and out the way we'd come.

•

R. F. My concern was to get my team in, then clear the ground floor and as far as the stairs. We had gone in through the library, then checked some other rooms and been lucky not to have run into anyone. So I sent two men to secure the stairs, but we couldn't go any further because it wasn't part of our zone of limitation. All of this took seconds, no more. Just getting as far as the stairs was a bonus because it was straight after that we heard people coming down. Then I heard a radio call from upstairs, but I couldn't hear the message clearly.

I saw someone pointing and that's when I saw a guy in a dark-green jacket. Something about the way he was always looking back up the stairs, when everyone else was just interested in getting down and out of the building, told me he was one of them. When he got to me, he tried to shield his face, twisting away with his jacket up, but I grabbed him to try to get a proper look. I just knew.

•

Mack I was at the top of the stairs, and I saw this bloke wearing a green jacket push past me, with hostages in front and behind, and I remembered that we had previously been given descriptions of most of the terrorists. I realized that he was one of the fucking baddies. I shouted over the banister, 'There's one coming now!' I pointed at him as I shouted, 'That's fucking one of them!' Minky had also seen him and shouted as well. Rusty heard me and so did Snapper, who'd come up from the cellar.

•

Snapper The guy drew level with me and I saw the grenade in his hand. I could see the detonator cap, but I couldn't fire because the call signs at the bottom of the stairs were in my line of sight. If I'd fired, the bullets would have gone through him and into my mates. So I clubbed him on the back of the neck with the MP5 as hard as I could and down he went. Rusty pushed him and he rolled down the stairs and on to the carpet.

•

R. F. I saw the grenade, pushed him and fired twenty-two rounds at point-blank range into him and he went down the stairs. I went down to check his pulse and confirmed he was dead. I didn't have time to check the pin in the grenade until later, but even so I could not touch it, since I didn't have gloves on. If it had gone off, it was too late to do anything anyway, and there are operational procedures that have to be followed. It was a Russian grenade. Later I picked up the grenade and passed it to one of the senior members of the team for safety reasons.

●

Mack And that was it. No more shooting. Then we found that one of the baddies had got past us and got ready to take him back inside and finish him off. As he was being dragged back in, one of the women hostages put her arms tight around his legs and begged us, 'No, no, no, please don't. He was really good to us.' I guess she had formed some kind of bond with her captor. Other people were now watching and he was kept alive. That's the only reason there was a survivor.

The boss appeared and checked we had finished the job, then everyone was ordered out of the building, which was now burning fiercely. Some of the guys got souvenirs. I got PC Lock's hat as a memento. Sek noticed that the guy with all the bullets in him was wearing a Rolex. There was a bullet clean through it. What a waste.

●

R. F. I looked around to check who had got out. I was one of the last ones out and, looking around, I knew we'd done our job, which was the main thing, but it was hard to tell who had got injured and who was okay. All you can do is look for your men, pick up your kit and head off.

●

Snapper Sek and I went back through the library and out, past the hostages who had been laid out and trussed up, ready for documentation. As we walked into Number 14, through the french windows, Gonzo took off his respirator and asked the police sergeant on duty what the snooker score was. The man couldn't believe it. He just stood there shaking his head.

It was 8.07 p.m. The whole thing had taken just over half an hour.

As I began to take off the assault equipment, I felt suddenly exhausted. The accumulation of the assault and the days' waiting was taking immediate effect. The Toad came up to me and said he was getting too old for this sort of thing. So was I. At thirty-three, I was far too ancient to be going around attacking besieged embassies. After about a quarter of an hour we were back in civvies with our MP5s in plastic bags for forensic examination. Then in came Willie Whitelaw. Old oyster-eyes. He was in tears as he thanked us for what we had done. 'This operation,' he said, 'will show that we in Britain will not tolerate terrorists. The world must learn this.'

Very emotional, but no wonder: it was his job on the line.

•

Of the total of twenty-six hostages, one was executed, another was killed in the assault and five had been released beforehand, which left nineteen who were rescued by the men of Red and Blue teams. The terrorist who threw the grenade at Mack was shot by a sniper as he ran into Hyde Park. The surviving terrorist, Fowzi Bavadi Nejad, was given a life sentence for manslaughter and is now in prison in the UK. That night, back in the barracks, the men who'd put the SAS on the next day's front pages were packing their kit ready for the trip back to Hereford.

•

Mack We were just finishing packing up our stuff when someone came in and said, 'There's some beer in the main hall.' We arrived in the big room and tucked into the cans and started chatting away – about everyday things, not just the attack. The tension was wearing off and we were coming back down to Planet fucking Earth.

One of the guys came in with his hand bandaged. He had had one of his fingers creased by a bullet. It wasn't very deep but fucking painful. Then we heard that Tom, one of the Fijians, had had to be taken to hospital. When he got hung up on his abseiling rope he'd been very badly burned: whole sections of the flesh on his leg were completely burned away. Yet he went ahead with attacking the Embassy after he had been cut down. Most people wouldn't even have been able to stand, having been as badly burned as he was. People asked if it was adrenaline that kept him going, but I think he thought to himself, I don't want to fucking miss this for anything. He got the George Medal for it.

Then I saw Tommy, who told me that his hood had caught fire as he abseiled through the flames at the back of the building. His respirator was so badly burnt he took it off and went through the whole attack without a gas mask. He was the only man I knew who could run through CS gas and be completely unaffected by it. Poor guy got killed in a car crash in Northern Ireland.

In the corner of the room there was a television which some of us were watching. Some bloke came in and said, 'Lads, lads, there's a visitor who would like to speak to you.' It was Maggie and her husband. She thanked us and said a few words and as she was speaking someone shouted 'Hey, look, it's on the TV.' Up until that moment we did not know that it had been filmed. Maggie was blocking my view of the screen, so without thinking I shouted, 'Fucking sit down, Maggie, I can't see.'

'Oh, sorry,' she said and sat down out of the way.

I remember saying, 'Fuck me, there's me,' as they showed a news flash of us attacking the first-floor front balcony.

After that Maggie and the rest of them went around chatting to all the lads. She was with us for about half an hour. Then about midnight we loaded up the wagons and left in packets. A couple of vehicles at a time, some going one way, others going another. I was driving the lead vehicle of our packet. As soon as we hit the old M4 I put my fucking foot down.

Sometimes, when needs be, we would do what is known as a

fast drive, with the police providing escorts front and back. Eight wagons in a convoy at over 100 miles an hour, all talking to each other, and the police escorts giving each other advance warning of the oncoming road situation. The front car would drive, sirens and blue lights on, in the middle of the road, giving a running commentary: 'Road clear, road clear, approaching roundabout, take second option to the left,' and he would then pull his car across the junction to block off other cars from coming round the roundabout. We would race forward, and then another escort car would move to the front. It was very efficient and we had some laughs too. But this time we were on our own.

If you don't have an escort, you always inform each police area you are travelling through of your presence. As an anti-terrorist team we worked with the police a lot and usually wanted them to know where we were. However, in this exceptional case we had forgotten to inform the local police. We had police radios in our white Range Rovers and we were listening in to the traffic coming from the scene of the Embassy. Suddenly I heard a police siren and saw the flashing blue lights. Next minute a police car was pulling us over. As we pulled up, the other two Rovers waved and pointed at us as they sped on past. They were pissing themselves that we'd been caught speeding.

The old copper swaggers over – you know what the traffic cops are like – 'Do you know what speed you were doing, sir?' As he said it, he clocked our police radio. A look of dawning understanding spread across his face and he said, 'Fuck me, you're them, aren't you?'

'Yes.' We grinned.

He held his head in his hands, shaking it in disbelief, and wandered back to his car muttering and swearing and mumbling to himself. He was quite within his rights to stop us but he didn't charge us. Extenuating circumstances, you might say.

We got back to camp, and as we were refuelling the Rovers and packing away our gear, one of the ruperts came over and said, 'Lads, you don't have to worry about coming in tomorrow morning until nine o'clock.' Half an hour extra time!

When we went into the mess virtually nothing was said. Just

a couple of the others gave us a nod and thumbs-up as if to say, 'Good job done, lads.' It was enough. We knew. We knew.

•

R. F. After that we had two days off, and then the police came to us for statements, and we had to go through them a couple of times. It was serious, particularly if you had killed someone, and we might have had to go to court. Snapper appeared at the inquest, though he hadn't killed anyone. Those of us who had were kept in London during the court case in case they needed to question us.

After a while the significance of the TV coverage, and the profile it gave to the team, hit me. It made me realize, particularly in terms of my IA, just what would have happened if I had had to send everyone in and it had all gone horribly wrong. I understood then that there would have been only one person to blame. Me. But being allowed to go and do what we were trained for was amazing. I firmly believe only Maggie Thatcher would have allowed us to go and do that.

It really put the regiment on the map. Nothing like that has taken place since, and I think it genuinely put terrorists off. At the time there were hijackings and the like, but it must have sent a strong message out – just don't try it any more!

Several weeks later the second in command of the operation presented a lecture to a large number of very senior British Army officers in the main theatre at the Royal Military Academy, Sandhurst. The first few rows were filled with top brass: rows of medals, gold braid, you name it. The Commandant of the Academy was there right in the middle. The theatre was full to capacity. All the officers being trained were there too.

While our boss was giving the lecture, which included slides and all sorts, we were waiting in the wings. Four of us. We were wearing the same black overalls, masks, belts, etc., that we had worn on the day. We knew the signal which would launch our attack. I kept thinking to myself, This is the first and last chance I will ever have to wipe out the most senior ruperts in the army all in one go.

It was a long lecture. No one had seen us enter. We came in via a back entrance after it had started. On the lawn outside a chopper was waiting, its blades turning in anticipation. The audience couldn't hear it, but we could. The lecture came to an end with the words, 'Right, gentlemen, any questions?'

That was our signal. 'GO, GO, GO,' we yelled. A couple of flash-bangs went off, and we sprayed the audience with blanks from our MP5s. It was fantastic. Half of the front row jumped out of their seats with surprise, while the rest dived for cover. We snatched our officer and disappeared with him. Next moment we were in the helicopter and away. There were no questions.

•

In the weeks following the siege the regiment received hundreds of cards, telegrams and letters of support from members of the public as well as numerous gifts. It also received over 2,000 applications from regular soldiers wanting to join the SAS. Of those 2,000, ten were eventually badged.

6
NORTHERN IRELAND

NORTHERN IRELAND

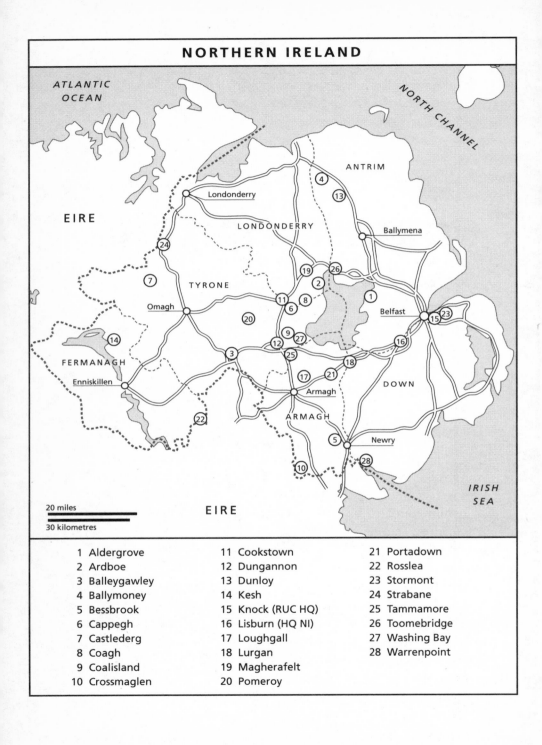

ATLANTIC
OCEAN

NORTH CHANNEL

ANTRIM

EIRE

Londonderry

LONDONDERRY

Ballymena

TYRONE

Omagh

Belfast

FERMANAGH

Enniskillen

Armagh

DOWN

ARMAGH

Newry

IRISH
SEA

EIRE

20 miles

30 kilometres

1 Aldergrove	11 Cookstown	21 Portadown
2 Ardboe	12 Dungannon	22 Rosslea
3 Balleygawley	13 Dunloy	23 Stormont
4 Ballymoney	14 Kesh	24 Strabane
5 Bessbrook	15 Knock (RUC HQ)	25 Tammamore
6 Cappegh	16 Lisburn (HQ NI)	26 Toomebridge
7 Castlederg	17 Loughgall	27 Washing Bay
8 Coagh	18 Lurgan	28 Warrenpoint
9 Coalisland	19 Magherafelt	
10 Crossmaglen	20 Pomeroy	

The sickest, most horrific thing I've seen in my life was the murder of the two signallers who had strayed into that funeral procession, yet none of us took the law into our own hands. None of us went out and took any retaliation or retribution. None of us. That's part of the training of the regiment and the calibre of the regiment and the professionalism of the regiment. We are not above the law.

Johnny Two-Combs

I've got no time for any of them because they're not professional soldiers. If they would come out on the streets and fight man to man, I might have some respect for them, but the way they do business – no time, no time.

Snapper

On 7 January 1976 Prime Minister Harold Wilson publicly committed the regiment to patrol South Armagh, the district having recently been described by Home Secretary Merlyn Rees as 'bandit country'. In 1969 and 1974 first D Squadron and then B Squadron had been tentatively introduced into the Province, but now the Prime Minister was making it clear that the SAS were in business.

An advance party from D Squadron set up a base in Bessbrook Mill and within weeks the full squadron of sixty-four men plus support had been deployed. Later the SAS strength was reduced to two half-troops – with a back-up team at the camp known as Screed that could be helicoptered over to the Province within an hour of a request being made.

From the late 1970s the SAS deployment in Ulster was one

troop at Bessbrook under the command of 3 Brigade, one troop in the Belfast area under 39 Brigade, one under 8 Brigade in Londonderry and a fourth under the personal control of the Commander of Land Forces.

In the 1980s this was changed. To make the SAS presence more effective in Northern Ireland, a new organization was established. Called the Intelligence and Security Group (Northern Ireland) – or the Group – it reduced the total number of SAS soldiers from a full squadron to a troop of just over twenty men called Ulster Troop. But they were consolidated, and they worked very closely with the 14th Intelligence Unit, a covert intelligence-gathering body whose recruits were trained by the SAS.

Snapper was first posted to Northern Ireland in 1974.

•

Snapper Belfast was a nervous breakdown waiting to happen. To most of us, all that was needed to solve the problem was take out the ringleaders and that would be it. The revolution would have been set back twenty or thirty years. Anyway, the Head Shed kept on about working by the book – going on about the democratic process and working within the law of the land. Belfast was a job for the police, not Special Forces. You needed people who knew all about rules and regulations; yet there we were, issued with strict rules of engagement: 'Minimum force to be used, with firearms as a last resort; challenges to be given unless you or others in the immediate vicinity are being engaged by terrorists; you may open fire only if an act is being committed likely to endanger life and there is no other way to make an arrest.' It was classic rules of engagement – up against an opposition who felt no need for any constraints.

The SF [security force] base was bleak. The January weather was bleak. Our weapons were state-of-the-art Japanese cameras. Instead of taking out the opposition, our job was to photograph them. This tour was going to be frustration, with a capital F.

On my second Sunday night I went out in a battered Vauxhall Viva heading for West Belfast, driven by Taff who had been around the town for a long time and knew it backwards. We each had a 9-millimetre Browning pistol and I put mine on my lap, hidden by the *News of the World*. It was freezing, so cold that the windscreen-washer liquid had frozen up.

We drove around the city all the next morning. Belfast reminded me of photos I'd seen of London during the air-raids: terraced houses with windows and doors boarded up, gardens like bomb sites and groups of youths staring at us as we drove around. All the time Taff was filling me in on the history, telling me where an RPG had been fired, where a guy from the reconnaissance force had been shot, etc., etc.

About midday we stopped at traffic lights outside the Royal Victoria Hospital. We were in the outside lane. Two youths were standing in a doorway, clocking the traffic, and for some reason I sensed trouble. It was the same instinct I'd developed in Oman, sniffing out the *adoo*. There was just something about the way the two of them were standing, one jerking his head from side to side watching the traffic, the taller one staring straight at us. Then he pounced, rushed through the inner line of traffic and yanked Taff's door open.

'Get out of the car,' he said, 'or I'll blow yer fuckin' head off.' His right hand was inside his bomber jacket. I thumbed the safety-catch on my pistol and looked at him. Where was his shooter? Show me a shooter, you bastard. He was a perfect target, but I couldn't do anything. If he was unarmed, I'd be up for murder. I glanced at the other one, still standing there, giving no clue of his intentions. To shoot or not to shoot?

Then Taff, in that instant, took the decision for me. 'You can fuck off, you wanker,' he said as he pulled the door towards himself, then smashed it back at the youth, cracking him in the guts and the knee. The guy staggered back and his hand came out of the jacket. No gun. Whether he had one inside his jacket, I'll never know. Then Taff was off, screeching the car on to the wrong side of the road, burning rubber, getting the fuck out of the place, the door still flapping, traffic coming at us, then he swerved right and we were back on track.

I radioed over: 'Attempted hijack corner of Springfield and

Falls,' and realized that I was shaking. This was a different type of fear than in Oman. This wasn't nervous tension before a contact, followed by the old adrenaline rush. This was a sudden shock, and I'd been close, very close, to appearing in the dock on a murder charge.

That evening we watched from the car as four youths were brought into the Castlereagh detention centre. The police had trawled the area and came up with this group – the wrong four, as it happened. One toot of your horn meant a positive ID; three meant a waste of time. I pressed the horn three times and we drove off.

Month in, month out, the killing went on, and all we did was take snaps, then one day we were put on stand-by for an assault on a flat in the Andersonstown area. Four armed PIRA [Provisional IRA] men were in position on the top floor of a block of flats preparing to snipe at one of our patrols.

For hours we waited in the RUC station on the Springfield Road, ready to go. I checked and rechecked my Remington pump-action shotgun and the 9-millimetre Browning. I was number three in our unit. It was my job to blast the door open and cover numbers one and two as they assaulted the flats armed with Heckler & Koch MP5 sub-machine guns. The word finally came and we all fought our way into our body armour – which stopped anything up to a .357 magnum – with high-velocity inserts which protected us against even 7.62-millimetre bullets. Assault gear on, gas masks in our hands, we climbed into the two pigs [armoured personnel carriers] for the short dash to Andytown.

Nothing was said on the journey. There was no need. There would be no orders given. We had practised the drill often enough. Then from the driver: 'Two hundred metres.' I adjusted the straps of my gas mask. 'One hundred ... fifty ...' and then we were out and running across a muddy verge and a concrete walkway. Two boys of about ten stared at us for a moment. Even through the misted-over eyepiece, I could see the hatred. Then they were off, with a warning that the SF were coming. We ran up the eight-step concrete flights to the first floor, then the second and finally to our target on the third floor. Numbers one and two were in position. I blew the lock away and kicked the door in and they were inside. I heard screams and shouts, followed by the sound of the flash-bang going off, then I went in after them. A man and a woman were sitting on the sofa, coughing and vomiting.

'The bastards aren't here,' one of the guys said. 'There's no fucking terrorists in here. We're going across the landing.'

Same again. Same procedure. Shotgun, stun grenade, yells and roars but still no gunfire. In my earpiece I heard a voice: 'All stations. This is Jake. The birds have flown. Endex. Lift off.'

I cursed, long and loud. (There had been no time for the two kids to warn the terrorists.) The green slime's tout had got it wrong. Simple as that. I wondered how much he'd been paid.

Belfast. Frustration city. Eighteen months of misery.

•

R. F. I went out on a five-month tour to Northern Ireland in '77 straight after Selection and Continuation Training. I'd been before, in 1970 with 49 Regiment. There had been a particularly bad spate of bombings then, and I'd gone round the streets picking up parts of bodies and putting them in plastic bags. You'd find a finger 400 metres from where the bomb had gone off. Once I climbed on to the awning of a hotel because we'd seen bits and pieces up there. I found someone's scalp. That's what we did. We went round with the police picking up scalps and putting them in the bags. None of that was done by the regiment, though. It wasn't an SAS job. Bagging bits of bodies was for crap-hats.

I was in B Squadron and the atmosphere among the lads was great. The bosses left us alone. We knew what jobs we had to do and we did them. There was a lot of inter-squadron rivalry, which is good because it keeps you on your toes. On that first tour I was really under scrutiny. When you join the regiment, you go back down in rank to trooper, and my boss gave us a real chance to prove ourselves. Instead of just letting us look like patrol members, he gave us patrols to run. You would have a senior corporal along with you, but you were in charge some of the time. It was a different way of testing us, but they must have liked what they saw because after two years I was promoted to lance-corporal, which was quite unusual. I think only two of us managed it. After all, we hadn't even done a course between us.

Our brief was principally mobile patrols and intelligence gathering by observation. If the OP is in a house, the longer it lasts the more uncomfortable it gets. You have to seal your shit in bags and bottle your piss because the noise of the lavatory flushing – and the smell – can give you away. Everyone's issued a piss bag with a one-way valve on it. You obviously can't shit into that, so if you are unlucky enough to be taken short and you do have to have a shit, then you use a plastic bag. Subsequently you won't use that bag to piss in. You will have tied it up. Some of the lads like to use cling-film. You shit on to a sheet of cling-film, roll it up, put another couple of sheets around it to seal it, and that's it.

You don't want dogs and rats sniffing around. You put the Bergens in one spot and don't move them. You put on soft shoes. You can't talk or eat or drink anything hot. No smoking, of course. On an OP no one changes their magazine each day. Unless you actually unload the ammunition from the magazine, there would be no point. Changing magazines is noisy, so you wouldn't do it for that reason alone. Also, if anything went down with the terrorists while you were changing magazine, you could be compromised if you were delayed in firing off the first rounds even by a second.

OPs are always changing. An OP is always recced, occupied at night and up and fully operational by daylight. A standing OP is a four-man patrol, where two of you actually move forward into the OP while the other two act as back-up. Other times you'd have four people lying under a hedge or hiding together in a building. Three of the four might be sleeping, or doing nothing but lying completely still in order to minimize noise. The fourth man is doing the actual observation. You swap over at regular intervals in order to keep maximum concentration. And there

THE IRANIAN EMBASSY

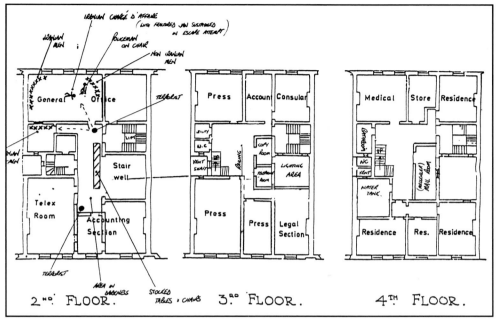

2ND. FLOOR. 3RD. FLOOR. 4TH FLOOR.

Above

RF: 'This is the plan of the upper
floors of the Iranian Embassy
which we were given as part of
our briefing packs.'

Right

RF: 'Before we knew that the
terrorists' leader was called Salim,
we were given this ID poster.
It turned out to be a pretty
good likeness.'

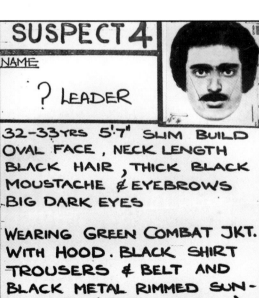

SUSPECT 4

NAME

? LEADER

32–33 YRS 5'7" SLIM BUILD
OVAL FACE, NECK LENGTH
BLACK HAIR, THICK BLACK
MOUSTACHE & EYEBROWS
BIG DARK EYES

WEARING GREEN COMBAT JKT.
WITH HOOD. BLACK SHIRT
TROUSERS & BELT AND
BLACK METAL RIMMED SUN-
GLASSES (MOST OF TIME)
VERY POLITE & CALM. V. GOOD
PERSIAN & ARABIC, PASSABLE
ENGLISH, RIGHT HANDED.

WEAPON: MACHINE GUN

Abseiling down the back of the Embassy, Tom the Fijian troop commander got tangled in his rope and the whole operation was put in jeopardy.

RF: 'Going in at the back of the Embassy. I'm in the middle with no gloves on.'

RF: 'The telex room after we'd eliminated three of the terrorists.'

RF: 'The aftermath. You can see bullet holes in the table on the right of the picture.'

RF: 'The Embassy after we'd finished with it.'

On patrol in South Armagh's 'bandit country'.

David: 'The Pucaras [top] and Aermacchi MB-326s [bottom] on Pebble Island after we'd seen to them.'

Matt: 'An hour into enemy territory and one of our Land Rovers was written off due to the arduous terrain.'

Matt: 'After our first contact we had to camouflage the Iraqi vehicle while we waited for a chopper to take it out. Of course, it proved to be too difficult to do that and we had to dispose of it on the ground.'

Matt: 'Two and half weeks inside enemy lines. It was freezing most of the time, especially at night, and these Arab coats proved a lifesaver after the resupply.'

Matt: 'Me in my woolly hat behind enemy lines about twenty-five miles north of the Iran–Iraq border. The operation had been satisfactorily concluded and we were having a brew before heading back to base.'

Matt: 'Safely on our way home.'

will always be a back-up. It might be a mile away; it might be 20 metres away.

You take enough gear for as long as is needed, and with luck you'll get an LLB [live letter box] coming to visit – this being a car appearing at a prearranged RV so that you can get rid of bags of waste and pick up what you need to continue. And you have to be careful about communications because the VHF can interfere with TV sets nearby and maybe someone will get suspicious.

Some ops go on for weeks and weeks. You take photographs and observe meetings. All you are really doing is getting information for possible use later, anything that will help, like licence registrations, routines, contacts. Of course, there have been times I've been compromised while on an OP: courting couples who happen along, or drunks looking for somewhere to take a piss, and they nose into where you are stationed. Not only is your cover blown but you have to be 'hot extracted'. Normally OPs are extracted in a very controlled operation which leaves no sign that you have ever been there. Hot extractions are danger-ous because there's no time for that kind of caution – you've been compromised and you have to get out.

One time we were stationed in Omagh and were hidden in a barn at the back of a pub. We'd moved a slate at the corner of the roof so we could see everything. We hadn't been there very long, hadn't set up anything. Just before closing time two fellows walked in and climbed up on to the upper floor, so we shouted as loud as we could, and they raced off. God knows what they thought. We told base we had been compromised and got them to pick us up. There is nothing that can be done about that sort of thing, and they don't ask questions. It just happens.

Once we surrounded a house in which we were told terrorists were hiding. There must have been ten or twelve of our men waiting. Sod's law: someone jumped out of a window between two of our lads and ran into the darkness. As I recall, no shots were fired because the person jumping from the window was not identified and no weapon was seen.

B Squadron did an operation in the Andersonstown area. Our

information was that we were to go to an upper-floor flat. A meeting was taking place there between known terrorists. This was to be a house assault. Two of us were dropped off by civvy car, and we walked towards the flat in dirty old clothes, carrying a bag containing high explosives, grenades, gas, etc. We had 9-millimetre Brownings and MP5s under our coats. Our task was to ID the flat and bring in the remainder of the assault team. We ID'd the flat, then waited while the rest of the assault team got into position.

We heard noises from the flat. One of our men opened the door with his MP5. Inside there was one little old lady.

We cleared the flat, climbed into cars and drove back to base.

Car chases have been carried out, but nine out of ten are pulled off. In none of the towns in Northern Ireland where I have served have I been faced with a terrorist with a weapon. All those man-hours on operations – have they been warranted? I would say not. The chance of being involved in contact with armed terrorists was very slim.

But, deep inside, you always felt that you were in with a chance of coming face to face with armed terrorists while serving in Northern Ireland.

•

In the seven years between the SAS first going in to Northern Ireland and the mid-1980s only two of their number were killed. The first was Captain Herbert Westmacott. On 2 May 1980 he led a patrol which stormed a house in Antrim Road, Belfast, where an IRA team was hiding. They hit the wrong door, Number 369 instead of 371, with their sledgehammers. The IRA unit had a 7.62-millimetre M60 machine gun in the house next door and two bursts were fired. Captain Westmacott was killed. He was wearing body armour, but he was shot in the throat. The IRA men eventually surrendered. The door, riddled with bullets and known as the Westmacott door, is now displayed at Stirling Lines.

Then, in December 1984, five IRA men mined a restaurant

near Fermanagh with 1,000 pounds of explosives packed into beer kegs. Lance-Corporal Al Slater and two fellow SAS men intercepted the radio message to blow the bomb. But the bomb did not go off. The men approached a car parked nearby, unaware that three IRA men were hidden in a ditch behind it. When Slater challenged the driver, he was shot. Despite being fatally wounded, Slater returned fire, and in the subsequent firefight the driver was killed and another man drowned as he tried to swim the River Branagh. The others were later arrested. Within hours of Slater's death, his friend Johnny Two-Combs took over as his replacement.

•

Johnny Two-Combs I was on the CT team training when I got paged and was told that Al had been killed. I went over by helicopter that evening and moved in to Al's room, sharing with a good friend of mine called Jocky. It was very depressing, but you've got to get on with it.

Everybody volunteers for Northern Ireland because it's known as a constant operations theatre, but there are only so many positions available and not everyone is suitable. You have to have the aptitude to operate in the environment that Ireland produces. Those who are picked spend six months with the Northern Ireland Training Wing. You are assessed throughout for any weaknesses. We don't go to Northern Ireland to run round the streets killing people. You have to have people who can operate under extreme pressure and not take things into their own hands. You have to be able to contain your emotions.

You learn covert photography. If we find weapons or bomb-making equipment, we go in, using infra-red cameras to get the evidence. We do helicopter fly-pasts, photographing approach roads of operations and then making a montage. We do a methods-of-entry course, going covertly into all sorts of build-ings, and we become good at lock-picking. Driving is crucial too, and it's a pat on the back to be selected as a driver – very prestigious. You have to be able to drive very fast, either pursuing terrorists or intercepting them. Such operations are called fast-balls. You've got to get from A to B in a very short space of time and not injure innocent people.

You are issued with normal, tracer and armour-piercing ammunition. It is normally up to the individual to decide how to mix his ammunition. Sometimes the patrol commander would remind us that we were going to do a vehicle intercept and that we should remember to have armour-piercing rounds as the first two in the magazine. In the same way, there is a lot of individual choice as to which weapon you use, but sometimes the commander will stipulate that everyone should carry a particular weapon. And there tend to be certain common-sense rules that relate to choice. For example, Drumnakilly was an 'outdoor' job, so it was the G3. You wouldn't use a G3 in a confined environment – say, from the back of a car – because it is just too big and bulky.

As far as specific operations are concerned, we are involved in source protection, target substitution and what we call Op Cleans, which occur when anybody reports suspicious activity. Maybe someone has seen a truck or a van parked near a culvert. Someone might be putting a bomb under it. Everyone's suspicious in Northern Ireland. It goes to the hot line and through to the powers that be. If it's decided that it requires our interest, then we go in. It's very rapid. You get paged, check your map and any aerial photography. It normally involves four people and a dog to sniff.

The first thing to think about is where the device might be detonated from. Ideally you approach the ground overlooking the target site because there may be someone there. It may be a come-on, someone waiting to ambush you or detonate a device. It's very dangerous. Once that is okayed, you clear the area. If it's a big culvert, you just get under there and take a look. If you find a device and a command wire, you follow it and set up a reactive OP. You select a ground of dominance. You and whoever you are with select your ambush position, send your sit rep back and you'll be joined by whoever else is deemed necessary to complete the task. You could be in that position for several days. You always try to arrest people, but there have been situations where terrorists have been killed.

The classic situation is a bomb in a culvert, a command wire leading to a detonation point or remote-control detonation device. The terrorists turn up either to check their bomb or to move into trigger position. We challenge them and more often than not gunfire is exchanged because they are always armed and they don't want to be captured. When contact is made, there's a firefight, which doesn't last long. When it's over, we pick up the pieces, and if a terrorist is wounded, he will be arrested and his wounds will be treated. We don't murder people. Contrary to popular belief, we don't give people the double tap or the third eye. A firefight is very furious and all you're concerned about is yourself. Once it's finished and you have dominated the area, if you come across dead terrorists, so be it. But if they are wounded or in hiding, you arrest them, and terrorists do surrender. We do not take the law into our own hands.

I've been asked whether it is possible to shoot to wound a terrorist in order to take him prisoner. The answer is that there is only one way to shoot a person and that is to shoot at the centre of him. You can only shoot a terrorist if your life or the lives of the people it is your duty to protect are in danger. You have to make a split-second decision, and that's bloody hard to do. However, that is part of our training and we never over-react. We have been involved in numerous operations where people have been shot and wounded and been arrested. You don't shoot to kill. You don't shoot to wound. You shoot to save your life or other people's lives. If the terrorist survives, then his wounds will be treated and he'll be taken to hospital. Once he is no longer a threat, we cease to take action against him other than to restrain him.

We do a lot of combat shooting, room combat and pistol work in every imaginable scenario based on previous live operations and with live ammunition. We do radio procedure, plan tactics and gather intelligence. But our primary role is at the sharp end. There are others who can gather intelligence. There are a lot of normal units who are perhaps not qualified to go against armed terrorists who have been involved in murder. Our task is to bring these people to justice – and it can be as frustrating as hell.

I was involved in an operation which lasted for ten months. We had intelligence from the police unit E4A that there was a bomb-making factory in a barn in the Newcastle area. We checked it out and found bomb-making equipment in there, so an operation was mounted to survey it and catch the bomb-makers and, more important, the people who were going to plant the bombs.

All the agencies were involved (SAS, the RUC, Special Branch), and we did job after job after job over those ten months in 1988. Each time we would crash out of our accommodation, zoom up to the barn and lie up overnight. Nothing. Frustration.

Then it happened. It culminated. We were sat one night in a police station a few miles away when finally the bombers turned up.

Black masks on, operational kit on and we crashed out in the cars. We had two assault teams. I was to be the first entry man and I was going in with Jocky. We went screaming out of the police station. It was nighttime. We had a large, fast car with an engine upgrade and we thought: Right, this is it. We've got them. All we expected was to go in there and arrest everyone inside, but we knew that they were extremely brutal people. We definitely expected them to be armed. However, we were not quite sure. We had to gain entry and take in the situation. We were in a reactive role. There we were, weapons cocked, one in the spout, balaclavas on, ready to confront them. Jocky and I were psyching each other up, saying, 'This is it. We're going to do it.' We knew it might result in a firefight.

About half a mile from the place we heard 'Stop, stop, stop' in our earpieces.

'What?'

'Stop, stop stop. Abort. Come back.'

We couldn't believe it. After ten months of sitting around. What an anticlimax. What also pissed us off was that, when you have terrorists around, they have dickers on the look-out and checking the approach roads. They couldn't have missed us. We had our weapons. We had our hoods on. We were screaming down the road, so we'd probably compromised our situation anyway.

That was it. We obeyed orders, turned back and sat in our private room in the police station, deeply upset. In ten months this was the only time we'd got 'Go, go, go'. After an hour one of the head men from the Special Branch came in (he was one of those who were killed later in the helicopter crash in Scotland). He said he was very, very sorry, but word had come from the highest level not to engage these terrorists. There would have been a bloodbath. We were never given another explanation. Maybe the source of the information might have been present in the barn. We didn't know.

Next day there was an open search of the area by the military and the police and the terrorists were arrested, either at home or at their place of work. The job was wrapped up.

If any testament were needed that we obey the law, this was it, though sometimes, like when the two signallers were murdered, you really have to keep a grip on your self-control. That was the sickest, most horrific thing I've seen in my life.

It was just after the business in Gibraltar and these two signallers, Corporal Derek Woods and Corporal Robert Howes, based at NI headquarters, strayed into the funeral procession in Belfast. Woods was a specialist and the other guy was his relief. Woods was due to leave in a few days and he was showing the other chap around these locations. They just ended up being in the wrong place at the wrong time. They should never, never, never have been anywhere near that bloody funeral. The RUC and the military had pulled back, allowing the mourners to have their procession. It was policed by their own people, the official IRA. They had their own stewards. They had put up their own road blocks and closed off roads.

I was in an RUC station with a patrol from the regiment. We had unmarked cars, quite a bit away from the funeral. The first we knew was at the same time as the rest of the world – the news flashes on TV.

'Fucking hell,' I said. 'Is that one of ours?'

We were trying to account for ourselves, looking at the car, checking the number plate, and realized it wasn't one of ours. At first, like everyone else, we thought it was a Loyalist hit team that had gone in to do a job and fucked up. But because streets had been closed off, the guys had ended up going down a couple of streets they didn't know. They got spooked and panicked and suddenly reversed into that funeral procession. They were blocked in by black taxis. Because they hadn't been trained and were slow to react, they allowed themselves to get boxed in. Had they been trained, they could perhaps have got out by ramming the taxis.

One of the guys drew a pistol and fired in the air. That again showed lack of confidence, lack of training. By that stage, surely, the game was up. When you are confronted by an angry mob like that, they are going to rip you to pieces. If you're going to draw a weapon, then bloody well use it, because the moment they fired in the air, they got leapt on. Had they fired and shot somebody, they might even have been able to shoot themselves out of it, although I doubt it because they did not handle the situation well enough. Lack of training: nothing more.

I'm sure that if those two soldiers in that car had been SAS, things would have been very different. In fact, it would never have happened because we would never have allowed ourselves to get into that situation. But just imagining the impossible, that we had found ourselves cornered by a rioting mob, then the streets would have been flowing with blood. For a start, we would have been armed to the teeth, including automatic weapons. Had they come at me, and it was clear that they were going to kill us, I would have issued the correct warning and then opened fire. The world would not have liked it, but I would have been covered legally. Do you honestly think I would stand there, knowing that I was going to be ripped to pieces, limb from limb? Have you ever had a rioting crowd coming at you? It is horrific. It is terrifying. It is very, very frightening.

The signallers ended up being dragged from the car by the mob, then they were dragged through the gates that led to a park. An army patrol got to the waste ground at the back of the shops in the Falls Road within minutes, but it was after the two guys had been shot. We got back to our hangar still thinking, What the fucking hell's going on? It was quickly established that it was two signallers who had been murdered. We were very upset about it.

Next morning we were buzzed to assemble in the meeting room. All the troop were there. None of us knew what was going to happen, then an Int. officer appeared and told us that the helicopter had videoed the whole thing. I think that the pilot, the cameraman and all those involved, and the people getting the live broadcast at Group, were severely reprimanded because surely the helicopter should have come down and buzzed but it just stood there monitoring. We were all slightly pissed off about that.

The officer warned us that the video was dreadful and that he was going to show it to us there and then. We needed to know what had happened because we were going to have to mount a major operation to bring those people to justice. You could have heard a pin drop in that briefing room. It was horrible. We had to sit and watch while the soldiers were beaten unconscious, thrown over a fence and bundled into a taxi, which drove to some nearby waste ground. Then they were shot, repeatedly.

After seeing the video, we were absolutely dumbfounded, mortified, outraged. I personally felt physically sick. No one spoke. We were just so horror-struck. It was obvious that we had to bring these people to justice. We were the SAS. Yet none of us took the law into our own hands. None of us went out and took any retaliation or retribution. None of us. That's part of the training of the regiment and the calibre of the regiment and the professionalism of the regiment. We are not above the law.

We continued normal ops, and a long-drawn-out operation was mounted. People were identified. One of the guys, the one who smashed the soldiers' car window, was an OTR [on the run], and eventually all the people guilty of murdering those two young lads were brought to justice.

•

Mack Most of the time in Northern Ireland we got pretty much nowhere, but on two occasions we had contact, the first time a fuck-up, the second time very sweet.

The first was a tip-off that a mobile attack was going to be made on the Queen Street police station in Belfast. We knew very little else. We didn't know what weapons they were planning on using, but the police station was quite heavily protected, so we assumed they would use something with a bit of punch. There was a building under construction directly opposite the main entrance to the police station, which gave us a good view of the road both ways, so we set up our position there. We had been informed that the attack was to be on a Wednesday night so we mounted our operation. Nothing happened.

The next night we mounted it again but had to fly four blokes over from Hereford who were on the back-up team because the rest of my troop were off on another operation that also seemed to be about to come off. The second night we decided to take up a position within the police station. We posted two of their operatives, dressed in ordinary police uniforms, on the gate house so that they could deal with enquiries from the public and so on. Of course, you never know when you see someone approaching you whether they are part of the enemy attack team or what. They often sent apparently innocent pedestrians in to ask questions of the blokes on the gate just to ensure how many police targets there were in position. The pedestrians would then go on their way and send a signal to their associates to carry out the attack.

Several people came and went during the evening and, of course, each time my heart beat a little bit faster. By about quarter to midnight still nothing had happened. We had cars out on the road looking for our targets (we knew who they were), but they had seen nothing.

I was just making myself a cup of tea when one of the lads at the window says, 'Fucking hell, they're here.' I looked out of the window. A Volvo was coming down the road towards us with this bloke standing up through the sun-roof with a fucking RPG7 on his shoulder. They drove past our position and stopped. The bloke turned around to face our position and took aim. Everybody down on the floor, because RPG7s do make a mess. It blew a good hole in the wall, but it could have been worse. I was already outside the door when the blast hit, so that put me on the floor, and as I was getting up, I realized there was incoming fire. One of the terrorists was firing an Armalite on automatic in our general direction, and it was coming through the metal fence all around me.

The gate we had planned to exit through had been buckled in the explosion, so it took us a few seconds to get into the street. As we were doing this a couple of our blokes had fired at the car from inside the building which had been hit. As I came out into the street, I saw one of them taking off on foot down an alleyway. As we approached the now abandoned Volvo, I noticed a taxi parked nearby with a woman in the back, screaming. The poor man driving had been hit in the cross-fire. One of our lads fetched a trauma pack and we had a drip into him double quick, but he was in a terrible state and it was obvious he was on his way out, so we made him as comfortable as we could. Meanwhile the rest of the team were chasing the terrorists. Soon our net met with the police line heading towards us. Nothing. The three people had disappeared in the maze of back streets. They must have had another car close by. The only good thing was that we recovered two RPG7s and other weapons that they had left in the Volvo.

•

Other SAS operations were much more successful. Following information collected from a telephone conversation between two IRA men concerning a planned attack on the RUC station at Loughall, for example, the regiment was able to prepare a carefully planned ambush. The IRA's notorious East Tyrone Brigade was going to carry out the attack, but the SAS knew the day of the attack – 8 May 1987 – and it brought over reinforcements from England to back up Ulster Troop. These were a sixteen-man troop from D Squadron, who joined the men of Ulster Troop in and around the RUC station at Loughall and waited for the terrorists. The eight IRA men arrived in a Toyota van and a mechanical digger, in the bucket of which was a large bomb.

After the digger had been crashed through the gates of the police station and abandoned and the bomb had been detonated, the IRA men began firing at the buildings with their personal weapons. Then the SAS opened up, and within seconds all the terrorists had been killed, cut down in a deadly crossfire.

Over a year later, Mack's second contact with the IRA at Drumnakilly in August 1988 was similarly successful, and very different from his first encounter.

•

Mack We received information that a coal-delivery man, who also worked part time in the security forces, was going to be murdered by the IRA. Many people in the province do two jobs for the extra money. We knew that this particular hit team, the two Harte brothers Gerald and Brian and a big fat bastard called Brian Mullen, had killed before. They were bad fucking people.

We put a reactive OP on the coalman's house. We watched his house twenty-four hours a day, as we were expecting the hit team to arrive at his house and shoot him at his own front door. The reactive team is on stand-by to take immediate counter-attack measures in the event of the hit team arriving on scene. We did this for nearly three weeks. After some time it seemed obvious that the murder attempt wasn't going to happen and this particular operation was temporarily suspended.

Some time later we were on patrol, following the coalman round as he made his deliveries. He had just driven into a house where he was dropping some coal and the hit team appeared in a car. We weren't sure if they were tooled up or not, but it looked like a fucking mobile hit was about to go down. For some reason they peeled off at the last minute. God knows why, but it got the whole operation going again. After that, it seemed likely that they would hit him when he was out working rather than at his home, so we decided to substitute one of our men for him in his lorry.

We knew the area where this guy worked, so we looked for a location out of town, on a back road. I did a bit of map study and identified a good place. We didn't know the area very well, so I went and spoke with some of the DET guys. They had done several operations in that area, including using an old farm house as a base. We decided that it would make an ideal place for our OP. We checked it out one night and realized it was ideal. So the plan began to take shape. We would secure the area around the farm house and move there the evening before we moved the lorry into place. The next morning one of our men would drive the coal lorry to the prearranged location and feign having broken down.

During the night we discussed final operational details and before first light we moved into position along the hedgeway beside the road where the lorry was due to 'break down'. There were two parallel roads and we placed blokes from the DET out actually covering the road junctions, so as to be able to give us advance warning of the arrival of the hit squad. Plus we had three cars up and about, driving around looking for the enemy. Finally there was a quick-reaction force of covert police also in the area, ready to move in and provide assistance if needed.

Geordie was the substitute. He looked a bit like the coalman, being a similar size and shape. Once we were in position we gave the okay via the radio and Geordie drove the lorry to our location. We were all wearing the green kit: camouflage top and bottom, which looked funny, given that some of us had really long hair and beards and all sorts. We also wore a special brassard which you could flick down to reveal a coloured band which was our ID. We were in communication with Geordie, who was using a covert radio, so we were chatting away to him while he was on his way and when he first arrived. He was disguised as the coalman, wearing one of those leather jackets like a mat. When he arrived, to my surprise, four more of our lads emerged from the back of his lorry and also positioned themselves along the ditch in under the hedgerow. We still didn't know if anything was actually going to happen.

I positioned myself right underneath the truck and chatted to Geordie from time to time. We were aware that our base could hear everything we said (and that it was being tape-recorded) and that our boss and several very senior anti-terrorist police officers were also monitoring our operation. We'd been in position for more than an hour. Suddenly the radio crackled to life with a voice I hadn't heard before that moment.

'X-Ray One spotted.' And then, after a few seconds, 'Heading your way. Over.'

This was our target. A grungy orange car appeared in the road coming directly towards our position. Geordie was working on the offside front wheel, looking as if he was repairing a flat tyre. As the car approached, it slowed right down. It was fucking obvious. I remember thinking, Here we go. But you can't do anything. We knew they were fucking bad bastards but you can't just shoot them. They weren't doing anything wrong. They drove right up and had a good look at Geordie. They carried on up the lane and then, still in full view of our position, turned around and came back towards us.

I thought, This is it. Something's going to happen. Gerald, the older brother, was driving, his brother was in the back and the big fat fucker was in the passenger seat. They drove past us and off the way they had originally come. The cunts disappeared. They went through a couple of checkpoints and disappeared.

Over the next half hour three or four cars stopped beside Geordie to ask him if he needed a hand. He was polite to them but said, no, he didn't need them. Of course, each time a car slowed down, we were all ready because we didn't know if they were going to use a different car for the attack. And if they had appeared, we didn't want anyone else around for fear of them getting caught in the crossfire.

After several hours in position we were talking over the situation with Control. Geordie seemed to have been changing a wheel for more than two hours and it was starting to look a bit fucking obvious. It doesn't take that long. We agreed that we would stay for just half an hour more. So Geordie started taking the wheel off again.

Suddenly the radio came to life. 'There's a white Ford Sierra just pulled into the farm not far from your position.' They gave us continual updates on all movements in the area. A few minutes later the same white car reappeared with our three targets in it. They had been waiting in this farm to hijack the car.

The radio continued, 'Yep, white Sierra approaching the junction. It has now turned right towards you.'

I'd been lying under the truck, facing out between the two front wheels. When I knew they were coming for the actual attack, I crawled to the back of the truck and stood up behind it in order to have some cover and also to be able to get a clear line of fire.

'Still coming, still coming,' the radio warned. There was a dip in the road and the car was temporarily out of sight. Just as it came back into view, about 100 metres away, this dick-head was hanging out of the back window fucking shooting off bursts of automatic fire from an AK47, which slammed into the lorry. They were approaching at about 40 miles an hour. Geordie was fucking funny. He hot-footed it round the back of the truck like a cartoon character. He wasn't running properly. More kind of lurching. He dived head-first into the bushes behind me to get out of the way.

We were using Heckler & Koch G3s. As the car came level with me, I put a burst into it. The weapon does ride up a bit as you fire it, so I had to put a good line up the side of the car. As this was happening, I honestly thought to myself, There's no way they are going to fucking stop. But after the car had only gone on another 10 metres, it stopped. I couldn't believe it. I had put about nine rounds through it. I didn't know if I had hit anybody. The next second the rest of the guys opened up from their positions in the hedge. It was nice. Very nice.

Johnny Two-Combs was waiting in the hedge.

•

Johnny Two-Combs I was in the hedge a few feet in front of the lorry and the first I knew about the op going down was the sound of a vehicle coming towards me, a high screech, then *whack-whack-whack*, a burst of AK47 machine-gun fire went over the top of my head. It sprayed the front of the lorry too. I ran into the road because I was sure the person I was there to protect had been hit. The first sight that greeted me was a man in a blue boiler suit, black balaclava and black gloves getting out of the front passenger seat. He had an AK47 with two magazines taped to each other and brought up to the aim. I had a G3 and I was quicker to the draw. I fired a short burst into him and he fell. I knelt down and fired an accurate burst into him. I turned my attention to the others and they had been dealt with. I looked at the person we were there to protect and found that he was okay. It was a successful conclusion to the operation.

I was absolutely ecstatic, overjoyed. Someone had fired at me. I'd gone to confront that person to protect an unarmed man. I'd been confronted by a terrorist. I'd beaten him. I was happy it was him and not me. He was a known murderer engaged in an act of attempted murder and I was justified, knowing that he could never be in a position to do that again. I was okay. My family didn't have to worry about me.

It was the training that made the difference between him and me. SAS training is very dangerous. There are accidents, fatalities. We train for real with live ammunition. When you go to a live operation, the reactions are just the same. The fact that this was a terrorist and not a target was just the same.

•

Mack As the others were firing, I stepped into the middle of the road and pumped rounds into the back of the fucking car. It was all over in seconds. Just after we stopped firing, two of our own cars came screeching down the road to block it off. There was a woman and her kids approaching in another car and someone shouted to our guys, 'Stop that car before it gets any closer.' They were stopped and turned away.

I got on the radio. 'Hello, we've just had contact.'

We checked all the lads to make sure everyone was okay. Check your mags. Safety catches on. I went across to the car to make sure they were all dead. The guy in front had half his fucking head gone. The one in the back had fallen on to the ground and the third one was also shot to fucking pieces. Then I got back on the radio. 'QRF [Quick Reaction Force], please move in.' The guys who had been hiding in bushes and on up the road appeared and so did the scene-of-crime officers. They asked us all to move back to the exact positions we had been in when the attack began. One of them marked each of our positions. Once he was finished, I asked if we could leave and he gave us the all-clear. A few minutes later two choppers appeared in the field next to us. They took most of us, while the rest left in our vehicles.

Once we were back in barracks we had some tea and some food. The police arrived and took our weapons from us. It's standard procedure. The weapons are used as evidence and in the forensic reports. Soon afterwards we were again taken by chopper back to our own base and we were joined there by police who had been involved. I did my written notes straight away while everything was fresh in my mind. I always used to do this. Afterwards we spoke to various officers and had a drink. We didn't go mad. We knew it was straight back to work soon afterwards. We also knew that we would have to give police statements about the incident the following morning.

That was the Northern Ireland score as far as I was concerned. In five years, three baddies on the plus side, one poor taxi driver on the minus side. Hopefully, that'll all be history soon.

•

The deadly cat-and-mouse game between the SAS and IRA continued into the 1990s. Ulster Troop continued to have more successes, testimony to the intelligence-gathering methods of the intelligence agencies. In 1991, for example, the terrorist Peter Ryan was killed while on his way to murder someone, and a year later four IRA members, Kevin Barry O'Donnell, Sean O'Farrell, Patrick Vincent and Peter Clancy, were ambushed and killed in Coalisland after machine-gunning a police station.

The ceasefire announced by the IRA in December 1994 appeared to signal the end of the war in Northern Ireland, but the bombing of Canary Wharf in February 1996 cast doubts on the prospect of a permanent peace. Whatever the outcome, the SAS stands ready to tackle the IRA.

7
THE FALKLANDS WAR

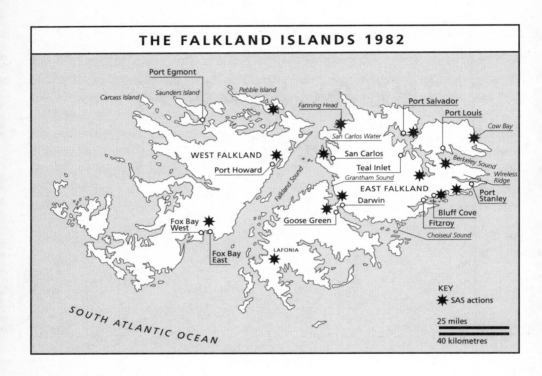

THE FALKLAND ISLANDS 1982

Port Egmont

Carcass Island *Saunders Island* *Pebble Island* Fanning Head Port Salvador Port Louis

Cow Bay

San Carlos Water

WEST FALKLAND San Carlos *Berkeley Sound*

Port Howard Teal Inlet *Wireless Ridge*

Grantham Sound

EAST FALKLAND Port Stanley

Darwin

Fox Bay Bluff Cove
West Goose Green Fitzroy

Fox Bay *Choiseul Sound*
East

LAFONIA

SOUTH ATLANTIC OCEAN

KEY
✸ SAS actions

25 miles
40 kilometres

Falkland Sound

The Falkland Islands had been under British sovereignty since 1833. However, Argentina had long-standing claims over the islands, and in April 1982 the leader of the Argentine military junta, General Galtieri, decided that the time had come to honour those claims. His forces invaded the Falklands on the 2nd of that month, and immediately the British government of Margaret Thatcher resolved to get them back, by force if necessary. A task force was soon assembled for this job.

As soon as the Argentinians had invaded, the Director of the SAS Group, Brigadier Peter de la Billière, and the commander of 22 SAS, Lieutenant-Colonel Michael Rose, lobbied hard for the regiment to play a part in the campaign. Their efforts paid off: when the carrier HMS *Hermes* left Portsmouth harbour on 5 April, a small party of men from D Squadron were on board. Other members of the squadron were flown south to Ascension Island on the same day. The next day G Squadron and the regimental HQ were on their way there.

Some of the men had anticipated their first chance of action.

•

David I remember lying in bed on the Saturday night. It was just after eleven when the phone rang and I was told to report for duty in the morning. I knew straight away. I turned to my wife and said, 'That's it. We're off.' She simply didn't believe me.

At the briefing we learnt that the Argentine junta was planning a full-scale invasion of the Falkland Islands and we were told to get our kit ready as soon as possible. Later that day we were told that our mission was to retake South Georgia.

On the Monday we were given a send-off briefing by Brigadier de la Billière. I'll never forget his final words of advice to us. 'Keep your Bergen weight below 45 pounds, and don't throw away your biscuits from your twenty-four-hour ration pack.' The full significance of this brilliant advice only really struck us when were in action later. Our Bergens seldom weighed less than between 80 and 100 pounds because of the conditions we were facing, and G Squadron were subsequently almost reduced to eating the soles of their boots they were so hungry. They were required to do ops with two weeks' rations that actually lasted four weeks.

The whole of D Squadron was halfway to Ascension Island by late Monday afternoon. We flew in a VC10 and were the first troops to arrive there.

One old soldier however was left behind.

•

Jock Thompson When I first heard on the news that there was going to be a war for the Falklands, I immediately got all my kit together. I went to the camp and saw the adjutant. By this time I was out in Civvy Street, but I never felt like I'd left.

'Sir, my Bergen's packed, I've got my parachute hooks and my helmet. All I need is a weapon. I'm coming with you.'

'Oh, no, not another one. We've been inundated with ex-members of the regiment. We don't need you. You're about number bloody sixty.'

'Right then, suit yourself. Fight your own war.'

So that same day I got my Para beret out and got my arse down to Plymouth. I had all the right kit on. I marched up the gangplank with all the rest of them. At the top they had a checklist.

'And who are you?'

'Staff-Sergeant Thompson, 15 Para,' which is one of the Scottish Para TA units. 'Beach Master.'

'Oh, a Beach Master. Fine, fine. Move along.'

I found my way to the canteen and sat down to have a cup of coffee with some of the lads. I knew quite a lot of the 2 Para blokes. Several of them came to say hello.

'Fucking hell, Jock, I thought you were out.'

'Aye, I am. I am. I'm 15 Para, TA. I've come down as a Beach Master.'

'Oh, good. Nice to have you on board.'

Some time later, just before we set sail, I heard a tannoy announcement. 'Staff-Sergeant Thompson, 15 Para, please report to the bridge.'

I marched into the room. Three military police officers looked at me.

'Thompson, the game's up,' said one of them. 'We're taking you back to Hereford.'

My wife had phoned the police in Hereford who in turn had contacted the military police. 'Look, this mad bastard, my husband, is trying to get down to the Falklands. He's going to try and get on to the *Canberra*.'

They only just got me in time.

•

David On Ascension Island nobody knew who we were and nobody asked. We moved into an American base on the island and waited until a suitable mode of transport appeared. After a couple of days we learned that a Royal Fleet Auxiliary ship called the *Fort Austin* had docked. It was headed to resupply Royal Navy ships *en route* to the South Atlantic from the Mediterranean. Once our troop commander had worked that out he found the captain and asked if we could hitch a lift until we could transfer to a Royal Navy ship.

It was a fine ship with loads of room. Good facilities and very friendly crew. This was our first exposure to any form of navy, so we were a bit naïve. There was a big tank deck below the top deck, wide enough for fork-lift trucks to manoeuvre, so it was a bit like a greyhound track, and we used this as a training circuit. The conditions were perfect for training and we really sweated hard as we started to acclimatize. We were just wearing shorts and T-shirts.

About three days out to sea, an announcement comes over the tannoy.

'Attention, attention, this is the captain speaking. Would all the army personnel aboard please wear tracksuit leggings and full PT clothes while training because your present state of undress is exciting the crew too much and is likely to lead to problems. Thank you.'

This was the first time we had any warning that merchant sailors are a little bit different from us regular soldiers. That same evening I was standing at the bar when I noticed some of the lads sniggering. I turned round and one of the sailors, who was built like a brick shit-house, was standing behind me in a pair of skimpy cut-off white denim shorts, a tight torn T-shirt, a bloody great love heart sewn over his crotch and a nasty twinkle in his eye – which was fixed on me. There was no trouble as such, though I did find it all a little bit disturbing. And we were all very pleased when we caught up with the nearest Royal Navy ship, HMS *Antrim*, because the regular Navy doesn't allow such goings on.

We crossed deck by Wessex helicopter. There were two other ships in convoy with us, HMS *Brilliant* and HMS *Plymouth*. The first thing that hit me, and really shocked me, especially as I was a young trooper wanting to go to war, was the extreme apathy of the naval ratings. I had expected everyone to have the same attitude as me. They just were not interested. They had been at sea for a long time and just wanted to get home to their wives and sweethearts.

After a voyage lasting several weeks, we arrived in the waters off South Georgia and rendezvoused with HMS *Endurance*, the Royal Navy's Antarctic Survey ship, and cross-decked on to her the same day. The captain, Nick Barker, was a great bloke, very positive, and he believed in what we were capable of achieving between us if we worked as a team.

There was an Argentine submarine called the *Santa Fé* in the area, which meant that the three other ships kept away from the coastline. *Endurance* was perfect for sneaking in and out of small bays and fjords undetected by the submarine, so it was an obvious choice for most of us to be based on her. It was also extremely cramped, as there was no extra living accommodation whatsoever. I was stuck in with two mates in the Number One mess, right up in the bow.

•

The first operation the SAS was involved in was the retaking of South Georgia, located some 1,400 kilometres south-east of the Falklands. The government had decided that it provided an excellent opportunity to demonstrate to the Argentinians that Britain was willing to use force to get her possessions back. The ships detailed to carry out the operation were the destroyers *Antrim*, *Brilliant*, and *Endurance*, the frigate *Plymouth*, the tanker *Tidespring* and the Fleet Auxiliary *Fort Austin*. D Squadron, under the command of Major Cedric Delves, would be the first unit of the SAS to have a crack at the enemy, though a bigger foe was the weather on South Georgia, which was like the Arctic.

•

David After a few days we got the order to retake South Georgia. A Nimrod came in close to us and dropped into the sea a canister containing a top-priority encoded Flash Message. A Flash Message is sent when an order requires immediate action.

The plan was that Mountain Troop would be inserted on to Fortuna Glacier to do a covert approach march across the back of South Georgia to establish an observation post so that we could see what was actually going on. We had no information coming out of the five settlements, although officials from the British Antarctic Survey had come up with plans of the settlements, including room-by-room descriptions of the houses where the Argentinians were thought to be living. There was some objection that the weather was too bad, but none the less the plan was approved.

On 15 April fifteen of our guys, including Captain John Hamilton, who was in command, were issued with their skis and snow-shoes and a pulk [a sledge for carrying equipment]. At noon they left HMS *Antrim* in three Wessex helicopters.

White-out conditions made the first two attempts impossible, but they got down on the third flight in winds of over 50 mph.

Each man carried 80 pounds of equipment and took turns in hauling the 200 pounds of gear on the pulk. Their GPMGs soon froze up, and it took them five hours to cover less than half a mile. They sheltered in a shallow crevasse behind an outcrop of ice and tried to erect two two-man tents. One was swept away and five men slept in the other, while the remainder went under the pulk.

Next morning Hamilton asked for evacuation, realizing that they would not get through another night. At 1.30 p.m. three helicopters reached them through a fifteen-minute window of clear weather. Soon after take-off one of them crashed in a white-out. Only one of the seven men on board was injured.

The other two choppers got back to pick up the rest of the troop, but on take-off, in another white-out, one of the helicopters hit a ridge of ice and tipped over. The pilot of the remaining chopper, S., dropped his passengers off on the *Antrim* and returned for the others. It took him five attempts to get them on board. The machine was designed to carry five people and, with seventeen men, was seriously overloaded. With that sort of weight S. could not hover over the deck of the ship and decided to crash-land instead. He was later awarded the DFC for getting the troop back intact.

The result of all this was that we had to completely rethink the attack plan. At dawn on 25 April circumstances changed dramatically. It was down to luck and Lieutenant-Commander S.'s excellent flying and battle skills. Just by chance he happened upon the *Santa Fé*, recognized an opportunity target on the surface and immediately attacked it, making a direct hit. He landed back on the deck of the *Endurance* and we helped him reload his air-to-surface weapons. As soon as we were through, he took off again and went back into the attack. He did this for a third time and again got direct hits, damaging the sub so much that it had to make a run for Grytviken Harbour.

With the threat of the submarine attack removed, a new plan could be drawn up. We knew that we could now take South Georgia without much loss of life. There were seventy-five of us:

four SAS troops, an SBS team and some Marines plus a Royal Artillery officer who was going to get behind enemy lines and direct naval gunfire. Once we were ready to attack, the Navy started a bombardment. It was amazing to watch the three ships lined astern, pounding the shore positions. The first British naval bombardment since World War Two. They started shelling the hillside beyond the perimeter of the settlements and gradually brought the targets closer and closer. The message was clear, and a white flag went up before a single one of their side had been injured. There was then a mad dash to see who could be first in to raise the flag. It was actually Mountain Troop, D Squadron, 22 SAS.

A company of Commandos then went ashore and occupied South Georgia, and my troop got orders to cross-deck to HMS *Brilliant*.

We turned north in order to join the Task Force which was heading for the main Falkland Islands. The rest of the squadron were divided between two other ships. Once we reached it, we all crossed-decked on to HMS *Hermes*. Now there were two full SAS squadrons, D and G, all on one ship. G Squadron were preparing to do long-term intelligence-gathering operations all across the islands. I remember sitting chatting to my mates, wondering when the action would begin. We didn't have long to wait.

At first light on 1 May I stood on deck, watching the Harrier jets take off to attack Goose Green and Port Stanley. I watched that journalist file his report for the TV news, counting them all out and counting them all back. While he did that a few of us stood on the gallery deck, taking photographs of the Harriers as they came past us, ready to take off. It was an amazing sight.

For the next two weeks G Squadron gathered intelligence information to provide us with our next target. It came sooner than we expected. It started with a couple of fighters on combat air patrol picking up some strange emissions from what they thought might be a radar site on a place called Pebble Island. Once they started having a closer look, they realized that there was an airstrip to the north of West Falkland. The question had to be posed: was this a dispersal site that could damage landing operations on the mainland or pose a threat to the fleet? Although apparently reluctant at first, Sandy Woodward was persuaded that it was a real threat, particularly as it was not clear what aircraft they had there. The order came for Boat Troop to make a covert landing and obtain better information about the Pebble Island airstrip.

•

Pebble Island is situated off the north coast of West Falkland. The enemy had placed a number of ground-attack aircraft there which would be a major threat to British land forces that were to be put ashore at San Carlos Water. The SAS was therefore ordered to destroy them. The ships involved were *Hermes*, *Broadsword* and *Glamorgan*. The raid took place on the night of 14 May.

•

David On 11 May Boat Troop inserted two four-man patrols by Sea King helicopter to the north of the main island. Their purpose was to get as close as they could to obtain enough information to make a proper plan. They carried with them wooden kleppers, which clip together to form canoes. Once they were dropped, they marched at a fair pace to the far shore, closest to Pebble Island, and paddled across. Half the team stayed guarding the boats; the rest went forward to gain the information. They were quickly able to confirm that there was an airstrip with eleven aircraft but they could not identify a radar installation, so the pilots had been mistaken. There was no radar, but there was a village nearby containing a military garrison, air force pilots and crews and an unknown number of civilians. They had the greatest difficulty maintaining an OP during the daylight, as it was very exposed. They had to lie completely motionless in the elephant grass at great danger to themselves and, indeed, to the whole operation had they been caught. As they bugged out, the information was being processed aboard *Hermes* and an assault plan was prepared.

The first idea was to attack the garrison as well as the airfield, but this was abandoned for several reasons. The launch of the operation was delayed due to several factors. There was some confusion as to the time it would take to bring the ships within helicopter range of the target. As a result the ships had to sail fast into a high wind, which meant, in turn, that movements and preparations on the flight deck could not take place until the carrier arrived on target. As a result of that there were delays in getting the helicopters up onto the deck. From then on the whole operation was rushed. Then the assault troop were not at the forward RV, so that caused an extra delay while a new troop were briefed to do the assault. Consequently we had only thirty minutes on target. We had to get back to the RV in time. If we had had any more time, we would have made some form of contact with the garrison, not knowing at that time just how many enemy troops were there.

For the twenty-four hours prior to the assault I had a high fever. I'd got flu. I asked to be isolated in sick bay, where I knew they would be able to get my temperature down. I wasn't going to miss the operation for anything. A couple of hours before we launched a mate came in and gave me the nod. I discharged myself from sick bay, got my kit together and jumped on to the back of a chopper.

We studied the reports and maps. Pebble Island is long and narrow. The airstrip and the village were at the south of a narrow piece of terrain, and we were to land 7 kilometres to the east and tab across at a fair pace. We reckoned the march would take about two hours. That 7-kilometre march was really difficult for me. I felt absolutely terrible. The boys were as supportive as ever: 'Oh, you're ill, David. You can carry *four* mortar bombs!'

My troop's task was to clear the village, house by house. A few families lived near the airstrip, which was one of the reasons why the original suggestion to bomb the airstrip was turned down. Using maps, we had numbered each house and estimated which ones might have been used by civilians and which ones were most likely to be used by military personnel. We did not know if any civilians were being held hostage, so we assumed the worst. Our brief was to contact the civilians, locate the enemy and keep them busy while the other lads got on with doing their stuff on the airstrip. One of the problems was that, like all the Falklands, the ground was so bare. Pebble Island was desolate even by Falklands standards. No cover at all. It was going to be hit and run – run like hell.

A total of forty-five of us landed in three Sea Kings in the early hours of the morning. We met with Tim, the commander of Boat Troop, who had done the OP. He did a bloody good job of persuading Major Delves, the officer in command of the special forces in the Falklands, that we should do the operation because right up until the last minute it was still not definitely going to happen. Timing was critical. We were already an hour late because the third Sea King had been below deck and it took some time to get it ready to fly. We knew that we had a 7-kilometre march to the target and back again, perhaps slowed down with casualties, and that we had to be back exactly on time to rendezvous with the helicopters. We also knew that they could not wait beyond the RV time because as soon as dawn broke they would immediately be vulnerable to air attack. We were attacking an airfield that had eleven aircraft on it. We did not know how many we would destroy successfully or if any of them would escape. If the Pucaras had managed to take off, they would have been able to attack the helicopters. But the Pucaras had no night-flying capability, so we were safe as long as it stayed dark.

Daylight would have meant the nightmare scenario of an entire squadron very exposed with the sun coming up, possibly having failed to destroy all the enemy aircraft, which would then undoubtedly come and do their worst. After a fifteen-minute last-ditch discussion with the head shed, we got the go-ahead.

Boat Troop led us in to the target in small groups. We were carrying a lot of kit. We all carried as much extra ammunition as we could. Most of us had between 200 and 400 rounds of GPMG ammunition in addition to the ammunition for our rifles. The machine gun was your fire-power, and if you ever got in the shit, that was what was going to get you out of it. In addition to all our usual operational kit, weapons, grenades, we all carried two bombs each for the 81-millimetre mortar. A lot of it was illuminant, so that we could see what we were doing. This was probably the single most important piece of kit for the attack, as it was our only support.

One troop carried most of the explosives, as it was they who were actually going to attack and destroy the aircraft on the ground. Some of the others had also managed to get their hands on explosives but not many. There were not enough Boat Troop troopers to lead all the groups in, so some of them had to manage on their own. We knew the route was clear because the Boat Troop lads had already been both ways. We moved initially to where we were going to set up the mortar, which, of course, provides indirect fire and is therefore held back behind the attack position. One by one we dropped off our mortar rounds.

At this point it became apparent that we had lost the troop that was supposed to carry out the attack on the actual planes. In all fairness to them, it is sometimes quite hard to locate a six-figure grid reference in the pitch-dark in the middle of nowhere in a place where everything looks the same. And they were one of the troops who did not have a guide. Nobody knew they were missing until we arrived at the forward RV. We had assumed they were out in front of us. We had to change plan immediately. We waited for a bit to see if they would reappear but they didn't. We now had exactly thirty minutes to complete the assault.

Mountain Troop, led by John Hamilton, was designated to do the assault. My troop became the fire-support team for the assault. Thank God for that. We were so lucky. It meant we didn't have to do the house-clearing assault on the settlement. We later found out that there were 200 Argentinian soldiers in the wool shed, which was the starting point for our operation. There were sixteen of us. That would have been interesting.

The attack opened with a naval bombardment on to the feature directly overlooking the settlement. Then our own mortar opened up, lighting the whole place up like it was bright daylight. The mortar man was having a lot of trouble. Every

time he fired the bloody thing, the whack of the pipe was kicking
the base plate further into the ground. If the angle of the plate
changed, he lost his trajectory and elevation. Despite this he
kept up continuous fire, eventually giving the order 'check fire'
before we withdrew.

After a few more minutes the assault troop went in. As they
reached one end of the airstrip they got into a firefight. An
Argentine officer and an NCO were in a bunker to the side of
the strip and opened up. They were rapidly dealt with. After
that there was virtually no enemy fire on us, so the boys got
stuck into the planes.

They split into seven two-man teams. It was a bloody big strip
and they had a lot of ground to cover. It's not as if the planes
were all parked in a nice neat row. They were all over the strip.
And all the time the boys were running against the clock. Five
planes were destroyed using the explosive charges that they had
with them. The Pucara was the tallest of the aircraft. As they
approached each plane, one bloke would give the other a leg up
on to the wing. Once up, he then leaned down and hauled the
other one up to join him. The Skyvan was not a problem. The
Mentors were very small, and with one great leap the guys got
themselves up on to the wings.

The other six planes were attacked at close quarters by hand.
It's not like in the movies, when you shoot the fuel tank of a
plane and it explodes. Planes are built to withstand bullet holes,
at least up to a point. Still, the lads used their initiative. They
riddled the planes, especially the cockpits, with machine-gun
fire and chucked in grenades for good measure. Some of the
lads, including Paddy A., got so worked up with adrenaline and
enthusiasm that they actually ripped instrument panels out of
the cockpits with their bare hands.

During the withdrawal there was suddenly this almighty
explosion. The Argies had planted command-detonated mines,
and as we were leaving someone on their side decided to get
brave and initiated one of them. We had no knowledge that they
had even been planted. The guys who had done the assault were
withdrawing in groups of four. Fire and manoeuvre. One team

of two is on the ground providing cover for the other two as they move. One foot on the ground, one moving. Leap-frogging. Two of our guys were caught in the blast of the mine. One had shrapnel wounds and the other was just winded. They were recovered and helped to the original central rendezvous point near the mortar. The base plate had to be dug out, it had sunk so deep. As soon as we could, we set off back to the coastline. There was so little time.

I was in the last chopper to leave. As we were taking off I remember looking back over my shoulder. I'll never forget it. The whole place looked as if it was burning. It was terrific. We all went nuts.

As we approached HMS *Hermes*, I looked down from the chopper on to the deck. There were loads of matelots on deck, waiting to welcome us home. As we landed they all swarmed around us, slapping our backs and cheering and carrying on. We were still all hyped up and carrying loaded weapons; it was really quite dangerous. One of the blokes fired off a negligent discharge. The bullet passed straight through the upper deck and burst through the ceiling of the sick bay. Our casualty with all the shrapnel wounds had been loaded in just a few minutes before. Next minute there's a friendly bullet rattling around his head.

The operation had been a fantastic success. We had two casualties and no dead. They had lost six Pucaras, four Mentors and a Skyvan, and the destruction of the Pucaras was particularly satisfying as they were slow-flying, ground-hugging aircraft that posed a particular threat to ground forces.

No sooner had the job been done than we began planning for the next operation. We were all delighted because we had proved to the Navy that what we were doing there was serious, and that we could do it. We were trying to form a working and trusting relationship with an organization that, even in 1982, knew virtually nothing about the Special Air Service. Yes, they knew about these blokes in black who had stormed the Iranian Embassy in Central London, but they really had no idea about our potential and power in a war setting like the South Atlantic.

On 18 May the main invasion fleet rendezvoused with the

carrier group. G Squadron were still working on reconnaissance, while we were preparing for our attacks on the four separate targets, designed to make the main garrisons think a much larger force had landed in order to cause a significant diversion while the beachhead was established further north at San Carlos Water.

The next day we moved from HMS *Hermes* to HMS *Intrepid*, which was an assault ship. Most of us had crossed, but there was one last group still on *Hermes*. They threw all their gear into the back and climbed into a Sea King helicopter at about 9.30 that night. The two ships were about half a mile apart. It was only a five-minute flight. The equipment, and there were tons of it, was all piled up high in the back and many of the guys had to sit on top of the gear. In order to save time, no one was wearing a survival suit.

There was a very heavy sea and, as usual, a strong wind. Suddenly, from about 400 feet, the Sea King ditched into the sea. One of the survivors later said that he had felt 'something like a sledgehammer blow' just before the chopper began to ditch. It stayed on the surface for a short time but had already capsized and was rapidly filling with water. There were thirty blokes on board, plus the pilot and co-pilot. Twenty of them died in that freezing water.

The loss was fearsomely tragic to everyone. It affected us all very personally. The first couple of days after the loss were terrible because we were just sitting around. Luckily, after that we were flat out almost all the time and had to put our own feelings of grief and loss to one side. There was work to be done. Nevertheless we had sustained a major loss. We had lost both squadrons' sergeant-majors, the two most senior soldiers. We had lost a lot of experience and expertise in the crash as well as friends. For months afterwards I kept on getting images of some of my friends at the bottom of the sea. Every time we got on to a helicopter there would be a scramble for the seat by the door in case that chopper came down in the sea as well. But we had to get on to make it up for the lads we had lost.

•

SAS and SBS parties had been put ashore on East and West Falkland since the beginning of May. SAS activity was concentrated around Bluff Cove, Stanley (the capital), Cow Bay, Port Salvador, San Carlos Water, Goose Green and Lafonia. The teams reported back to the Task Force on the day-to-day movements of the Argentinian forces and of the enemy aircraft and helicopters which were on the islands. One four-man team from G Squadron established a camouflaged OP on Beagle Ridge overlooking Stanley. He reported back that the enemy had a secret dispersal area for helicopters between Mount Kent and Mount Estancia. The location was then hit by two Sea Harriers from the Task Force and three of the helicopters were destroyed.

•

David A full beachhead landing was planned, and we had to get on to the mainland ahead of the invasion force and carry out diversionary raids: classic special forces stuff.

That first night was probably the most painful of my entire life. We were dropped off in troops of sixteen at various points around the island. We all had a long approach march into our targets, as we wanted to get in quietly rather than assault direct from the helicopters. We were carrying a lot of kit, well over 100 pounds, because we had to be prepared to stay on the ground for an unknown and potentially extended period. We did not know how long it was going to take the main forces to establish a beachhead. In addition to the belts of machine-gun ammunition we were carrying the Stinger ground-to-air hand-held missile, which was a new piece of kit given to us by the Americans, along with a consignment of night sights. We had never seen it before.

Two of the blokes in my troop, Carl and Kiwi, were particularly competitive. The morning after our first mainland attack, we were marching back towards San Carlos. By now it was broad daylight and we still had a long way to go. We felt very vulnerable to air attack, as we still didn't have total air supremacy at this stage and were definitely under air observation. Suddenly one of their Pucaras began to come towards us. Kiwi decided to try and take it out using his Stinger. None of us had actually fired one or even seen one being fired, and as far as we knew they had never been used in anger anywhere in the world, so we had no idea what it would be like or how effective it would be. Kiwi fixed on the battery unit, and when he heard the lock-on signal he fired the trigger. *Whoosh.* Away it went. To our amazement he hit the plane and blew it out of the sky. Then we saw this lone parachutist floating down to the ground. First plane kill to Air Troop. We were all very chuffed. It was great. And it was 1–0 to Kiwi.

Carl was now desperate to even the score. Once we had shot down the first plane we decided to lie up and wait to ascertain whether it was safe to proceed. The trouble was that the pickets and the defence forces being set up around San Carlos did not even know who we were or what we were doing, so we had to be very careful on our approach. We decided to wait at the main rendezvous for the rest of the squadron. While waiting, we were buzzed by two more Pucaras. They came quite low over our position, flew around in a large circle and then came in again. Carl grabbed the Stinger and rushed to fire one off. It nosedived into the ground right in front of us, sending up an enormous cloud of smoke, which was as good as sending the pilots a clear message, saying, 'HERE WE ARE!' Then they flew past us so low that I could see the pilots quite clearly. More important, I could see that all their rocket pods were empty, so they obviously didn't even have any ammunition for their machine guns. But it still felt like they were telling us something: 'We know where you are and we'll be back.' We felt incredibly vulnerable but they never did reappear, thank God.

Eventually the entire squadron regrouped. We moved down into San Carlos and on to *Lancelot*, sister ship to the *Sir Galahad* that went down with the Welsh Guards.

Lancelot became our home for most of the rest of the war. It had received a hit from a 1,000-pounder early on but had not sunk. We used it like a floating barracks and launched the rest of our operations from there. It was certainly better than living on the ground under a poncho. It worked out really well because each time we did our operations, for however long it was, we would come home to a ship's crew, mostly Chinese, cooking us really good scoff.

Once we were committed to the mainland we virtually never stopped moving. We also did patrol missions, gathering information on both East and West Falkland. We planned dozens of diversionary raids based on intelligence provided by G Squadron. We hit numerous small targets around the outer perimeter of San Carlos to make it look as if we had come ashore by air. We wanted the Argentinians to think there was already a large force on the ground in order to stop them from moving troops to defend the possible beachhead position at San Carlos.

After dealing with the Pucaras and the diversionary raids we had to tackle Mount Kent. We were tasked with locating a helicopter landing site that could be used to start bringing forward the rest of the ground forces' kit. So while the troops began their famous yomping, we looked for the best site. Eventually we settled on Mount Kent and set about trying to hide ourselves.

This wasn't easy. You can't dig deep in the Falklands – you just hit granite or water – so our 'scrapes' were only 18 inches deep. We covered them with hessian camouflaged by peat and tussock grass. They were lined with plastic, but we were still constantly soaked. Most of us got trench foot. There was no tree cover. We couldn't cook, of course, and even taking a piss was problematic – the steam might give you away. And transmitting was really dangerous because the Argies had direction-finding equipment.

On our first day nine enemy helicopters came out of Stanley in formation, obviously going to disperse, and flew low over our position. They were a beautiful target, coming within 150 yards of us, virtually directly above our heads. We just wanted to blow them out of the sky but we had to stay hidden as we could not compromise our position or the helicopter site. Shortly afterwards a Huey helicopter full of Argentinian special forces landed just below our position. We hadn't been seen. We were sure of that. I suspect they knew that Mount Kent was exposed and wanted to defend it against possible attack, without realizing that we were already there. They disembarked and began to move towards our position. We formed a classical linear ambush. But it didn't go quite according to plan. Some of our squadron moved unexpectedly and met them head on. All hell broke loose, and we opened up, not realizing that some of our troops were in among them. Two of ours were hit, one quite badly. Most of theirs just ran away but a few of them hid and actually infiltrated 17 Troop's position the following night. They attacked, mainly with grenades. Some of our blokes took some shrapnel but the enemy were all killed in a matter of minutes.

One time we went off as a four-man patrol to West Falkland. We had to make our way to an OP in the shittiest weather conditions I have ever had to work in. One of the patrol developed the early symptoms of hypothermia. A combination of individual soldiering skills and team work meant that he was okay. After three days we were offered the chance to be extracted and had to make our way to a helicopter landing point. It failed the first night, due to the weather conditions, so we went back again the next night. We were so pleased to see it coming in and were really looking forward to getting back to our ship and some warm scoff. But when I climbed into the back of the chopper I couldn't believe it: there were the rest of my troop plus the first lot of B Squadron troops who had just arrived.

They chucked us three days' worth of rations and briefed us during the flight that we were being flown to a new drop zone that our intelligence believed was going to be used by the enemy as a major drop zone for an airborne reinforcement from the mainland of Argentina. This mass drop was literally imminent. The plan appeared to be that they were intending to establish a fresh strong force on West Falkland, to try and hold that and to negotiate from a position of controlling at least half the Falklands. Just to cheer us up, we were told to expect anywhere between a battalion and a brigade strength of the enemy forces' regular soldiers. There were twenty of us who were going to stop them. Fucking crazy. A brigade is almost 2,000 men.

I remember someone said, 'Fuck me, who's got the ammo?'

And then, as we started thinking about the reality of what we were about to take on, someone else said, 'If they get the chance to get even half decent numbers clear of the aircraft, we're going to be in deep shit. Our only hope will be to blow 'em out of the sky with these Stingers.'

That wasn't very comforting, as so far I had seen one successful hit and several misses.

Once we were in place on this supposed enemy drop site the principal enemy was, as usual, the cold. The 2,000 men never showed up. It would have been a slaughter.

●

While D and G Squadrons were carrying out actions under the noses of the Argentinians, B Squadron, including Snapper, was making its way south.

●

Snapper B Squadron's war got off to a false start but none of us complained. The plan was for us to fly from Ascension Island straight on to the runway at Port Stanley and end the war. The head shed told us, 'This is the most important operation that the SAS has carried out since the Second World War.' His thinking was one squadron of men in two C130s coming down among 11,000 Argentinians and with anti-aircraft guns and ground-to-air missiles to contend with; at the briefing I reckoned it would be Arnhem all over again, and I suggested, as an alternative, hitting the Argentine mainland airbases with a Polaris missile. It didn't go down very well, though once the colonel had finished swallowing his tongue he did concede it was an option.

By the time we got to Ascension we were fully committed to an Entebbe-style raid on Port Stanley, but then there was a rethink. The OC launched in. Port Stanley was scrubbed and mainland Argentina was our new target. Same plan as before. Same problem as before. Same stunned B Squadron sitting in the briefing room. Being SAS, you pays your money and you takes your choice. I thought to myself, The Argies won't be expecting us. It wasn't Port Stanley, where they were dug in, hyped for an attack. We'd get away with it on the surprise factor. Whether we'd get through the radar was another question, but perhaps we could have a Spanish speaker in the cockpit of the C130s to fool the guys in the control tower. It wasn't the raid so much. In the confusion we would probably get away with it. The problem was escaping and evading across 40 miles of open countryside to the Chilean border.

Come H-hour, the sergeant-major got us all together: 'It's a go. Prime the grenades, charge the magazines, get the gear ready. The trucks are outside. Load up and we'll go to the C130s, de-bus and do the job. You can name your medals.'

So we get the gear, load the weapons. This was not going to be a good day out. The trucks were loaded down with spare ammunition, spare machine guns, spare medical packs. We climbed on to the trucks and sat there, waiting in the sunshine.

I watched the C130s gearing up about 200 metres away and began thinking about the battle ahead. You begin to have your reservations, begin to weigh up the options. You're hoping your weapon won't jam when you need it to be 100 per cent. You remember how you rehearsed the attack. You try and remember if you can fire the M202 properly. Will it do the business? You're just sat there, waiting and bloody waiting. It's the worst bit.

Then suddenly the OC appeared with the sergeant-major. There was a brief conversation in the lead truck. Then it rippled down through the blokes, from truck to truck. Operation scrubbed. That's it, boys, you're off the truck.

At first I was disappointed. We were so hyped up, ready to go. I just wanted to get on with it, do the job. Then I started to think. Good old SAS common sense. They'd realized it would have been a suicide mission. And the SAS are not suicide troops. Relief hit me. It was going to be a good day after all. But it had been a close call.

The next day we were retasked. We had to fly two C130s to do a para-drop in the South Atlantic and rendezvous with HMS *Andromeda*. From there we'd sail to San Carlos Waters, meet up with what was left of D Squadron and reinforce them.

The flight took all day, sitting for hours cramped with only a couple of meal breaks to relieve the monotony. Then, finally, came 'action stations'. I put on my diver's suit and made sure that the guy next to me zipped me up properly. In the freezing South Atlantic, a quarter inch of unzipped flesh could prove fatal.

I was first in the stick at the tailgate, my fins handy, both chutes checked, a distress flare strapped to one wrist. As ever, there was a touch of comedy. Someone had told the despatcher that there was a missile on the way and that he had to eject chaff – immediately. He was panicking until he realized it was a stitch.

I got to the tailgate and looked down. It was a low drop, just 800 feet, a very short time in the air. Red on. Green. Go. I jumped, counted out the three seconds it took for the canopy to open, sighed with relief, as always, as I checked it, then looked down. I was directly above the *Andromeda*. I couldn't release my reserve. It would have hit the ship square on. So I took avoiding action, kicked away and went into a spin, but I managed to clear the ship.

It's hard to judge distance in poor light when you're coming down into a high swell, so I just got rid of my harness immediately, which was lucky, as I went straight in; but there was no drag from the harness, nor did the canopy come down over me. I got into my fins and popped my life jacket. I was safe in the water and felt exhilarated as I watched the others float down, some kicking out of the twists.

Once again I felt the surge of adrenaline. Now and again, as I bobbed up and down, I could see the *Andromeda* and one of the rigid raiders [marine assault craft] about 250 metres away picking up one of the lads; then I saw it heading back towards the ship.

After fifteen minutes my hands and face were numb and my neck was sore from being pushed back by the life jacket. I shouldn't have inflated it fully, just blown it up a little by mouth. I cracked open the tube of my distress flare and it began to glow, but no one saw me. I saw the rigid raider going back with another load, then it vanished again.

After thirty-five minutes I was getting seriously fatigued and was in danger of exposure. I began to worry. Then the rigid raider appeared 100 metres away and I waved my flare. They saw me. The big Marine, leaning towards me, said he thought he'd lost me.

'So did I,' I said. 'I'm starving. Got any scram?'

Once on board there was a problem. One of the pallets containing our personal kit hadn't been recovered, despite a radar scan, and the search had been called off. I went to a petty officer and asked for it to be resumed.

'No way,' he said.

'Fuck you,' I replied and went off to see the captain, who told me that he had to get under way in order to reach San Carlos Bay by morning. I asked what the point was of being flown all the way out here. Without our kit we'd be a liability to D Squadron. I said we may as well have stayed on the piss in Ascension.

He took the point, gave me another two hours and eventually, just past midnight – I had to keep awake all evening and argue that the search must continue – we found the bloody thing.

•

While B Squadron was heading south to join the Task Force, D Squadron was hitting the enemy. On the night of 20 May, for example, forty men of D Squadron, led by Major Delves, mounted a diversionary raid in the Darwin/Goose Green area to support the main British landings at San Carlos. Supported by gunfire from HMS *Ardent*, the SAS soldiers laid down such an amount of fire-power that the Argentinians reported back to Stanley that they were being attacked by a battalion.

Towards the end of the war, on the night of 13/14 June 1982, 2 Para was to attack Wireless Ridge, a few kilometres west of Stanley. To take the pressure off 2 Para, the SAS volunteered to put in a diversionary raid from the sea. The target was a large Argentinian oil refinery. Two troops from D Squadron and one from G Squadron made the attack. Facing them were 8,000 enemy troops in and around Stanley.

•

David There are plenty of other stories about supposedly top-secret missions on the mainland of Argentina, but as far as I am concerned these are total fantasy. I was there and I know who was there from the regiment and what they did. I also think that both strategically and politically it would not have made sense to attack forces openly on their mainland.

Just before the end of the war there was another plan of attack that was almost as suicidal as B Squadron's crash landing. From our position on Beagle Ridge we overlooked a sound. Stanley was beyond the sound and the town's oil refinery was on the peninsula opposite us. On the basis of intelligence coming to us from staff, we were ordered to attack the oil refinery. We were told it was 'lightly defended'.

Part of G Squadron had joined up with us. Boat Troop prepared to assault from the water, together with a Rigid Raider Squadron of the Royal Marines, while we provided fire support from a flank 200 metres away on the shore opposite the refinery. They moved to the shore line to get into the boats. Unknown to us, there was an Argentinian observation post behind and above us. They waited until we were most exposed before acting.

On the signal the boats were to cross the sound in full view of Stanley, cut their engines, float on to the beach, go ashore, recce it, make the assault and then blow up the refinery. Away they went. As they hit the beach, the whole fucking world opened up on them and us. It was horrific. Far from being lightly defended, there was a minimum of a full battalion against us. That is a lot of fire-power. Our position had obviously been communicated to the defensive forces from the observation post above us which we had not known about. Then I heard the crack of high-velocity weapons being fired at us from behind and above. So we were getting it from both sides. Just to add to the fun and games, the Argies then turned ground-mounted Roland anti-aircraft guns on to our position.

I took a patrol to try and find them but they were very well hidden and we just could not locate their position. As a result the whole squadron was rendered ineffective. Their fire was so accurate, we were all pinned down, and anyone who had shown his head clearly would have had it taken off. This left Boat Troop very exposed. They had to fight their way out and back to the boats. The bravery of the guys in the rigid raiders was amazing. They risked their lives to get the blokes out. If they hadn't gone in when they did, the troop would have been wiped out. The ground fire was so intense, the only way they could evade being blown out of the water was by using the Argentinian hospital as cover. They went underneath the bow of the ship and the enemy stopped firing. The rigid raiders were literally riddled with holes. We had two blokes hit. One had a chest wound, which I patched up. The other was hit in the upper part of the leg and testicles. Two Gazelle helicopters came in to casevac them. That was brave flying too, as there was a lot of shit still flying through the air. I went with them to Fitzroy settlement. The aid station was attached to the back of a house. After the injured boys were settled in, I went and sat down in the kitchen of this house. The lady who owned the house took pity on me and said, 'Why don't you relax a bit? Have a cup of tea. Take your boots off. Come and sit here in front of the Aga.'

I accepted her hospitality, which was a big mistake. To my horror I discovered that I had trench foot and frost nip. It is a horrific feeling. After a few minutes of warming up my feet in front of the fire, the warmth got the blood trying to flow into my toes and I was virtually crippled with pain. Most of the capillaries in my toes were dead. Trench foot comes from having your feet permanently submerged in water. Frost nip is a lesser form of frost bite, giving you no circulation in the toes as a result of all the capillaries having been killed off. It's bloody agony.

The following day, still crippled, I took out the two injured blokes' gear in a chopper. That same day the Argentinians surrendered. The following day we moved into Stanley. We moved on to another ship for a couple of days until the airport was officially reopened. The first C130 out took all the press, which pissed everyone else off. We were on the third plane out to Ascension and from there boarded a VC10 back to the UK.

We were the stand-by squadron, so there was no time off apart from a few days' local leave. We had to be ready again for immediate response anywhere in the world.

•

The SAS war had been extremely successful. As well as well-known operations such as the retaking of South Georgia and the Pebble Island raid, teams from the regiment had, in the weeks before the main landings at San Carlos, relayed a continuous stream of intelligence from their covert OPs on the Falklands. They, and the SBS, were the eyes and ears of the Task Force. This high-risk work resulted in a number of awards after the war. Delves received the DSO; three SAS captains won Military Crosses; and two other soldiers from the regiment won Military Medals. For the SAS, though, operating 13,000 kilometres from home in an enemy-occupied, desolate, freezing land was nothing to write home about.

8
THE GULF WAR

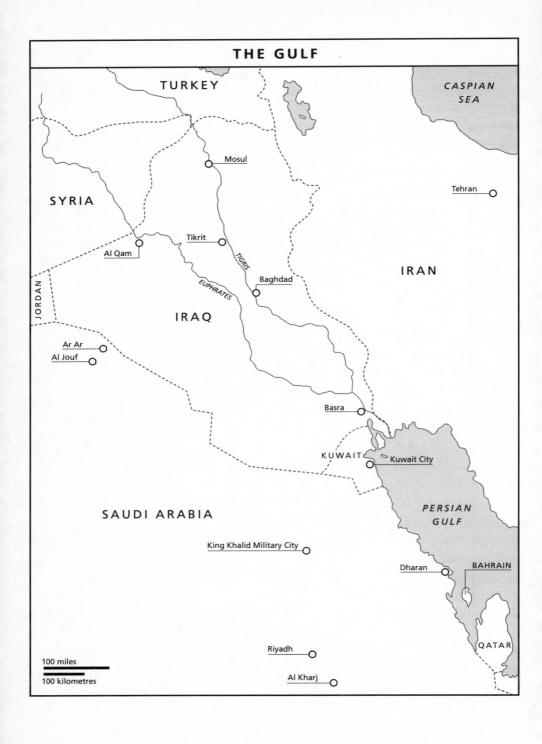

THE GULF

CASPIAN SEA

TURKEY

SYRIA

Mosul

Tehran

Tikrit

Al Qam

IRAN

EUPHRATES

TIGRIS

Baghdad

IRAQ

JORDAN

Ar Ar

Al Jouf

Basra

SAUDI ARABIA

KUWAIT

Kuwait City

PERSIAN GULF

King Khalid Military City

Dharan

BAHRAIN

Riyadh

QATAR

Al Kharj

100 miles

100 kilometres

We don't know the true tally of Scuds taken out by a combination of ground and aircraft. It's an open-ended question. We believe we contributed a great deal: we did make contact with the enemy – it was our role. We did it from the ground, and we all came home together, which meant more to me than finding a couple of Scuds.

David

On 2 August 1990, 100,000 Iraqi troops invaded the small, oil-rich state of Kuwait. Saddam Hussein's Iraq was $80 billion in debt as a result of fighting an eight-year war with Iran. He owed Kuwait $65 billion, for which Kuwait wanted payment, and to add insult to injury Kuwait was involved in the over-production of oil, which further reduced oil prices and hence Iraq's ability to service her debt. There were other disputes, such as over the border and drilling into disputed oil fields, but in essence Iraq was broke and Kuwait was too rich a prize to pass by.

But Saddam had badly misjudged international reaction, and soon his men were facing thousands of soldiers from all over the world as part of the United Nations Coalition sent to Saudi Arabia. Part of the Allied contingent were men of the Special Air Service. Unfortunately, the UN theatre Commander-in-Chief, General Norman Schwarzkopf, was a veteran of Vietnam, and he had seen special forces in action. He thought they were overrated and used up valuable resources when they had to be extracted from trouble. The prospects for any SAS campaign appeared remote.

When Iraq invaded Kuwait D and G Squadrons were already in the Gulf, training, but would they get a chance to test their skills? Luckily, the regiment had a friend in the Gulf in the form of the commander of the British forces and ex-SAS veteran, Lieutenant-General Peter de la Billière. The latter persuaded Schwarzkopf that the regiment could be useful, especially in resolving the most urgent problem: getting the Western hostages out of Iraq and Kuwait.

Saddam Hussein had hundreds of Western hostages, and he deployed them around his military and strategic installations as 'human shields'. The SAS and US special forces drew up plans to rescue them using helicopters, but even de la Billière himself thought many would be killed during the rescue missions. However, on 6 December 1990 Saddam released the hostages and the regiment was spared a nightmare scenario.

The regiment was then tasked by de la Billière with creating diversions and cutting roads in western Iraq to draw Iraqi forces away from the front. The SAS was also tasked with attacking Scud surface-to-surface missiles and their mobile launchers, although this was not a primary objective until they started falling on Israel. In the end A, B and D Squadrons were used in the Gulf (though not G Squadron).

The war started on the night of 16/17 January 1991, and the SAS waited like a coiled spring at its remote base at Al Jouf in western Saudi Arabia. The air war went well: the Iraqi Air Force was shot out of the skies, and soon the Allies had complete air superiority. However, on 18 January the first Scud missiles fell on Israel. If the latter retaliated, then the Coalition would fall apart. The Scuds would have to be found and destroyed, and quick.

At first aircraft were detailed to hunt for the launchers, but they had limited success. So the SAS was sent in. The regiment attacked the Scud threat in three ways. First, road-watch patrols would be mounted to report on Scud movements. Second, mobile Land Rover columns would be sent in to attack the Scud convoys. Third, SAS teams would cut Iraqi concealed communications cables to stop orders from Baghdad reaching the Scud launchers.

The road-watch patrols were made up of three eight-man

teams from B Squadron and would observe the three Iraqi main supply routes (MSRs) that went from the Euphrates valley to the Jordanian border. They were called the North, Central and South road-watch patrols respectively, and they went into western Iraq on 22 January. The South and Central road watches were soon abandoned, but the story of the Northern road watch – codename 'Bravo Two Zero' – has since entered legend. The eight SAS men, led by Sergeant Andy McNab, were landed in the middle of an area swarming with enemy troops. They tried to escape to the Syrian border, but tragedy struck. Sergeant Vince Phillips got separated from the rest and died of hypothermia, as did Lance-Corporal 'Legs' Lane. Trooper Robert Consiglio was killed by enemy gunfire, while McNab and three others were captured. Only Chris Ryan made it to Syria, after an epic 300-kilometre walk.

At the same time the mobile fighting columns went into Iraq on 20 January. There were four columns in all: two from A Squadron and two from D Squadron.

•

Matt (A Squadron) Initially, the regiment was tasked with rescuing the hostages who had been taken by Saddam Hussein to be used as human shields. They were mainly Western, though they included some Japanese as well. When they were released we were ordered to go into western Iraq, behind enemy lines, to carry out search-and-destroy missions. We were to hit any targets we could find and cause maximum mayhem. In this way, it was hoped, we would draw Iraqi forces away from the front in Kuwait, thus making it easier for our front-line troops when the ground offensive started.

Then the top brass started to talk about the mobile Scud launchers and taking them out. But before the air war started in mid-January 1991 the Scuds were well down the list.

I was in Mobility Troop, and the plan was to mount the whole squadron on vehicles and divide them into mobile fighting columns. That meant all the guys from Air, Boat and Mountain troops brushing up on their vehicle skills. We split the squadron into halves, one group learning how to drive behind the lines and the other half honing their weapons skills on the ranges. Obviously, the guys in the Mobility Troop were split up to teach all the others the fine art of desert driving. We didn't have much time – about thirteen days, I seem to remember – which meant each half squadron had six days on the vehicles and six days on the ranges.

It was amazing. Blokes who hadn't had much experience of driving suddenly became very proficient with a steering wheel in their hands. The hardest part was training up on the motorbikes. It's very tiring driving motorbikes in the desert because you've got to concentrate all the time and it's physically demanding. Nevertheless, we managed to get a few of the blokes up to speed on the bikes – well, sort of.

Supplies are always a problem with mobile fighting columns: you can't have enough. We had a Unimog which acted as a mother vehicle. It's like a fucking great truck which can go anywhere – a useful bit of kit. We loaded it with everything: mortar rounds, spare rations, ammunition for the guns, NBC (Nuclear, Biological and Chemical) kit, the works.

The other vehicles in each column consisted of eight Land Rover 110s, each one armed with .5 Browning heavy machine guns, American M19 40-millimetre grenade launchers and Milan anti-tank missiles. The Milans had thermal imaging sights, which meant we could pick out targets up to 8 kilometres away. In addition, you could use them at night.

Then we were tasked with going some 400 kilometres into enemy territory, into the southern central region of Iraq, moving up towards the Euphrates just to the west of Baghdad. But that all changed when the Scuds started falling on Israel.

Before we went in morale was terrific. We knew we were going in, and we were pleased – it's what you train for, after all. Even before we went, though, we were sending out patrols near the border to recce everything, and that made everyone very tired. But our spirits were high. I remember the night before we went in everyone was shaking each other's hand. No one knew what we were going to encounter, but we were all ready to get stuck in.

As ever on SAS operations, each man had a lot of personal equipment. I carried an M16 assault rifle fitted with a 40-millimetre M203 grenade launcher. I also had a 9-millimetre Browning high-power pistol on me, just in case. I had as many spare magazines as I could carry – 16 or 17, I think – each one filled with thirty rounds. I had two or three mags for the pistol, plus six or seven grenades for the launcher. Naturally, I had my survival gear and escape and evasion kit – you never go anywhere without them.

We fucked up on the clothing side, though. Intelligence had told us that it would be warm. So a lot of the guys went out in their bog-standard SAS smocks, which were useless in the cold weather we experienced.

There were massive intelligence gaps concerning the exact nature of the enemy we were likely to encounter. We were told that the Iraqis at the front were very professional and well armed, especially the Republican Guard, but no one knew about their rear-area troops. We didn't worry too much about this. We took the pragmatic approach – anyone we came up against, we would take them on! We knew we were better than anyone we would meet; it would be tough shit for them, that's all.

No one in the regiment considers failure, no fucking way. Roving around behind the lines in heavily armed vehicle columns is the best type of operation because you're in charge. They've got to find you, and meanwhile you're shooting up everything you can see. They don't know where you are. But in quieter moments, just before we started off or when driving at night (we always drove at night), you do think about the possibility of being killed. It's only natural. Then I'd say a little prayer, both for myself and for the rest of the lads.

We crossed the border at a Saudi fortress. Their forces let us through, which was just as well because up to that point we had had a nightmare of a time trying to find a crossing point. The whole border was one big minefield. Fortunately, the enemy seemed very lazy – we could tell their morale was low after we had watched them for a few days. They just stayed in their trenches and kept their heads down.

The actual night of our crossing we had scanned the area with the thermal imagers. We saw nothing, but the adrenaline was still pumping. The boss came up to us and said: 'We're going for it.'

The whole column drove down the hill from the fortress and straight across the border. The border wasn't even marked, save for a massive sand berm which had a gap in it. So we just drove straight on through. I was driving the lead vehicle and began thinking, This is too good to be true. It was, because just as we hit a track I went over a sand mound and stalled the engine. Fuck! It was only nerves, but it seemed like an eternity before I could get the engine started again. The boss simply turned to me and said, cool as a cucumber: 'Just turn off the engine, put it into neutral and turn it over again.' Bingo, the engine chugged into life and we drove on.

At first we didn't know if we would be operating during the day or at night – we had trained for both – because of the terrain. We had eight Land Rovers and the Unimog, which we always had in the middle of the formation to protect it, and two motorbikes that would be our eyes and ears up ahead, to recce in front and on our flanks, so we wouldn't be surprised by the enemy. The bikes were also useful for finding little tracks and routes which we could use. That's what I mean about it being demanding riding them – they're always out on missions. For example, if we came across a *wadi* or stream bed we could send the bikes up to have a look.

We used one bike for scouting and the other for passing messages from vehicle to vehicle. Don't forget that nine vehicles will be spread out over a distance of up to 300 metres. The front vehicle always had a thermal imager to allow it to see in the dark (we quickly decided it was safe to lie up during the day and move at night).

Western Iraq itself was a mixture of terrain types. It was a lot different to what you imagine a desert to be – you know, sand and oases. We came across lots of lava-like beds, and the *wadis* were very deep with steep sides. We'd often drive into them, which could have been tricky if we had been bumped because there was only one way out. That was an exception, though, because standard operating procedures state that you always try to work on high ground so you can dominate the terrain, not the other way round.

The weather was piss-poor most of the time, and it was made worse by the fact that we didn't have the proper clothing. Therefore we had to improvise as best we could. Remember that we were driving around in tropical combat gear and at times it was snowing. I began to get terribly frozen fingers because the gloves we had been issued weren't good enough. As time progressed my fingernails started to crack, which was really painful. So I had to wrap socks around my hands to keep them warm. Even now, five years afterwards, I still suffer from my hands. I used to grit my teeth a lot because of the cold, cracking a few in the back of my mouth in the process. I didn't realize this at the time, but when I got back I had a lot of dental treatment.

The first four or five days were quite uneventful. We'd seen some enemy patrols but had given them a wide berth. We were in lying-up points during the day. They were camouflaged, of course, and we had sentries on the high ground to keep watch. When choosing an LUP we went for dead ground, a depression, for example. Then we'd put camouflage nets over the vehicles and then sort out administrative matters. These included cleaning weapons, eating, sending signals and getting some sleep.

We had been lying up one day when one of the sentries on the high ground spotted an approaching vehicle and reported it. It drove straight towards us and we didn't know what to do. It was obviously Iraqi, but the question was should we take it out? It stopped about 30 metres from us, and the driver got out and went to the front of the vehicle. The rest stayed in the back. The driver then lifted the bonnet and started to tinker with the engine. Unknown to him there were about thirty SAS soldiers all with their assault rifles and Land Rovers' machine guns trained on him.

Suddenly, the commander in the Iraqi vehicle jumped out and started to walk towards our position with his hand on his pistol. One of our guys then left our position and headed towards him. He was wearing a *shemagh* [Arab headdress] to disguise the fact that he was European. Anyway, the Iraqi commander spotted him and went to grab his weapon. Our chap hit the deck in an instant and we opened up. For a few seconds the air was filled with lead as our rounds tore into the Iraqi vehicle. We hit everyone in it, no problem, but then we had a major headache: we were on a deniable mission and had to get rid of any evidence of our existence. But what to do with the vehicle and its occupants?

Immediately after the contact we rushed forward to inspect the vehicle. When we got there the scene was bad. One bloke had been hit many times and there was a big jet of blood spurting from his body. It wasn't like in the movies, nice and neat. This stream of blood was spurting out over a distance of 15 metres. The companion next to him was, remarkably, unhurt, but he was massively traumatized and in shock. Imagine it: one minute you're driving with your mates deep inside your own territory, far away from the front, the next everyone around you is cut to pieces in an ambush that lasts just a few seconds – unreal.

It turned out that one of the dead – the one I had shot – was a divisional commander. The information he had on him concerning troop movements was very useful, and we radioed it back as quickly as possible. (When we got back to friendly territory we were informed that there had been 30,000 enemy troops in our area and that we had been surrounded at one point.)

We knew we had to get rid of the vehicle and bodies so as to avoid being compromised. When all the fuss had died down, the boss decided that we couldn't bury the bodies there because the graves would be found, and in any case we could dig only shallow graves in that particular terrain. So we decided to take them and the vehicle with us and to put them in the back of the Iraqi vehicle (the prisoner was bound and gagged and also taken with us). One of the lads volunteered to drive the vehicle with the bodies in it. He had an ulterior motive: it was covered with a soft skin and it had a heater. Crafty bastard!

The rest of us stashed the cam nets in the vehicles and prepared to move out. We covered over the blood that had spilt on the sand and picked up as many of the empty cartridge cases as we could find – we were determined to leave as little trace of our visit as possible. Then we bugged out at speed.

We headed in the opposite direction to the one the Iraqis had come from. We moved 10–15 kilometres east, then headed south for a good distance. At that time we were 150 kilometres behind enemy lines, but we drove nearer the border in the hope we could get rid of the bodies. The journey that night was a nightmare; the whole area seemed to be full of enemy troops. We had the upper hand, though, because our night sights allowed us to see.

We had been driving for about an hour when I saw something through my night-vision goggles. It turned out to be ten Iraqi soldiers, but they looked in poor shape. They had their heads down and were carrying their weapons idly in their hands. Beyond them we could make out a large group of vehicles heading towards us, so we turned right and gave them a wide berth. We kept on avoiding enemy patrols until we ended up in a depression, from where we reported our intelligence back to base.

We thought about burying the bodies there, but the boss decided to keep them with us. We moved off and eventually arrived at this disused Scud launch site. It consisted of sand banks constructed in such a way as to deflect the blast from the rockets when they took off. From here we sent out another situation report and requested a helicopter to evacuate the prisoner and the dead bodies. The guy who had been driving the vehicle with the dead bodies in the back now smelt quite badly.

We had confirmation that a chopper would be sent to get the bodies and prisoner, so we deployed in all-round defence and waited for the helicopter. We put the bodies into body bags ready for their journey.

Helicopters always arrived under cover of darkness. They were usually Chinooks, and they would fly very low – around 10–15 feet off the ground. The pilots were fucking good. Anyway, this Chinook swept in and right past us. I thought, Shit, he's missed us, but it turned out that he was resupplying some other SAS teams operating further north. It was quite amusing because we had pushed the Land Rover with the bodies in the back out of the Scud position ready to unload them onto the chopper. When it didn't materialize we had to push the vehicle back. It was like a bloody *Carry On* film!

Finally, the chopper came in to land. The engines and rotors made a massive amount of noise as it got close. Then the resupply started to be unloaded: 50-gallon drums of petrol to refuel the vehicles – six or seven of these – ammunition, rations and clothing. The last was very welcome, especially the thick Arab coats, which proved life-savers. They were thick, woollen affairs. Champion.

Anyway, it was time to load the bodies. But the load master decided that the Iraqi vehicle wouldn't fit into the chopper and he refused to take it. So there we were, stuck behind enemy lines with this Iraqi vehicle and three dead bodies in the back (the prisoner had been put on the helicopter and flown away). By this time we were really worried about being captured with the three stiffs. If we had have been, we would have certainly been executed on the spot.

We had to get rid of the bodies, and quick. So we drove the vehicle into a gully and dug a hole for about half an hour. Then we drove the vehicle into it and placed two massive anti-tank mines inside it. The spare fuel we had we poured around the vehicle, together with a large can of petrol which we put inside with the bodies. We set a timer on the mines to go off around 5 a.m. the following morning. That gave us five or six hours to get as far away as possible.

We drove all night to find another location, and as we did so we saw a flash on the horizon – we had disposed of the evidence at last!

One day we identified an enemy position and reported it back to base. The brass decided to order an air strike. It was about 20 kilometres from us, but when the aircraft hit we could still see the billows of smoke and the aircraft – A10s – circling above. I think a lot of us were glad to see the aircraft, to know that we could request air support if we needed it.

We used to get sit reps every night from headquarters back in Saudi, telling us what was going on. One report stated that there was a big microwave tower to the north of us. We were ordered to do a recce on it because they had little hard info on it. So four vehicles were dispatched from the column to go and take a look. That night the rest of us drove towards the target, not really knowing what we would run into. We drove for about 30 kilometres, but it was like the M1! It was no different to the roads back home, apart from having an irrigation ditch on either side 3 feet wide and 2 feet deep.

We advanced stealthily to see if there were any enemy around and to get closer to the installation. There was too much enemy activity at that time, so we pulled back and viewed the tower through our thermal imagers. It looked like a large, square building with a massive antenna on it. The antenna was about 200 feet high, and we could see the building was defended by a perimeter wall and fence. Around the building itself was a collection of Portacabins, vehicles, small buildings and the like.

There seemed to be few guards and other military personnel, which wasn't surprising, given that we were behind enemy lines.

The plan was for an assault group to breach the wall and fence using explosives or anti-tank missiles, then to hit the main building itself. According to intelligence there were three floors below ground, so the idea was that the nine-man assault group should split into three-man teams, each team taking a different floor. Everyone would be carrying a lot of explosives to destroy anything they came in contact with. Timers would be used with the explosives to allow for a safe evacuation of the teams (giving everyone about ninety seconds to get out and away before they blew).

We didn't have any information on the garrison, so we would use speed and superior fire-power to overwhelm the defences and achieve the task. I was one of three assaulters in the first group. Once we had breached the defences, all the SAS groups would take out enemy soldiers as and when they came across them.

One man in each team was detailed to be the explosives guy. He carried the explosives and it was his job to plant them and engage the timers. While he was doing it the other two would provide cover – all nice and simple.

The actual attack took place in the dark. We got to within 1,500 metres and then did a close recce just to confirm what we were up against. When we drove close to the site, though, we had a bit of a nightmare getting across the drainage ditches beside the road. We had to use sandbags to fill them in so we could get the vehicles across. All the while the clock was ticking and we were losing valuable time. Eventually, though, we got across and moved towards the target.

The boss decided to drive almost straight up to the perimeter, which we did, hiding the vehicles behind a big sand berm. We them recced forward on foot. When we got near to the wall we could see a tarpaulin sheet across the part where we were supposed to make our breach. It was obvious that we wouldn't have to blow a hole in the wall. It looked as though an aircraft had dropped some bombs and done our work for us.

My group was therefore retasked to keep an eye on a couple of vehicles that were inside the compound. They looked like fuel trucks or such-like. The rest of the lads moved forward and went under the tarpaulin. Unbelievable! There wasn't a sound – you could have heard a pin drop.

I moved up to the side of one of the tankers and hit it accidentally with my 66-millimetre anti-tank weapon. Shit! However, nothing stirred. I thought that anyone in the cab up front must be asleep. So two of us rushed up to the cab and yanked open the door. Although someone had tied a piece of wire to it, it gave way and the door opened. It was dark, but there was a lot of ambient light, and I saw immediately a young Iraqi soldier. He was looking at me in total shock. Beside him was another, older soldier.

I tried to indicate to the younger one to stay quiet, but he started to jabber in Arabic. Fuck! My mate covered me as I pushed the barrel of my rifle into the lad's stomach, which made him push himself back off the seat. I then realized that he had a rifle and was trying to reach it, so I had no alternative but to pump two bullets into him. Or at least I tried to shoot two rounds, but the second jammed in the breech. My mate screamed, 'Stoppage!', rushed forward and sprayed the cab with bullets, finishing off its two occupants.

At that point the whole place erupted. Our fire support must have thought we had been bumped because they put in a fearsome amount of fire. There were a number of bunkers in the compound with heavy-calibre machine guns and what sounded like an anti-aircraft gun. There were tracer and rounds going off all over; none of it seemed to be aimed at anyone. Then I saw an Iraqi dart across from one of the vehicles. I had cleared my stoppage by this time and brought my weapon to bear, but I didn't shoot him. At the briefing we had been told that there might be a lot of civilians in the compound, and I didn't want to shoot any unarmed civvies.

By now our guys had got into the building and had placed their charges and were coming back. There were ninety seconds or so to get away. But, of course, that was from when the charges had been set. As the demo teams got to within 100 metres of where I was, the explosions started to go off. There were three or four very loud bangs. Then the tower started to move! We found out later that the lads had gone in and decided to place all the charges on the legs of the tower. When the charges went off they severed the legs and the tower collapsed at a 45-degree angle.

We all moved back to the vehicles, giving covering fire all the time. At one point a group of figures became silhouetted. I shouted out, 'Who the fuck are they?' Someone yelled back that they were civilians. Like hell: they started firing at us. We all hit the deck, but not before one of the lads got a round through his trouser leg. We were taking a lot of incoming. I shouted to one of the men on our vehicles to fire the M19 grenade launcher at them, which he did.

By this stage some of the blokes had decided to withdraw. There was a danger of the group being split up, which would have caused major complications. We laid down a lot of fire and the enemy seemed to pull back, but in fact they regrouped and started putting down a load of fire on our right flank. Suddenly there was a lot of tracer heading towards us – red hornets flying at you out of the darkness. It was obvious that it was too dangerous to stick around. We started a headlong flight, some guys running and others on vehicles. Amazingly, no one got hit and neither did the vehicles.

The operation was a real 'Who dares wins' type. I mean, we had the bottle to go in and do it. We caused a massive amount of damage but didn't lose anyone – that's what I call a good mission. Okay, so our fire support was left behind, but one of the lads got on a bike and went to fetch them and we all rendezvoused safely.

The boss used a satellite navigation system to get us out. He was a cool character – while we were totally disorientated, he kept his head. We drove straight through an enemy position. The opposition must have thought: Who the fuck are this lot? But we just kept on driving. They must have thought that all the commotion was an air strike and we were just poor Iraqis like them, about to get a pasting from the aircraft of the infidels. See, that's the thing. If you've got the nerve, the bottle, you can get away with anything. When we got back to base a few weeks later we were told that there had been 200–300 enemy troops at the location we hit, which was 600 metres in diameter.

When you're withdrawing you try to reach what we call a reorganization position, and that was our intention. Once we hit it we travelled along the tarmac road, roughly where we had come off it earlier. The blokes had started to calm down by this stage. I was sitting on the back of the rear vehicle, very nonchalantly. Suddenly it shot forwards and I was thrown off the back. I thought, Fuck, I'll be left behind. I screamed as hard as I could and started to run after the Land Rover. That caused great hilarity among the blokes when we got back.

Another story concerned one of the guys who manned one of the GPMGs on a Land Rover. He didn't have a thermal imager, but his mate manning the Milan did. So the bloke with the Milan guided the machine gunner. During the battle the Milan operator had seen an Iraqi having a shit, and he decided to scare him a little. So he told the other bloke to fire a couple of short bursts near him, just enough to get him moving with his trousers around his ankles – great fun.

Another of the Milan operators at the reorganization point spotted a barracks building some way off (he had seen troops coming out), and he decided to take a pot at it. *Whoosh!* The Milan missile streaked towards the building and hit it. The explosion blew the roof straight up, and then it came crashing down. Flaming figures came staggering out and collapsed on the ground.

We knew that the Iraqis were communicating with each other via fibre-optic cables. They were buried deep, but they had service shafts at frequent intervals, covered by manhole covers. They were easy to spot, but we knew that a lot had been rigged with alarms – open one up and a microswitch would indicate that it was being tampered with. A patrol would then be on our arses very quickly. We got round that by blowing the manhole covers with explosives combined with a can of petrol. In this way the explosion would burn everything in its path, including the microswitch. Remember that the cables were often up to 30 feet down. The petrol would soak down and the explosion would also destroy the cables. This knocked out the Iraqis' communications big-time.

We hit any cables we came across, even D10 wire, which is just like your average telephone cable. Sometimes we'd stop and dig up 20 feet of cable and drive off with it to cause more confusion.

Occasionally the Iraqis would pursue our patrols, and one of the regiment's blokes was lost in such a contact, God rest his soul. Fortunately, the enemy was pretty crap during contacts, just content to keep at a distance and fire at us. Stuff that for a game – we were off just as soon as we had a chance!

After the attack on the communications tower – codenamed Victor Two – our morale was A1. You know, thirty guys against a major enemy force. At the same time, though, we were all tired. By that stage we had been behind the lines for nearly a month. It takes its toll: not much sleep – two or three hours a night. You need at least four to work properly.

Resupply became a major problem. The RAF couldn't fly in choppers because of the change in light conditions, so they hit upon the idea of para-dropping supplies to us. Only thing is that the kit can go over everywhere, and if the opposition finds it, your deniable operation goes out the window. So base organized a convoy of vehicles to bring supplies to us. They loaded up about fifteen 4-ton trucks and then drove them 75 miles into enemy territory.

They were very blasé about it. OK, they had some of B Squadron's Land Rovers for escorts, but even so it took a lot of balls. They actually identified a couple of enemy positions on the way in and called down air strikes, then they put little marks on the side of the trucks – cocky bastards!

We made the rendezvous in a *wadi*. It was like Santa's grotto. They had fuel, rations, ammo, the works, even down to little chocolate bars. In total we stayed five days at the resupply point, then they left and headed back to Saudi. They had done a fantastic job, and we couldn't have stayed in Iraq for the amount of time we did without their help.

At this stage D Squadron took over from us while we moved north and took up their former position.

We all had short-wave radios, and we used to listen to the World Service. By that time the ground offensive had started and we were ordered to move back, closer to the border. We were all eager to get the job done to be truthful, and were a little concerned that we were becoming too casual.

We made efforts to keep our concentration up, but at times it got a little ridiculous. On one occasion, for example, we thought we had spotted an enemy position, but it turned out to be an abandoned mining site. We continued towards the border, and eventually we could make out the Saudi fortress marking the spot where we had entered Iraq. We then spotted an enemy position. We didn't want to take it on, so we laid up and monitored it. Very soon we realized that it was deserted. However, there was a cable nearby, so a couple of us jumped off the vehicles, cut it and dug it out with a shovel.

As we neared the fortress we fixed our large Union Jack flags (which we used for aircraft recognition – although from 10,000 feet they look like small dots) on the vehicle posts and rode up to the border. The Saudis were cheering us – we felt good.

Of course, there are always casualties in war, and this one was no different. In the regiment you are issued with what's called a NAAFI number – every SAS guy on ops has one. If someone is killed, HQ can say that NAAFI number 32 has been killed; it maintains security, you see. On ops no one is allowed to carry identification. Anyway, when we got back we found out that one of our close friends had been killed, which deflated the triumph somewhat. The others took part in the big celebration, but me and a few others just sat quietly and thought about our mate.

Relationships can get strained on ops in the regiment. It's only natural. Tempers get frayed and everyone is living on their nerves to a certain extent. I myself became quite distant from my mate, though we are close again now. That said, some people stay very calm under all the pressure. The commander of my vehicle, for example, was the coolest man I've ever worked with in my life – I can't sing his praises highly enough. Naturally, when we got back the tensions were released: we were hugging each other and shaking hands. We had taken part in something that hadn't been done since World War II, and we had done it with minimal casualties. We had the upper hand all the time because of our mobility. The Iraqis didn't have a clue.

After it was all over Schwarzkopf paid us a visit. He shook every man in the squadron by the hand. It was weird: we'd seen and heard him on television, and then suddenly there he was, a monster of a man, standing in front of us. He made a speech to us, one of the most exhilarating I've ever heard. He said what we had achieved was phenomenal, that we had caused massive damage to the enemy's communications. In addition, he said that our campaign against the Scuds in western Iraq had prevented Israel from entering the war, which had saved the UN coalition.

•

David of D Squadron has a similar tale to tell. His recollections cast an interesting light on the minutiae of missions behind the lines and show that even SAS soldiers are human after all. He illuminates a little-known aspect of the SAS's war in the Gulf: their assault on Saddam's communications. The only way Hussein could talk to his men in the field after UN aircraft had knocked out his transmitters was via underground cables. So the SAS was sent in to find and disable them.

•

David (D Squadron) The initial concept was that we were going to deploy with two squadron groups in small columns infiltrating across the border into designated areas to conduct the operations and, if necessary, rendezvous to make larger-size formations to do any specific actions that we were tasked to do. In my particular squadron that was the case, although initially we deployed across the border at squadron strength because of lack of intelligence on the enemy directly in front of us. Then we split, in small, troop-size formations, into our designated areas of responsibility.

We initially hit communications in conjunction with air power to take out any reasonable target we thought would have a major effect on the war itself. Lines of communications in particular became areas of interest. Because we were a long way from the front, we didn't actually come across large formations of enemy troops so lines of communications and observation towers became key targets.

In addition, we hoped that by conducting missions we would

draw Iraqi forces away from the front, which is a classic SAS tactic. I was very positive we could do the job. The only problem we had, which is common to all small formations, is lack of fire-power. We would try to avoid fights unless they were of our choosing in deliberate ambush-type or attack scenarios – i.e. surprise was on our side.

As for getting killed, you always think about the possibility beforehand, but you don't dwell on it. It's only when you've got nothing to do that it creeps into your mind. Some of the blokes wrote what we call 'blood letters', in case they were killed in action, but I tried not to think about it. And when I did, I gave myself a big bollocking. You've got to put it out of your mind and get on with the job. Obviously there's a lot of tension around, but on ops you are too busy surviving, eating, sleeping and maintaining kit to think about bad things.

One thing that did get us down was the weather. For security reasons we weren't told the specific region we would be operating in. Therefore we were not prepared for the cold and the wet, which were made worse when we were in the vehicles because of the wind-chill factor. In training beforehand the weather conditions we were training for were your classic image of what people imagine the desert to be: open, rolling, sand-duney conditions with very hot days and fairly cold nights, but not too cold. I mean, you thought you could sleep on top of a sleeping bag rather than in it.

We had Goretex, of course, but even Goretex is only one layer, and when you're training in a desert environment, you're normally used to wearing one layer and perhaps two at night. There were times when I was wearing seven layers of clothes and still feeling the effects of the cold. The first patrols that went in reported that the issue clothing was inadequate, so the regiment got those big woollen coats that the bedouin sheep farmers wear for protection. They were life-savers: otherwise people would have gone down with exposure easily, and we would have had major problems trying to deal with that and continue operations.

Having said that, we didn't have any major medical problems on operations. Our blokes are very good at knowing their own bodies and looking after them. It's all part of the professionalism, you see. Everyone knows that if someone falls sick, then resources have to be directed at looking after him. So everyone realizes that prevention is better than cure and less time-consuming.

Morale was high generally, and I certainly didn't think about being captured. We didn't really worry about the Iraqis at all. We knew they used Soviet doctrine and so we were clued up as to the formations they would use. Our only concern was getting bumped by a large force. In such a situation we would be very vulnerable because we were riding in soft-skinned Land Rovers.

To minimize risks we would drive at night, in a column, with the drivers wearing night-vision goggles. The vehicles were well spaced out, so if one got in the shit, the others could stop in time. Similarly, if we got bumped by the opposition, we could provide covering fire for the front vehicle while he extracted himself, and we had enough time and space to get out.

A column is the best tactic when you're driving in a no-light situation. In a firefight, if you decide to take on the enemy, you can always deploy into line and bring all guns to bear. There weren't enough night-vision goggles, so the priority went to the drivers, particularly of the lead vehicles, who had to see ahead as they were driving. Any time we were unsure of the ground or sensed a threat we would stop, switch off the engine, listen, use the night-vision devices to their full potential and then move on again. We'd keep the chat down to a minimum. We very rarely used radios and things like that. Gradually we became more confident and drove at greater speeds. We knew that, apart from bedouin and the sheep that we might run over, the likelihood of running into an enemy convoy was pretty remote. We never really experienced holes like bomb craters or anything like that.

However, due to tiredness I once made a very bad decision when my driver, who could see ahead of me, was unsure of the ground. Although we were moving very slowly, he suggested we stop and do a full recon. on foot. I just told him to keep going. He did so and we ended up overturning the vehicle on a small incline. Suddenly there was a 10-ton vehicle on top of three really pissed-off guys. Luckily, nobody actually suffered any physical injuries because the gun mounts on the vehicle stopped us all from getting broken necks. We were driving without roll bars because taking them off reduces the silhouette of the vehicle – which can mean the difference between being spotted and staying unseen.

The vehicles we used were Land Rover 110s. They have a tremendous range because of the additional fuel that can be carried, and they can hump a lot of equipment. They can't move very quickly, though, but you can't have everything. We were carrying enough food, water, fuel and ammo for a fourteen-day trip. We carried anti-tank missile rounds and ammo for the personal weapons, the machine guns and the grenade launchers, a big load of kit. The reason for this was that we preferred to tackle any enemy at a distance, hence the Milan ammunition. However, if we had to fight close up, then we wanted plenty of rounds for the GPMGs and Brownings, as well as for the assault rifles – the M16s. Some of the Rovers had American M19 grenade launchers fitted to them, but not all, due to the problems of fastening them on to the vehicles.

We also took bar mines for laying ambushes on roads and tracks against armour. All in all, we were happy with the firepower we had. You rely on what you've got rather than what you think you're going to get resupplied with.

When we crossed the border everything went well at first, but 5 kilometres into Iraq one of the Rovers hit a rock and snapped a track rod. We had a Chinese parliament and decided to abandon it. The vehicle was stripped of all supplies and then we rigged it with explosives and set a delayed timer. So straightaway my command was down to three vehicles.

We arrived at the MSR – one of the main highways connecting Jordan to Baghdad – while it was dark. When it was light we had a good look around and saw we were laid up near an observation tower. We couldn't stick around, so that night we moved on unobserved. We were making for a rendezvous with the other half of the squadron, but they had been bumped by the enemy. The troop managed to break contact, although they lost some of their vehicles. They didn't lose any men, but they lost their mobility. Some tried to make the rendezvous, but because of distance they didn't do it. One particular group decided they would get home as quickly as possible, so that they could get back on operations, and they hijacked a civilian transport. They got back across the border, were debriefed, reissued and back in no time.

Once we had been at the rendezvous site for some time it was apparent they weren't coming. We were informed of their contact when we began to look for them. When we were parallel to the MSR – 50 to 100 metres off it – this huge Scud convoy came rolling past us. I remember sort of literally looking right and seeing armour, Scuds and support vehicles rolling along beside and I'm driving down the side of it. One of our guys wanted to attack it, which would have been a pretty stupid thing to do, bearing in mind we were so close to the missiles that if we had hit them, they would have exploded and taken us with them. In the end we decided to report it and call in an air strike. We were heavily outnumbered, and hitting this stuff with everything we had might have resulted in us all going up in smoke, but it was quite funny afterwards.

In the first part of February our mission changed – as we found out, as a result of political change in the strategic deployment of our regiment. We became Scud hunters, required primarily to locate and direct offensive air strikes to neutralize both mobile Scuds and, if located, fixed Scud sites. Fixed Scud sites are pre-surveyed sites where there are rails and you can drive vehicles in to raise your Scud and fire it in the minimum amount of time. When you're firing a mobile Scud, there is a time delay because you have to fix it in position.

We came across several of these places. The first time we drove straight through one. We didn't even know we were in it until we were challenged by some Arab guard, so we just kept on driving and ignored the challenge. We hoped he'd think we were bedouin, who moved around a lot at night in trucks, carrying out smuggling operations into Jordan. We got away with it and it turned out that these sites were open, with little or no defences at all. The next time we came across a fixed Scud site we didn't really think it was one. By this time we'd got quite comfortable moving around by day, knowing that there was limited opposition, certainly nothing that could restrict our mobility.

We were ordered to cover ground and move to a resupply rendezvous. The lead vehicle spotted what he thought was a bedouin encampment with improvised shelters, possibly on the edges of a fixed launch site. We went forward to recce it, and as we moved we started taking incoming fire. It was, in fact, a mobile Scud hiding in a fixed launch site. They knew that the Americans had bombed the shit out of it and wouldn't come back, so they hid their mobile Scuds there.

We decided to take it on. The only way we could do that was to withdraw and begin a containment operation to keep the Scud static while we called aircraft to bomb it. We waited for some time and their fire on to our vehicles was very accurate. We had to start thinking about our stand-off capability because we couldn't get close enough to engage with normal-calibre weapons. The only long-distance weapon we had that would give us protection from anti-aircraft fire that was being used as ground-rolled fire was the Milan. So we used it – with tremendous effect. The Milan operator did a bloody good job and was later awarded the Military Medal.

We got on the radio, saying, 'We've got one! Come and get it!' The only problem was that even though our message got through really quickly, the rolling aircraft were dedicated in western Iraq, and it took three hours to get them on to our target. We couldn't contain the Scud that long, and by the time they got there, it had moved a couple of clicks away from its original location. So there we were with a flight of F15s coming in, dropping 500-pound bombs directed from the ground on to a fixed grid site, and then we had to tell them that the site had moved.

Trusting that their equipment would give them the correct lat. and long. was a pretty big risk, but we were lucky. The first flight dropped on the original coordinates without communicating to the ground before they dropped. Once we established communications with him, though, he went back to refuel, and the second flight came in, controlled from the ground by us, on to the Scud – we think very successfully. It was tremendous use of the Milan, with our gunner illuminating the target by actually hitting one of the vehicles and setting it alight. The pilot was confused by it because from the air there was a lot of sand. It was night, so what he could see didn't necessarily relate to what we were telling him, but he dropped on to the target. We couldn't do a bomb-damage assessment because we couldn't hang around. It was now getting towards daylight, so we withdrew, packed up the kit and drove back into the desert to have a nice cup of tea.

In February we were told that HQ wanted more information from the area and were tasked to take prisoners, although we weren't certain who would be appropriate. Nevertheless, we plotted to capture a POW, and the observation towers lining the MSR were suitable targets. We deployed against two of the sites simultaneously, doubling our chances of actually capturing somebody, and made a typical covert assault on the observation tower in our area. We gained a lot of information about it. We decided we would try a covert approach to the target and go noisy if we had to convince them to surrender.

We achieved that by getting right up into the target itself. There were dogs barking, but there was no reaction from the targets. We later realized that they knew we were out there somewhere but hoped we'd go away and locked themselves into their little Nissen hut at night. We didn't know that at the time, but we knew they didn't move around at night. We knocked on the door of the hut and politely asked them to come out. They refused. Our linguist tried to communicate in Arabic with the Iraqis, who must have been shitting themselves inside the building, scared to death that we were going to shoot them. One of the lads went round the back to see if there was a way in there and tried to force an entry. He placed a phosphorous grenade inside to encourage them to come out, which they did. Unfortunately, they came out shooting and tried to disappear into the night. They were all shot and killed, but that presented us with a problem, as we didn't have anybody to take back as a POW.

The other troop was much more successful and brought back a guy who was later sent out by helicopter to Saudi to provide information, but it turned out to be information that nobody actually wanted.

We were later told that the intelligence HQ were after was from generals or higher-ranking officers. That was the end of that, really – there weren't any generals lurking in our immediate vicinity. They were probably all in Jordan by then.

All in all, we were very frustrated because we thought we were going to take on the classic role of the regiment and were looking forward to conducting offensive action and intelligence gathering. But we were directed to concentrate on reporting on Scud positions for air strikes to take out: that was the job, and those were the orders. We got on with it.

We don't know the true tally of Scuds taken out by a combination of ground and aircraft. It's an open-ended question. We believe we contributed a great deal: we did make contact with the enemy – it was our role. We did it from the ground and we all came home together which meant more to me than finding a couple of Scuds.

•

The SAS continued to hit Scud convoys and Iraqi communications systems right to the end and continued to bump into Iraqi units. On 21 February, for example, a column from A Squadron was involved in a series of running battles. The Land Rovers managed to beat off their attackers with a combination of Milan missiles and Browning heavy machine guns, though not before an SAS motorcyclist, Lance-Corporal David Dembury, was shot and killed.

When the UN ground offensive began on 24 February, the mobile columns had spent between thirty-six and forty-two days behind the lines. The SAS had achieved the remarkable, which was reflected in the honours bestowed upon the regiment's soldiers. No fewer than twenty-four awards were made to members of 22 SAS, including ten Military Medals (three posthumous) and another fifteen Mentions in Despatches. The words of Norman Schwarzkopf himself are testimony to the SAS's contribution in the Gulf War.

SECRET

UNITED STATES CENTRAL COMMAND
Office of the Commander-in-Chief
Operation Desert Storm
APO New York 09852-0006

9 March 1991

To: Sir Patrick Hine
Air Chief Marshal
Joint Headquarters
Royal Air Force Wycombe
Buckinghamshire HP14 4UE

Thru: Sir Peter de la Billière
KCB, CBE, DSO, MC
Lieutenant General
British Forces Commander Middle East
Riyadh, Saudi Arabia

Subject: Letter of Commendation for the 22nd Special Air
Service (SAS) Regiment

1. I wish to officially commend the 22nd Special Air Service
(SAS) Regiment for their totally outstanding performance of
military operations during Operation Desert Storm.

2. Shortly after the initiation of the strategic air campaign, it
became apparent that the Coalition forces would be unable to
eliminate Iraq's firing of Scud missiles from western Iraq into
Israel. The continued firing of Scuds on Israel carried with it
enormous unfavorable political ramifications and could, in fact,
have resulted in the dismantling of the carefully crafted
Coalition. Such a dismantling would have adversely affected in
ways difficult to measure the ultimate outcome of the military
campaign. It became apparent that the only way that the

Coalition could succeed in reducing these Scud launches was by physically placing military forces on the ground in the vicinity of the western launch sites. At that time, the majority of available Coalition forces were committed to the forthcoming military campaign in the eastern portion of the theatre of operations. Further, none of these forces possessed the requisite skills and abilities required to conduct such a dangerous operation. The only force deemed qualified for this critical mission was the 22nd Special Air Service (SAS) Regiment.

3. From the first day they were assigned their mission until the last day of the conflict, the performance of the 22nd Special Air Service (SAS) Regiment was courageous and highly professional. The area in which they were committed proved to contain far more numerous enemy forces than had been predicted by every intelligence estimate, the terrain was much more difficult than expected and the weather conditions were unseasonably brutal. Despite these hazards, in a very short period of time the 22nd Special Air Service (SAS) Regiment was successful in totally denying the central corridor of western Iraq to Iraqi Scud units. The result was that the principal areas used by the Iraqis to fire Scuds on Tel Aviv were no longer available to them. They were required to move their Scud missile firing forces to the northwest portion of Iraq and from that location the firing of Scud missiles was essentially militarily ineffective.

4. When it became necessary to introduce United States Special Operations Forces into the area to attempt to close down the northwest Scud areas, the 22nd Special Air Service (SAS) Regiment provided invaluable assistance to the U.S. forces. They took every possible measure to ensure the U.S. forces were thoroughly briefed and were able to profit from the valuable lessons that had been learned by earlier SAS deployments into western Iraq. I am completely convinced that had U.S. forces not received these thorough indoctrinations by SAS personnel U.S. forces would have suffered a much higher rate of casualties than was ultimately the case. Further, the SAS and U.S. joint

forces immediately merged into a combined fighting force where the synergetic effect of these fine units ultimately caused the enemy to be convinced that they were facing forces in western Iraq that were more than tenfold the size of those they were actually facing. As a result, large numbers of enemy forces that might otherwise have been deployed in the eastern theatre were tied down in western Iraq.

5. The performance of the 22nd Special Air Service (SAS) Regiment during Operation Desert Storm was in the highest traditions of the professional military service and in keeping with the proud history and tradition that had been established by that regiment. Please ensure that this commendation receives appropriate attention and is passed on to the unit and its members.

H. NORMAN SCHWARZKOPF
General, U.S. Army
Commander-in-Chief